Sister
Genevieve

Sister Genevieve

John Rae

LITTLE, BROWN AND COMPANY

A *Little, Brown* Book

First published in Great Britain in 2001
by Little, Brown and Company
Reprinted 2001

A CIP catalogue record for this book
is available from the British Library.

ISBN 0 316 85632 0

Typeset in Janson by M Rules
Printed and bound in Great Britain by
Clays Ltd, St Ives plc

Little, Brown and Company (UK)
Brettenham House
Lancaster Place
London WC2E 7EN

www.littlebrown.co.uk

For our children

Siobhan   Penelope   Alyce
Emily   Shamus   Jonathan

Contents

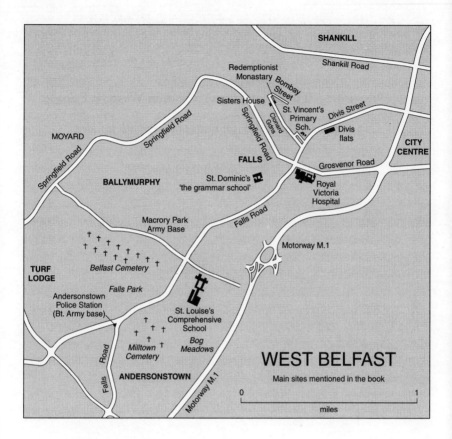

SHANKILL

Shankill Road

Redemptionist
Monastary
Bombay
Street

Sisters House

St. Vincent's
Primary
Sch.

Divis Street

Divis
flats

CITY
CENTRE

MOYARD

Springfield Road

Clonard
Gdns

Springfield Road

Springfield Road

FALLS

Grosvenor Road

BALLYMURPHY

St. Dominic's
'the grammar school'

Royal
Victoria
Hospital

Springfield Road

Falls Road

Macrory Park
Army Base

Motorway M.1

† † †
† † †
† † † †

TURF
LODGE

Belfast Cemetery

Falls Park

Andersonstown
Police Station
(Bt. Army base)

St. Louise's
Comprehensive
School

†
† †
†

*Milltown
Cemetery*

*Bog
Meadows*

WEST BELFAST

Main sites mentioned in the book

Falls Road

ANDERSONSTOWN

Motorway M.1

0   1

miles

Introduction

In the late Spring of 1987 I flew to Belfast to make a television programme about the problems young people experienced finding jobs when they left school. My role was to interview the principal of a large girls' school which had been so successful in placing its pupils in jobs that, even in an area of high unemployment, no girl left school and went straight onto the dole.

The producer met me at Aldergrove airport and we drove into the city. Although there was a police checkpoint outside the airport and British soldiers on the street in the city centre, there was little other evidence that this was the eighteenth year of the Troubles, but when we left the centre and drove along Divis Street and up the Falls Road, the signs that we were entering a war zone were unmistakable. This was Roman Catholic West Belfast. Here the soldiers travelled in Saracen armoured cars or, if they were on foot patrol, moved with the alertness of men who believed they were in enemy territory. If they had any doubt about their welcome, they had only to look up at the gable ends which bore the messages of Republican defiance – 'Provos', 'Smash H-Blocks', 'Up the IRA'.

St. Louise's Comprehensive College was at the top of the Falls Road, deep in Republican territory, a large complex of modern buildings on the slope of the hill, with fine views back over the city. Inside the main entrance it was so quiet that it was easy to imagine that the 2,400 girls had been given the day off. A nun approached. She was wearing a blue habit with a white turtleneck jersey under a blue jumper and a short blue veil covering the back of her head. Though I had been told she was in her sixties, she looked much younger. She smiled and held out her hand. 'I'm Sister Genevieve,' she said.

When Sister Genevieve discovered that I had been a head-teacher too, the producer had some difficulty keeping us focused on the subject of the programme. No one who has not been a headteacher can know how eager headteachers are to talk with others who have had the same experience; rightly or wrongly, they think it is impossible for anyone who has not done the job to imagine what it is like. So Sister Genevieve and I seized the opportunity, despite the fact that to the outsider we must have appeared to have little in common. She was a member of a Roman Catholic religious congregation, the principal of a large state comprehensive school that served one of the most deprived areas in Western Europe, and an implacable opponent of academic selection. I had just finished sixteen years as the headmaster of Westminster School, one of the most academically selective of Britain's independent schools, which until recently had barred Catholics from membership of its governing body and which charged fees higher than the annual income of most of the families whose daughters attended St. Louise's.

What Sister Genevieve and I had experienced in common easily outweighed these differences. We became and have remained good friends. There was however, one aspect of Sister Genevieve's work that was completely outside my experience and it was this that first made me think of writing a book about her: she was running a school in a war zone. The more I discovered about the impact of the Troubles on the school – the fathers and brothers killed or imprisoned, the senior girls who joined the IRA, the everyday mayhem and violence on the streets where the girls lived – the more I came to appreciate what a remarkable person Sister Genevieve must be.

Sister Genevieve and I met from time to time over the next seven years, in Belfast and in London, and always seemed to pick up the conversation where we left off in the manner of people who know exactly what it is they want to talk about. Then in 1994, at the age of seventy-one, she suffered a major stroke that left her unable to speak or write. Now she would never be able to undertake the task I knew she had had in mind of writing about her experiences as a headteacher in troubled West Belfast. Her story was too interesting to be left untold but was I the person to tell it? I had the advantage of having been a headteacher myself and had talked with Sister Genevieve about many aspects of her job. But I was a stranger to the life and outlook of a Roman Catholic sister whose religious vocation was to serve the poor and knew little about the distinctive culture of West Belfast, a Catholic ghetto in a predominantly Protestant city. I realised that I could not write convincingly about Sister Genevieve unless those who had known her and worked with her were willing to help. I was very fortunate, therefore, to have the wholehearted support and encouragement of Sister Genevieve's two closest friends in the congregation who had also been her colleagues in the school, Sister Ita Polley and Sister Declan Kelly. Sister Declan made sure my visits to Belfast were productive; she provided accommodation and arranged meetings with former pupils and colleagues of Sister Genevieve. She ensured that I heard the opinion of Sister Genevieve's critics as well as her admirers. Though some of the latter called her 'a saint', this book is not a hagiography.

The help I received from Sister Declan and other friends of Sister Genevieve should not be taken to mean that they all agree with my interpretation of Sister Genevieve's character and motivation. I know some of them do not but I hope they will accept that I have tried to produce a truthful portrait of a remarkable woman.

The portrait relies partly on personal testimony and anecdotal evidence, on tales told out of school. As a former headmaster, I know that memories of schooldays are notoriously unreliable and I would certainly not wish an account of my headmastership to be based on the uncritical acceptance of the opinions and recollections of my former pupils and colleagues. So while I have listened to many of those who were at the school in Sister Genevieve's time, I have been discriminating in the use of their evidence, double-checking the facts wherever possible.

I should add a word of caution, nevertheless, about some of the language in which the opinions and recollections are expressed. The popular mood in Ireland today is so inclined to be critical of religious orders engaged in education that people may read into familiar language more than the speaker intended. It is common-place, for example, for adults to say that when they were at school they were frightened of the headteacher. From the point of view of a pupil, the headteacher can be a frightening figure so that women who remember being frightened of Sister Genevieve are saying nothing more than that the relationship between the pupils and the headteacher was normal.

I was struck by the fact that one of the words most frequently used to describe Sister Genevieve by those who had dealings with her as adults was 'ruthless', another example of a word that is open to different interpretations. For the record, I was clear that these adults meant Sister Genevieve was exceptionally single-minded not that she was pitiless; 'ruthless' described how she pursued her ambitions for the school not how she treated individuals.

A rather different problem of the use of language arises from the nature of Sister Genevieve's religious community. The Daughters of Charity of St. Vincent de Paul is not a religious order, its members are sisters not nuns and they live in the world not in a cloister. But almost everyone I talked with in West Belfast called the sisters nuns and referred to the house where the sisters lived in the Lower Falls as Clonard Convent. I have tried to be consistent in using the correct terms but there were times when only the incorrect terms fitted the context.

Although the views and recollections of individuals provided me with much useful material for this book, I was also given access to a number of written sources, including school records, the archives of the Daughters of Charity, letters Sister Genevieve wrote, her notes for morning assembly and the talks that she gave. The latter were particularly helpful because in some of them she gave a detailed account of how she operated as a headmistress.

I am grateful to the large number of people who helped me gather the material on which the book is based. They include Sister Genevieve's childhood friends, fellow members of the Daughters of Charity, former pupils and colleagues of St. Louise's, former members of the security forces, former Republican and Loyalist prisoners Sister Genevieve helped, civil servants responsible for education in Belfast, priests responsible for education in the diocese and British politicians responsible for education in Northern Ireland under 'direct rule'. Most of these individuals were happy that their names should be mentioned in the text but some wished to remain anonymous and I have respected that wish. The latter included women who joined the Republican movement in their last year at St. Louise's or soon after leaving. Some of these women were willing to talk about their experiences but with two exceptions did not wish to be identified. Women whose fathers or brothers were active in the IRA while they themselves were pupils at St. Louise's were also willing to talk about their experiences, though once again some preferred to remain anonymous. Another group who wished to remain anonymous were the former Republican and Loyalist prisoners who became the focus of Sister Genevieve's vocation when she had retired as headmistress.

I am very grateful to all these individuals whether or not their names appear in the text.

I am grateful to Yvonne Murphy of the Linen Hall Library in Belfast and to the officials of the Belfast Central Library and the Catholic Central Library in London, for their help.

Peter Taylor, author of *Provos: the IRA and Sinn Fein* helped me to make contact with the Republican movement in Belfast and I am most grateful to him.

My very special thanks to Una McMahon (née Donnelly), one of Sister Genevieve's first head girls, who was unfailingly helpful in locating other former pupils. Without Una's networking on my behalf, much interesting information would not have come to light.

I am also most grateful to Mary O'Hara, the first of Sister Genevieve's pupils to go to Cambridge, who told me her story.

A number of people read parts of the typescript from the point of view of their experience or expertise and pointed out factual errors. They include the former pupils, Una McMahon and Mary O'Hara; Tom Hartley, a Sinn Fein councillor; former teachers at the school; members of Sister Genevieve's religious congregation, the Daughters of Charity; and a former Loyalist paramilitary who was helped by Sister Genevieve. While I am very grateful for their help, they are in no way responsible for any factual errors that remain.

My thanks, too, to my agent, Andrew Lownie, and to Alan Samson and Becky Quintavalle of Little, Brown, who had faith in the book and made helpful suggestions about its structure.

My greatest debt is to my wife, Daphne, who has been a friend of Sister Genevieve for many years – they visited prisons and prisoners in Northern Ireland together – and whose support and interest throughout the writing of this book has been invaluable.

1923–1958

1

'I did not like nuns to put it mildly.
Their whole secretive way of life
revolted me'

On a January morning in 1956 a sister wearing the blue habit and distinctive white collar and cornette or headdress of the Daughters of Charity of St. Vincent de Paul left Clonard Convent in the heart of Roman Catholic West Belfast to walk the short distance to St. Vincent's primary school in Dunlewey Street, just off the Falls Road. She was a few weeks short of her thirty-third birthday and, although she was an experienced teacher, this would be her first day at St. Vincent's. The sisters were familiar figures in the area but there was something about this sister that attracted the attention of the watchers in the windows and doorways of the small Victorian terraced houses that lined the street. For one thing she was tall and the 'butterfly' headdress of starched white linen made her look taller still. And she was beautiful. A former pupil remembers seeing her new teacher for the first time. 'I thought she was an angel. She was the most beautiful woman I think I've ever seen in my life. You look at a lot of nuns and you know why they're nuns. But she was stunning.' There was something else about the new teacher that former pupils remember. The way she held herself and the grand manner in which she swept into the school yard where the girls were playing skips, tig and kick-the-can to keep warm, made them think she might be proud not humble as a nun ought to be.

Over the next thirty years this tall and beautiful butterfly nun would become one of the best known, most loved and most controversial Catholics in Northern Ireland. As principal of St. Louise's Comprehensive College on the Falls Road from 1963–1988, she transformed out of all recognition the opportunities in education and employment for the Catholic girls from some of the poorest homes in the United Kingdom. She gave hope of a better life to people who for generations had been at the bottom of the heap. But the single-mindedness with which she pursued her goal made enemies: among the Catholic clergy whose male, middle-class status quo she threatened; among the Republicans of Sinn Fein and the IRA whose daughters and sisters she educated but whose control of West Belfast she defied; and among the other schools who resented and envied her success.

It is hardly surprising that it is difficult to find anyone who is neutral on the question of Sister Genevieve O'Farrell. As principal of St. Louise's, she inspired fierce loyalty among her pupils and staff. Those who would not or could not accommodate themselves to her vision have less happy memories. It is not unusual for strong personalities in positions of authority, particularly when the authority is exercised over the young, to divide opinion and inspire very different emotions. When a former pupil says of Sister Genevieve, 'the things that made us love her, made others hate her,' she is echoing what was said about the autocratic Victorian headmistresses.

Adults who had dealings with Sister Genevieve found it equally difficult to be objective. When you have discounted the petty jealousies of the academic world and the gullibility of men enthralled by an attractive nun, you are still left with a sharp clash of opinion about her personality and her methods. She infuriated officials by going over their heads and won the lasting gratitude of those who benefited from her refusal to take no for an answer. This is not to suggest that the different views of Sister Genevieve in some way cancel each other out or reach a bland equilibrium. 'On the one hand this, on the other hand that' was not her style, nor is it an accurate summary of her reputation. The weight of opinion is firmly on the side of admiration for her achievements.

An extraordinary mix of politicians, public figures and former paramilitaries were united in believing that Sister Genevieve possessed a touch of greatness, even saintliness. A former member of the Protestant Ulster Volunteer Force who served sixteen years in prison for his part in the murder of Roman Catholics called Sister Genevieve 'the greatest person I have ever met in my life'. To her friend, Mary McAleese, now the President of Ireland, she was 'a marvellous person', while Dr Rhodes Boyson, a British Minister of State in Northern Ireland, thought she was 'the nearest to a saint that I have ever been privileged to meet'. Brian Mawhinney, a less flamboyant politician and a Protestant Ulsterman, who was under-secretary of state in Northern Ireland in the 1980's, thought so highly of her that when she retired he singled her out for an unprecedented gesture by a British minister to a Catholic nun in the Republican heartland. To the annoyance of rival schools and the Church hierarchy who thought she had received enough attention already, and of the Republican movement who were openly critical of her pragmatic hob-nobbing with the British, Mawhinney appeared unannounced at her final assembly with television cameras in tow and, as the eight hundred senior girls stood and cheered, presented her with a bouquet of flowers.

Mary O'Farrell, the future Sister Genevieve, was born on 22 March 1923, in Tullamore, County Offaly, a small town fifty miles west of Dublin. The Irish Free State had come formally into existence three months earlier on 5 December 1922; the bloody civil war that accompanied its birth was almost over. What Mary's parents thought of these great events is not known. Despite its status as the county town and its position on the Grand Canal that linked Dublin to the River Shannon, Tullamore was the sort of quietly inconspicuous place that history passes by.

Mary's father William O'Farrell was farm manager and gardener to the Sisters of Mercy whose Sacred Heart Convent with its extensive grounds and fine gardens stood on the edge of the town. Her mother, Catherine, a small, firm woman, was said to stand in the shadows when visitors came to the door but was the unquestioned ruler of the domestic scene when the door was closed. Mary was their fifth and last child and only daughter. With four older brothers she might have been expected to feel that she had to assert herself to be noticed, but she grew up to be a shy child, content to let others do the talking.

The family went to Mass every day so that when Mary started school she was always able to tick the day's box on the sheet that hung on the notice board, the nuns' way of checking on their pupils' religious observance. But her parents' piety was not oppressive. They allowed her to go to the cinema on Sunday afternoons when she was a teenager, something of which the nuns strongly disapproved; on Monday morning the cinema-goers were made to stand against the wall to receive a warning from the principal on the dangers of this form of entertainment. If her parents hoped she would become a nun, they kept the thought to themselves. Of her four brothers, Peter, Patrick, Dominic and John, Patrick became an Augustinian priest and Dominic joined the Christian Brothers, a teaching congregation of laymen, but no pressure was put on Mary to enter the religious life.

Mary's two oldest friends in late childhood and adolescence, May McFadden and Bridie Byrne, have clear memories of the three girls growing up together in Tullamore. Memories of a Catholic girlhood have a habit of exposing dark episodes but these girls do not seem to have suffered anything more traumatic than a ban on leaving the house for being late back from a dance or a 'nice telling off' from the nuns for being caught smoking. The heartaches and confusions of adolescence must have been there but they were contained by the rhythms and routines of a Catholic community in a small Irish town in the 1930's.

The convent school they all attended was run by the Mercy nuns, with a mixed religious and lay staff. There was a modest termly fee which was waived in Mary's case not because her father worked for the nuns but because she had won one of the two scholarships. Mary was one of those unusual people whose high intelligence did not inspire envy or irritation, partly no doubt because her approach to school work was happy-go-lucky and she made her talents available to the other girls in her class. When there was difficult mathematics homework, Mary would sit on the bank of the Canal on the way home and work out the right answers so that the other girls could gather round and copy her solutions into their own exercise books.

The adolescent Mary, recalled by Bridie and May, is a bright cheerful girl, clever enough to sail through school without too much trouble, still rather shy and reticent, popular with her peers and loyal to her friends. As with some other individuals who become dominant leaders as adults, there was also a quality that, without conscious effort, drew others to her. May McFadden tried to express what this quality was. 'She was always the central figure. She was like a saint in the middle ages, she listened to it all, you didn't feel she was criticising, she had a great way with her, we trusted her completely.' In the photographs of the girls taken when they were about seventeen, Mary always appears at the centre of the group, an attractive young woman though a little round-shouldered as though anxious to disguise her height.

The girls' entry to the sixth form to study for their Leaving Certificate coincided with the outbreak of the Second World War. Ireland was neutral. Though the girls can hardly have been unaware of what was going on in the outside world, they had other things on their minds. 'We admired and criticised boys,' Bridie wrote, 'but Mary never had a boy friend.' When Bridie found a boyfriend, Mary did not approve and dismissed him as a snob. May had a boyfriend too, but agrees that Mary never did. She thinks this was because Mary was self-conscious about being tall and anxious not to upset her parents who were protective of their only daughter. When the school principal, Sister Dympna, wishing to impart some advice on relationships, took each girl aside and asked 'Are you company keeping?', Mary's answer was 'No'.

If the three girls were divided on the subject of boys, they were united in their dislike of nuns. When the Mercy nuns or nuns from other congregations spoke to the girls about the joy of receiving the gift of vocation, Mary and her friends were not impressed. 'The more cynical among us thought it was fun and a chance to escape from class,' Mary wrote many years later, 'the more outrageous responded to dares from friends to feign interest.' The cynicism of adolescence was reinforced by a positive rejection of the nuns' world. 'I did not like nuns to put it mildly,' Mary wrote. 'Their whole secretive way of life revolted me and I did not consider them normal women or in fact women at all.'

Bridie's recollection of their attitude at the time is very similar. 'We never spoke of being nuns, the life had no attraction for us. I am sure God was calling us but we didn't want to hear. The convent seemed to us a cold, formidable building and we always stupidly thought the nuns were looking out of the windows watching us. I assure you we didn't say nice things about them . . . whenever we saw nuns out walking, we hid until they were out of sight.'

Yet within a year of leaving school, Mary and Bridie had entered religious communities to which they would be committed for the rest of their lives. May was the odd one out; she trained as a teacher, married and raised a family. Despite the cynicism, eight of the sixteen girls in Mary's Leaving Certificate class became nuns and some of the others considered it seriously before deciding against.

Because God's call to the religious life is difficult to understand, it is tempting to explain it in terms that owe nothing to the supernatural: as a desire to escape from the world; as misplaced idealism; as a realistic career choice for girls when few careers other than teaching and nursing were open to them; or just as conformity to the expectations of others.

In the Ireland of Mary's youth, women in religious orders were the largest single group in the small field of professional women, outnumbering lay women teachers, nurses and midwives. As an alternative to marriage, the religious orders offered an outlet for the energies of thousands of Catholic women. The age of vocation suggests that it was a genuine alternative not a second best, most women entering the religious life between the ages of eighteen and twenty-two. Not that the prospect of marriage was all that attractive. There was no shortage of unmarried men but what many of them wanted was not a wife in the true sense but a skivvy to do the chores. It might be argued that as religious vocation was a phenomenon of late adolescence rather than mature adulthood, the girls who became nuns were making decisions they would later regret. But the same could be said of marriage, and in Ireland it was easier to leave a religious order than to obtain a divorce.

The trouble with Mary O'Farrell was that she did not want either alternative. For the time being at least, marriage was not on her mind and she was certain she did not want to join a religious order. Nursing and teaching did not appeal to her. She was an intelligent, strong-willed, young woman who in a later generation might have forged a successful career for herself in business or the professions but in provincial Ireland in 1941 the choice was limited.

Not that Mary or any of the other talented women who joined religious orders in what has been described as 'the golden age of religious life', between the French Revolution and the mid-twentieth century, would have seen it as a matter of choice. God called them to enter the religious life and they obeyed, joyfully in some cases, in others with initial reluctance, but always willing to sacrifice whatever prospects they may have had. Of Mary's near contemporaries, Bride Geoffrey-Smith, who as Sister Bridget was headmistress of St. Mary's School, Ascot, turned down a place at Cambridge in favour of her vocation to become a nun. In the previous generation, Agnes Berkeley, Sister Xavier, happily abandoned an aristocratic lifestyle because she was convinced she had been called to join the Daughters of Charity and to serve the poor in China, which she did for fifty years until her death in 1944. However much our secular, twenty-first century perspective seeks a down-to-earth explanation, the fact remains that some very able women committed themselves to God's service not as a career choice or for want of something better but in response to what they believed was divine guidance.

Mary, too, believed that her decision to enter the religious life was a step she would not have taken without supernatural intervention. She was certain that God had called her, even though at first she did not recognise His voice. She remembered the moment in detail. The girls in her class were discussing in their usual sceptical fashion the different congregations of nuns, when Anna Daly, whose brother, a Down's syndrome child, was being cared for by the Daughters of Charity of St. Vincent de Paul, turned to Mary, perhaps in response to a comment Mary had made, and said: 'Those French sisters really do serve the poor.'

That was it. Anna Daly's words did not seem important at the time but Mary soon became convinced that they expressed God's call to her. Far from being ecstatic as the nuns had assured her she would be, she was baffled and then resentful. 'The call came to me through that simple incident and I loathed it . . . I felt I was being pushed into unknown territory for which I had no natural taste.' Despite her feelings, she wrote to the Daughters of Charity and studied the literature they sent.

The Daughters of Charity, Servants of the Sick Poor, was a company of 'sisters' founded in Paris in 1633 by Vincent de Paul, 'Monsieur Vincent', a French priest, and 'the virtuous widow' Louise de Marillac. Their innovation was to found a religious organisation of women who would serve their vocation on the streets, in the hospitals and in the homes of the poor not in a convent. Instead of the medieval ideal of the female religious as the bride of Christ, a consecrated virgin whose life was suitably reclusive and devotional, Vincent and Louise saw the possibility of using the practical and pastoral skills of women to alleviate suffering in the world outside. Because the sisters would be exposed to that world, they would have to be more virtuous than cloistered religious, and because their lives would be hard and dangerous, their training would have to develop physical as well as spiritual resources, the exterior strength to undertake exhausting work as well as the interior strength of a life of prayer. 'As for those two girls,' Louise de Marillac wrote about two country girls who wanted to join the company, 'try them out very thoroughly in body and mind because you realise that a girl with a weakness in either is not suitable to us.' The qualities of the ideal candidate are suggested by the reference written on behalf of the future St. Catherine Laboure, a farm girl who applied to join in 1830: 'very devout, of good character, with a strong constitution, a love of work and a most cheerful disposition.'

It was not a life for the faint-hearted. Seventeenth-century France was a violent society almost continuously at war with itself or with its neighbours. The early Daughters of Charity were robust country girls who ran the gauntlet of the slums, the prisons and the battlefields to find in the faces of the poor and suffering the image of their Saviour. They cared for those at the margins of society, the orphans and the insane, and because their founders believed that charity should be accompanied by instruction, started Petites Ecoles for the daughters of the poor.

Some contemporary Catholics were critical. Instructing girls may have been women's work but going into the royal prisons, 'the ante-chambers of Hell', and onto the battlefields, was a job for male religious, if indeed it needed to be done at all. There was something unsettling too, about the cheerful manner in which the sisters embraced danger. One of the first, Marguerite Naseau, died of the plague because she had happily taken into her own bed a homeless woman desperately ill with the disease.

Selfless individuals do not make a great religious movement. Fortunately for the Daughters of Charity, Vincent and Louise, in common with many saints, were efficient organisers. Vincent had the additional skill of knowing how to win influential support, a skill that Sister Genevieve would also possess and use, like Vincent, to good effect. The company grew in numbers and reputation, opening houses all over France, including twenty-five in Paris, and sending the first mission 'abroad' to serve the poor in Poland. By the end of the eighteenth century, the Daughters of Charity had established themselves as one of the largest and most respected congregations of women in Europe.

This did not protect them from the politically correct logic of the French Revolutionaries for whom charity had connotations of aristocracy and selflessness might be privilege in disguise. The sisters were expelled from the motherhouse in Paris; other houses were closed or allowed to continue their work under the new title of *La Maison de L'Humanité*. When the more extreme revolutionaries introduced a programme of dechristianisation, those sisters who remained at work were at risk. During the Reign of Terror, four sisters in Arras were arrested, tried and guillotined on the same day, 26 June 1794, going to the scaffold in a tumbril wearing the habit and the white butterfly headdress of their company.

In the nineteenth century the Daughters of Charity quickly
re-established themselves. New houses opened throughout France
and overseas including the first house in China. By the time Mary
O'Farrell wrote to them, the Daughters of Charity had a world-
wide organisation with 43,000 members. The first house in
Ireland had been opened at Drogheda in 1855, but the Irish sisters
were still part of the company's English province with its headquarters at Mill Hill in North London.

What attracted Mary to the Daughters of Charity was that they
were not nuns. Vincent de Paul called them 'sisters who come
and go like seculars'; in other words they lived in the world not in
the cloister. Strictly speaking, the organisation that Vincent and
Louise started was not a religious order but a company or congregation, or in modern Catholic terminology, a society of
apostolic life.

For Mary, these were not just technical or semantic distinc-
tions. Given her antipathy to 'the whole secretive way of life' of
cloistered nuns, they were of fundamental importance. The
Daughters of Charity may have dressed like nuns, taken vows like
nuns and have been almost universally referred to as nuns by
bishops and canon lawyers no less than by the populace at large,
but the fact that they served God in the world made all the difference to Mary. As an adult, she was happy to be called a nun and to
call herself a nun, but at eighteen the distinction between the secular and the cloistered role was crucial to her decision to enter the
religious life.

So was the nature of the work she hoped she would be doing.
Like so many women who had joined the Daughters of Charity
before her, Mary was physically and mentally strong and not interested in the contemplative life. To work with the poorest and most
marginalised in society was a prospect that must have appealed to
her idealism as well as to her dislike of the bourgeois femininity of
the convent school. She knew she did not want to be a teacher and
she probably assumed there was no danger of the Daughters of
Charity pushing her in that direction against her will.

Over the summer months of 1941, Mary appears to have wrestled with the decision about her future without mentioning the

possibility of joining the Daughters of Charity to her parents or to her brother John who was closest to her in age and outlook. Her doubts about whether to enter the religious life seem to have been stronger than any doubts she may still have had about the Daughters of Charity. Her friend, Bridie Byrne, had already decided to join the Sisters of Mercy at Tullamore, and the sisters wanted to recruit Mary too: she was one of their star pupils. But for Mary it had to be the Daughters of Charity if she was going to enter the religious life at all.

At the end of the summer, when she was eighteen and a half, Mary applied and was accepted as a postulant with the Daughters of Charity in Dublin, but her doubts remained. Her family could not give her the wholehearted support she needed because they thought she was making a mistake. When she confided in her brother John, he told her she would be mad to join the Daughters of Charity. It was not her vocation the family doubted, it was the wisdom of joining that particular community. Mary's deeply religious parents considered a religious vocation the most marvellous thing that could happen to a member of the family and said so, but 'not in that hard order'. Popular prejudice identified the Daughters of Charity with a demanding physical life in which there was little room for spirituality. Or as a French priest put it: 'N'y allez pas, mon enfant, là-bas; ce n'est que bras et jambes.'

On the eve of Mary's departure for Dublin, a Jesuit priest who was a friend of the family made a similar attempt at dissuasion. 'Don't join that order,' he told her, 'it's not for you. I'll fix it even at this late hour.'

The attempts to dissuade Mary failed. On the morning of 27 November 1941, she put on the black dress, black stockings and black shoes that postulants were expected to provide for themselves, and after breakfast, she said goodbye to her parents. As she adored them both and knew that she had broken their hearts by sticking to her decision, the leave taking was sad and difficult. John accompanied her by train to Dublin. It was a foul day, raining ceaselessly. When they arrived at the Daughters of Charity house in the Navan Road, Dublin, it turned out to be a former workhouse, a large, forbidding building swept by the rain. John could control his feelings no longer. 'For God's sake come home,' he pleaded. But Mary shook her head and replied, 'I'll give it a try'.

The policy of the Daughters of Charity was to place postulants in small numbers in any one of their houses in the province so that there was an element of chance in the type of work they experienced. The house in Navan Road was a residential home and special school for mentally handicapped children. There were a few mentally handicapped adults left over from the days when the building had been used as an asylum and a number of illegitimate children who were perfectly capable of attending a normal school but who had nowhere else to live. In the long corridors the different groups occupied separate rooms, but their lives overlapped and their cries intermingled so that the task of meeting their diverse needs required exceptional stamina and patience.

The relationship between the sisters and the postulants was friendly but formal. Mary would have been addressed as 'Miss Mary'. Sister Gabriel McDonnell who was a sister in the house when Mary was a postulant, said that most of the sisters were soon won over by Mary's personality though some thought that the new postulant's attractiveness might be 'a handicap in the community'. For Mary, the postulancy was a tough initiation into the Vincentian life but the seeming impossibility of loving the poor and suffering as Vincent de Paul had done did not deter her. At the end of the three months, she was prepared to make the commitment necessary to enter the seminary but, true to form, she still had reservations. As Sister Genevieve, she wrote in 1990: 'I went into the seminary hoping that I would be sent away, as happened to others frequently, but after six months I changed course and wanted to take up the challenge of being in this tough army of charity.'

Mary entered St. Catherine's Seminary at Blackrock outside Dublin on 26 February 1942. She was still only eighteen. The seminary would be a sterner test of her vocation and of her willingness to submit to the disciplines of community life because, like the training camps of elite military units, it was partly designed to make or break those who aspired to join. The seminary was housed in a Georgian mansion called Dunardagh, a square, two-storey building set in thirty-five acres of grounds close to the sea and the ferry port of Dun Laoghaire. It was a far cry from the Navan Road. The twelve to fourteen months the sisters spent in the seminary was the only time they withdrew from the world. There were no sick poor or mentally handicapped children or orphans here, only the 'seminary sisters', as the former postulants were now called, and the 'habit sisters' who trained them for the hard life that lay ahead and sorted out the genuine vocations from those whose mental or physical weaknesses disqualified them.

The day Mary arrived was as wet and dismal as the one on which her brother John had accompanied her to the Navan Road, but this time she was alone. She was met by one of the Sisters of Office and taken upstairs to the dormitory to change out of her postulant's clothes and into those of a seminary sister. White curtains separated the beds. On Mary's bed were her seminary sister's clothes, folded neatly. With the help of the Sister of Office she changed, putting on the long black robe, tucked in at the waist and held with a pin, the white *fichu* or shawl and the white *coiffe* that fitted closely over her head. She was no longer an Irish girl but a French peasant girl of the seventeenth century.

The superior of the seminary was its Directress, Sister Philomena Rickard, a large, strongly built Dubliner, with big hands and a forthright manner. Like so many of those who are required to test recruits to the uttermost, she hid a kindly nature behind a tough exterior. She was supported by four Sisters of Office, 'non-commissioned officers', who were responsible for seeing that the seminary sisters were in the right place at the right time, supervising work, answering questions and giving permissions.

Two other postulants had arrived at the same time as Mary and the three 'new girls' now joined the continuous cycle of training on which the seminary sisters were engaged. At different points on the cycle some sisters joined and others left having received the holy habit, and their first *placement* or mission, while others left early of their own accord or were sent away. The comings and goings must have complicated Sister Philomena's job, but there were seldom more than thirty seminary sisters so she was able to keep her finger on the problems and progress of individuals.

At the end of the first week the three new girls went on a short retreat under the direction of Sister Philomena, one purpose being to determine their vocation date when they would formally be admitted as seminary sisters. The vocation date is of great importance to the Daughters of Charity because it is the date on which their response to God's call becomes a commitment and from which they calculate their membership of the company. Mary's vocation date was 9 March 1942. On that day, too, she took a further step away from girlhood. Miss Mary became Sister O'Farrell.

The daily routine of the seminary had not changed much in three hundred years. Before the war, Irish and English postulants had crossed the channel to join the large seminary in Paris where sisters from around the world trained to follow in the footsteps of St. Vincent and St. Louise. In the small Irish seminary at Blackrock, the spirit of the Paris seminary prevailed, and the sisters were never allowed to forget that they were in a French company. French terms were used at every turn: the superior was addressed as *ma soeur*, her office was her *cabinet*, insufficient modesty might be criticised as still too much *la tête en l'air*, and the successful completion of the seminary was marked by the *prise d'habit*. French customs had to be learnt – Mary complained that they even had to adopt French table manners – and French centrally imposed uniformity accepted. The old jibe about French education – that the authorities in Paris could tell what the pupils were doing any time of the day – could have been applied to the Vincentian seminaries.

The sisters got up at four in the morning as a French peasant girl would have done. A Sister of Office rang the handbell and called out: 'In God's holy name, please sisters arise', to which the watchful replied, 'Blessed be God's holy name'. When they had washed and dressed, the sisters vied with one another to be the first into the chapel for a period of meditation and silent prayer. After praying together for the sick and dying, the orphans and the insane, the sinners and the benefactors, the sisters spent the time until Mass at seven on housework or improving reading. There were no lay staff in the seminary so the sisters had to do everything from polishing the floors and cleaning the pots and pans to cooking the meals and doing the laundry. It was no good pleading lack of skill; if Sister Philomena sent you to the kitchen, you learnt to cook, instructed and supervised by a Sister of Office.

Idle moments did not occur. If a sister found herself with a gap in activity she was expected to profit from it by saying her rosary. That would have been normal in the noviciates of the day, but the Daughters of Charity added a sense of urgency to capture the spirit of the first sisters who hurried through the streets of Paris to visit the poor. Breakfast after Mass was taken 'on the run'; standing in silence, the sisters had a mug of steaming coffee and cut themselves a thick slice of bread from the loaf on the table. As they had already been up for three and a half hours, even this plain fare must have been very welcome.

After breakfast, the main part of the day was divided between instruction in the seminary and more hard manual work at your 'office' which changed in rotation so that if this month you worked in the kitchen, next month you worked in the laundry. Time was set aside for spiritual reading, meditation and prayer as well as for recreation. Much of the day was spent in silence but during recreation the sisters could talk to one another over their sewing about uncontentious matters – what a Sister of Office had said that morning or whether there would be biscuits as a treat on the next feast day. On fine days, a Sister of Office accompanied the sisters into the garden where they said seven Hail Marys at the statue of Our Lady before sitting in the sun and opening their sewing bags to work on their *trousseau*, the personal garments that needed attention. The long hours of silence, the intent listening at instruction and the hard physical work meant that by the evening the sisters were exhausted. At eight o'clock, two points for meditation on the following day were read out and the sisters examined their own consciences before retiring. Lights out in the dormitory was at nine thirty.

As Sister Genevieve, Mary was ambivalent about her experience of the seminary, proud to have endured, which was proof she thought of her vocation, but critical of the denial of individuality. 'The seminary, as the noviciate was called, made every attempt to

dehumanise us. Only a divine call could explain our survival.' It was
not the rigid routine that Mary found dehumanising but being
treated as a child who should be seen and not heard, who could not
be trusted to read a secular book or to go for a walk by herself, and
who was certainly not encouraged to have ideas. 'Who are you to
think what should be done?' she was asked. 'The community has
been in existence for three hundred years and did not need your
thoughts.' At each stage of her life, as Mary O'Farrell the
Tullamore schoolgirl, as Miss Mary the postulant, as Sister
O'Farrell the seminary sister, as Sister Joseph, her first religious
name, and as Sister Genevieve, she found it difficult to be obedient
to an authority she did not respect and there must have been times
in the seminary when, despite her growing understanding of Sister
Philomena's purpose, she found the whole rigmarole of petty reg-
ulations almost insufferable. The sisters had to ask permission to
do the simplest things and to ask pardon for the most trivial mis-
takes such as breaking a cup or a shoelace. For only slightly more
serious lapses the sister had to kiss the floor in penance and woe
betide the sister who let her mind wander. 'Sister, would you share
with us the virtuous thoughts with which God inspired you during
your prayer?' Then the sister would go forward, kneel before the
Directress and begin: 'Having placed myself in the presence of
God . . .' Sister Philomena must have seemed omnipotent and
omniscient to the young sisters. There was no privacy and no
corner of your life she might not inspect. Letters home were left
unsealed for her to read and incoming letters were slit open and
read by her before being placed in each pigeonhole.

Although most sisters had difficulty accepting the traditions
and disciplines of the seminary, their commitment carried them
through. Some were so eager to receive the holy habit they would
have done anything, including as one sister put it, 'eating breakfast
standing on my head', if it was required. Others submitted to the
regime but with reservations they managed to keep to themselves.
Mary was one of these. For all sisters there must have been
moments when the whispered encouragement, 'cheer up, this
won't go on for ever', broke the rule of silence and made all the
difference to morale.

Those who could not take the regime left. There was a coldness, even ruthlessness in the way the Daughters of Charity dealt
with its failures. They were seminary sisters one day and gone the
next. No comment was made when a sister left and no questions
were asked. An empty pigeonhole was the only way the other sisters knew she had gone for good. A similar coldness characterised
the community's attitude to those who left after making their
vows. One of Sister Genevieve's pupils who left the Daughters of
Charity after six years, wrote: 'At my departure, the coldness,
indifference and awkwardness of the sisters in charge hurt so
much. On the actual morning of my departure I was told to go to
a certain room at the front of the house where I would find some
lay clothes. A taxi would come for me and I should go when it
arrived. It broke my heart, no one said goodbye. I just left, stream-
ing with tears.'

The achievement of Sister Philomena Rickard was to use the
strengths and weaknesses of the old regime to inspire the seminary
sisters with the practical idealism of St. Vincent de Paul and St.
Louise de Marillac. She had lived the Vincentian life in the slums
of Manchester and Glasgow and like a battle hardened soldier
sent home to train recruits, she knew the conditions the seminary
sisters would have to face and was single-minded in preparing
them for the trials ahead. Of herself, she gave little away.

For Mary, as for others, it was Sister Philomena who made
sense of the months in the seminary. Any remaining doubts about
their vocation and about whether the Daughters of Charity was
the community in which they wished to spend the rest of their
lives were dispelled by the challenge of Sister Philomena's teaching. Every morning and afternoon, the sisters sat in their rows on
the narrow wooden benches as Sister Philomena instructed them
on the lives of St. Vincent and St. Louise, on what it means to
serve Christ in the poor, on the characteristics of simplicity, humility and charity that the sisters should strive to maintain, on the
vows of poverty, chastity and obedience that they would take after
they had left the seminary, and on the importance of a life of
prayer. The mainspring of her instruction, the text to which she
always returned, was the record of Vincent de Paul's 'conferences',

the spiritual teaching and practical advice that he gave to Louise and the early sisters at face-to-face meetings. Vincent's ideal of 'serving Our Lord in the person of the poor' combined with Sister Philomena's experience of trying to put that ideal into practice, at last convinced Mary that she had made the right choice. Serving the poor was what God had called her to do. There would be times over the years when her dedication to the religious life wavered but her belief in Vincent de Paul's teaching never did.

Vincent de Paul was a realist. He did not pretend to the early sisters that they would find the poor attractive or grateful, or that it would be easy to love them. The prisoners would scream obscenities when the sisters brought them food and the poor would resent their charity. If the sisters wished to fulfil their duties, they had to put out of their minds any thought that they were doing the poor a favour. In a famous phrase, he told them: 'The poor will only forgive us the bread we give them if it is given in love.'

It is not difficult to understand why those words caught Mary's imagination as they had caught the imagination of many idealistic young seminary sisters before her. They turned the conventional idea of charity on its head; they asked the impossible of those who took up the challenge, and they seemed to contain a call to fight inequality and injustice. Here at last was an ideal that Mary could dedicate her life to, a concept of what it meant to be religious that was a million miles away from the nuns who peered out of the convent windows in Tullamore and asked the schoolgirls whether they were 'company keeping'.

Fondness for the company of men was one of the temptations that Sister Philomena warned the young seminary sisters against because it was one of the hazards of secularity, of working in the world while trying to keep your distance from it. The sisters would find themselves working with male colleagues in schools and hospitals and visiting men in prison. By practising mortification of the flesh they would in time liberate themselves to work in the world without the distraction of 'entanglements of the heart'. Meanwhile they needed advice on how to avoid potentially dangerous situations. On 'persons of the other sex', Vincent de Paul warned against 'remaining alone with them at undue hours and places, seeking their company and prolonging useless conversations with them'. He urged the sisters of his day to 'be like rocks against any familiarities which men may wish to take'. As for the risk of falling in love, the sisters of Mary's generation were told to 'withdraw immediately when you hear the hissing of the serpent'.

The best defence against all the temptations of worldliness was as 'intense interior life'. Sister Philomena, who knew all about the problems of working in the secular world, told the seminary sisters that they could not expect to remain true to their vocation unless they developed a life of prayer. Vincent de Paul, speaking at a conference in 1648, explained: 'A Daughter of Charity cannot persevere if she does not pray. She may continue for some little time but at length the world will carry her off. She will find her mode of life too hard.'

Sister Genevieve acknowledged the debt she owed to the Seminary Directress and wrote that as a young sister she had worshipped Sister Philomena. For Mary, Sister Philomena, who had worked for years among the poorest of the poor, was a role model, epitomising those qualities that convinced Mary to 'take up the challenge of being in this tough army of charity'.

In the early Spring of 1943, when it was still too cold for the sisters to walk in the garden during recreation, Sister Philomena decided that Sister O'Farrell was ready to make her retreat of the *prise d'habit*, a final examination before God that would end in her taking the habit of the Daughters of Charity and being sent on her first mission in the outside world. For the time being she would remain Sister O'Farrell, the custom being that a new sister was only given a religious name when she joined her first house. Even that name could change if she moved to another house and found her religious name already in use there, a curious practice, now abandoned, that seemed to emphasise the unimportance of individual identity.

As a passing-out ceremony, the *prise d'habit* was deliberately low-key. In keeping with their desire not to be thought of as a religious order, the Daughters of Charity kept the chapel service, at which the seminary sister became a habit sister, business-like and free from the trappings associated with the clothing of a nun. There were no novices dressed as brides or proud, sad parents peering through the grille.

Mary put on her habit before the service under the eye of Sister Philomena. The heavy cloth was the exact shade of blue worn by French workers and was lined with black to protect the cloth when the sisters rolled up their sleeves. The collar and cornette of starched white linen were put on last. The collar, like a stiff white shirtfront, reached from the neck almost to the waist. The cornette, the winged headdress, was held in place by the 'obedience pin' which on the occasion of the *prise d'habit* was put in by the Seminary Directress, Sister Philomena's last duty before sending the young sister out into the world.

Mary's sense of achievement on becoming a habit sister was swiftly followed by a disappointment when she was told that she was to be trained as a teacher, the one thing she did not want to do. The decision was taken not by Sister Philomena but by Sister Anne Thomson, the Sister Provincial at the headquarters of the English Province in Mill Hill. Nearly half a century later, Sister Genevieve wrote, 'I joined that particular order because I did not want to teach', but at the time she was expected to accept this *placement* with 'holy indifference' to her own wishes.

Mary's objection to teaching was that it fell far short of her ideal of serving the poorest and most marginalised in society. She described her frame of mind on leaving the seminary as 'fanatically dedicated to the equality of all human beings' and she saw herself working in the slums of a great city as Sister Philomena had done, not teaching at a school like the Mercy Nuns of Tullamore. But her objection would have been of no interest to the Daughters of Charity. New habit sisters were sent where they were needed.

In the summer of 1943, Mary travelled from Dublin to Mill Hill and then north to Manchester, where her destination was St. Joseph's Technical High School for Girls. The Daughters of Charity ran the school and had a residential house on the site for the sisters. The plan was for Mary to spend a year in this house, gaining some experience of teaching while applying for entry to the ordinary degree course at the Victoria University, Manchester in the autumn of 1944.

On arrival in Manchester, Mary was given the religious name of Sister Joseph, an odd or perhaps deliberate choice for an attractive young woman. A year later she started at the university. For someone who made such a powerful impression on those she met at other periods of her life, Mary seems to have slipped through her three years at university unnoticed. There is no record of her attendance at the university or of her taking a degree. What few recollections of Manchester she was prepared to put on paper concentrate on her life as a sister and make few references to her life as a student. She lived during this period at the Daughters of Charity house in Rumford Street close to the university. While she attended lectures in the nearby arts building, the other sisters in residence worked with poor families in Manchester's slum districts. The contrast between the maturity these sisters had to display in their daily work and the dependent, almost childlike personalities they assumed when they returned to Rumford Street, struck Mary as extraordinary. They looked to their superior for a lead in everything with the result that the evening's recreation was stilted and artificial, and a young sister was not encouraged to express her opinions or indeed to say anything at all.

This was the old regime in the Daughters of Charity and Mary found it stifling. She was too strong a personality and had too keen a sense of humour to sit po-faced and silent through what passed for conversation in the community room; all her life, she enjoyed ruffling feathers and it is unlikely that the older sisters in Rumford Street were spared. Her obvious frustration with the dependency culture earned her the reputation of being, in the words of one of her friends, 'pretty wild in the community', but on her own account, she was no more at home in the university. 'Those of us who were lucky enough to be given a third level education,' she wrote, 'found ourselves almost freaks in a social setting outside.'

Other sisters, including Sister Margaret Cunnane, who was a year ahead of Mary and obtained her degree in 1946, coped with the difficulties of living in two worlds but Mary evidently did not.

Her reticence in Belfast about her experience as a student in Manchester was due to the fact that she failed her final exam. In the third year of her ordinary degree, she concentrated on two subjects, French and history, and it was her French papers that let her down. The Provincial Director of the Daughters of Charity, Father Joseph Sheedy, wrote to the university asking for an explanation but if he received one it is no longer in the archives. The explanation put forward by those sisters who knew her – that she failed deliberately because she did not want to be a teacher or that success in a convent school in rural Ireland had given a misleading impression of her ability – are unconvincing. It may be that she allowed herself to be distracted, that 'pretty wild in the community' meant more than just speaking out of turn during recreation, but it is hard to believe the story that her tutor arranged for her to fail so that he would have the pleasure of teaching her for another year.

Whatever the true explanation, the failure was a bitter and humiliating disappointment. Many of those who knew her as Sister Genevieve in Belfast described her as 'a driven woman' and there is little doubt that one of the factors that made her so single-minded, was a determination to prove herself.

The Daughters of Charity were not prepared to lose a potential teacher and Father Sheedy arranged for Mary to go to Sedgley Park College of Education to take a one year teaching qualification. Before that she could return to the seminary at Blackrock to make her vows. Despite the frustrations and disappointments she seems to have had no hesitation in doing so. She was required to make vows of poverty, chastity and obedience as well as an additional vow to serve the poor. The vows were simple not solemn; they were made without pomp and ceremony and were not ratified by the Church. Nevertheless, they were binding and it was a mortal sin to transgress them. All the sisters renewed their vows each year on the same day, the feast of the Annunciation, but the commitment was for life. As Sister Joseph, Mary made her vows at mass in the seminary chapel on 29 June 1947. She was twenty-four years old. A few weeks later she returned to Manchester to start her teacher training.

Sedgley Park College was run by the Faithful Companions of Jesus, another company of Catholic sisters that had its origins in France. The course it offered to potential teachers was highly regarded but it does not seem to have overcome Mary's lack of enthusiasm for the role. At the end of the year, her 'Ministry Final Mark' was B minus and the report on her teaching practice at Bury Convent speaks for itself:

> Found it difficult to get into contact with the young
> children – a difficult class. Inclined to take the attitude that
> there was nothing she could do about it in three weeks.
> Not very anxious to come for help or very ready to take a
> suggestion.

Mary's first *placement* as a qualified teacher was at an orphanage school for boys attached to the provincial house at Mill Hill and it was here that she was given a new religious name, presumably because the provincial house already had a Sister Joseph. Genevieve was the name of one of Louise de Marillac's earliest recruits to the company but it was also the name of a fifth-century saint who, by sheer force of personality, had rallied the citizens of Paris when they were on the point of surrendering to Attila the Hun. If Mary knew something of the saint's history, she probably welcomed the change but a new religious name did not reconcile her to the role that the Sister Provincial had chosen for her.

Genevieve – as she will now be called – still hoped that she would be sent on a more demanding mission, one that matched Pope Pius XI's description of the Daughters of Charity as 'consecrated heroines of the people', and that would enable her to test her vocation in the slums of a great city or in one of the company's missions overseas. But the Sister Provincial had other plans. In 1950, Genevieve was sent to Lanark, a market town mid-way between Edinburgh and Glasgow, where the Daughters of Charity ran an orphanage and provided some of the teachers for St. Mary's Catholic primary school nearby.

Genevieve spent six years in Scotland, teaching at St. Mary's and learning to love the country to which she would return whenever she could. She learnt to love the children, too, and even though she may still have dreamed of serving the poor in more 'heroic' circumstances, she began to recognise that the job she was doing was making its contribution to 'the equality of all human beings'. The recollections of those who knew her in Lanark suggest that she was now happier both as a teacher and as a member of her religious congregation. According to Sister Fidelma Archer, who had recently come to Lanark straight from the seminary, Genevieve's 'great sense of humour' helped transform evening recreation into 'an hour of happiness and fun'. Some of the orphans thought she was fun too. 'She was different,' one of the girls, who was a teenager at the time, recalls, 'she was a very warm person with a lovely smile; if only she had been looking after us.' Anne Mulligan, a contemporary on the staff at St. Mary's described Genevieve as 'a stunningly beautiful woman', a popular and respected member of staff, much loved by her pupils 'for whom she showed great love and compassion but also firmness when necessary'.

But Genevieve was restless. Towards the end of 1955, she heard that a secondary school in Dundee, run jointly by the Daughters of Charity and the Marist Brothers, was looking for a teacher and she told her superior at Lanark that she would like to be considered. Once again, she was to be disappointed. The Sister Provincial at Mill Hill decided that Sister Genevieve O'Farrell should be sent to Belfast not Dundee.

If there was a time when Genevieve thought about leaving the Daughters of Charity, this was it. Among her friends, opinion is divided. Some believe she would never have contemplated leaving but others think that being sent to Belfast was the last straw for someone whose constant criticism of the Daughters of Charity was that the sisters were never treated as intelligent adults. Genevieve herself said that while she could not have refused to go to Belfast, she made up her mind that she would only stay for six months. It was the postulancy and the seminary all over again. She would give Belfast a try.

In January 1956, she took the boat from Liverpool and was met at Belfast Docks by Sister Ita Polley, the principal of St. Vincent's primary school where Genevieve would be teaching.

'Had you a nice crossing?' Sister Ita asked. 'As well as can be expected,' Genevieve replied. The two sisters took a taxi from the docks across the city centre to the Falls Road. So many buildings have been destroyed during the Troubles or as the result of re-development, that the old Falls district that Genevieve was seeing for the first time, with its linen mills and warren of narrow streets, has vanished. But in 1956 the narrow streets, whose names, Cawnpore and Lucknow alongside Bantry and Tralee, might have been chosen to remind the Catholic population that although this was Ireland it was still part of the British Empire, were teeming with life. If Genevieve was seeking the poorest of the poor, she would find them here because Catholic West Belfast was one of the poorest districts in Western Europe.

Sister Ita had told her pupils how they should greet the new sister. One of the first to do so as Genevieve swept into the school-yard, so tall and regal on that cold winter morning, was ten-year-old Margaret Conlan who ran across the yard and said: 'Cead mile failte, Sister Genevieve, a hundred thousand welcomes.'

2

'There came a point when I just couldn't resist any longer'

The sisters teaching in the school and those who worked in the surrounding parish lived in the company's house in Clonard, a militantly Republican area in the Lower Falls. The superior or 'sister servant' at Clonard was Sister Vincent Wallace, a gentle, soft-spoken, refined woman in her early seventies whose courage, quiet authority and unsanctimonious holiness had made her a true 'heroine of the people' in West Belfast.

Sister Vincent appears to have understood Genevieve's personality correctly from the start. She bent the rules, allowing Genevieve to read secular books, not to indulge the new sister but to remove unnecessary obstacles to her remaining in Belfast. That might have caused dissent in another community but Sister Vincent was too well respected and her regime was anyway unusually enlightened for the time. She bought the daily newspapers for the community room because she thought that the sisters who were teaching should not be less well informed than the children about what was going on in the world. Although she was supposed to read the incoming mail, she just made a token slit at the top of the envelope and handed the letter to the sister unopened. In the summer, she hired taxis to take the sisters to Tyrella Beach, where the older sisters prepared a picnic on the sand and the younger sisters walked barefoot in the shallow waves.

Sister Vincent was too shrewd to imagine that Genevieve's rest-lessness in the company could be ended by permission to read secular books. The conflict between Genevieve's attachment to her own will and the obedience and indifference required of a sister might never be fully resolved but it could at least be con-tained if Genevieve's idealism and drive were harnessed to the cause to which Sister Vincent had dedicated nearly fifty years of her life.

'You do not understand the sufferings the people of this area have endured down the ages,' Sister Vincent said sharply on one occasion to a sister who had passed an ill-informed comment on the people of the Falls. But she wanted Genevieve to understand. In the evenings, when Genevieve returned from the school, Sister Vincent would take her round the Falls, the maze of streets that the security forces would one day video and photograph and know inside out, to visit the homes of the children Genevieve was teach-ing. In the overcrowded, two up, two down, terraced houses with no bath or hot water, the grandmother sitting by the open grate greeted Sister Vincent as an old friend while the children kept their mother between them and the sisters who they regarded as the real authority figures in the parish. Sister Vincent had taught generations of girls from these homes and she often knew the family history better than the families themselves, so that as the two sisters walked from house to house, Sister Vincent was able to tell Genevieve what it was the people of the Falls had had to endure.

On these evening visits, a close bond developed between the older sister who knew and cared so much about the people of the Falls and the younger sister who knew and cared little at first but who would eventually dedicate the rest of her life to completing Sister Vincent's work. It was not long before Sister Vincent's pas-sionate advocacy of her mission in the Falls and her gentle persuasiveness of manner won Genevieve over. 'There came a point,' Genevieve confessed, 'when I just couldn't resist any longer.' Although they were separated by nearly forty years, their friendship remained strong and vital to them both until Sister Vincent's death in 1970.

Ellen Wallace, Sister Vincent, had been born in Dublin in 1885 and had been sent to the Falls straight from the seminary at Blackrock. In 1908, at the age of twenty-three and only a few weeks after her *prise d'habit*, she had been appointed principal of St. Vincent's primary school in Dunlewey Street, a post she held for forty-two years. After her retirement, she remained in the Falls as the superior of Clonard.

The story of St. Vincent's primary school is part of the story of the Falls. Although it was called a primary school, St. Vincent's had been opened in 1900 to provide part-time education for Catholic girls aged eleven to fourteen who worked in the linen mills. The girls were known as 'half-timers' because they worked a ten-hour day in the mills on Monday, Wednesday and Friday and were released to attend school on Tuesday and Thursday, the days at work and at school being reversed on alternate weeks. On Saturdays they always worked in the mill for six hours. The over-whelming majority of workers in the mills were women and juveniles under eighteen, about ten per cent of the workforce being girls under thirteen. Though the minimum age was set at twelve in 1901, this was widely ignored by the mill owners who needed cheap labour and by the families in the Falls who needed the money.

The task of educating the half-timers had been given to the Daughters of Charity in 1900 by the Bishop of Down and Connor whose diocese included West Belfast. He provided them with a house – Clonard – in the Falls and a school building in Dunlewey Street. Clonard had at one time been a mill owner's mansion in spacious grounds but when the sisters moved in it was as much part of the mean streets of West Belfast as the terraced houses and the mills.

During the nineteenth century, the growth of linen manufac-turing, ship-building and engineering had transformed Belfast from a market town of 20,000 inhabitants into an industrial city of 350,000. Over the same period, the Catholic population of Belfast rose from 4,000 to 100,000 as Catholic families from rural Ulster poured into the city to find jobs. The majority settled in the Falls where there were linen mills and Catholic churches to keep body and soul together. But the Catholic families soon discovered that the jobs in the mills were for women and children and that the men were lucky if they found work as navvies or as unskilled hands in the shipyards and the foundries, thus setting a pattern of male unemployment that persisted for generations in the Catholic community. Some of the fathers of the children Genevieve was teaching at St. Vincent's in the late 1950s were the third generation of men in the same family who had never had a job.

The mills, huge box-like structures of red brick with smokestacks and steep glass roofs to give light to the machine rooms, had been built to the west of the city to make use of the small rivers that ran down from the Black Mountain. For a hundred years the mills dominated the Falls and the lives of the people who lived there. When Genevieve arrived in 1956, most of the mills had closed down but the buildings remained potent symbols of the world of the mill workers and half-timers, underpinning the Catholic community's sense of itself as always having been exploited and treated as second class or worse. When the latest round of the Troubles started in 1969, twenty-year-old Gerry Adams watched the mill building in Northumberland Street go up in flames and knew why the petrol bombers had chosen that target. His grandmother, too, had been a half-timer.

At the turn of the century, the so-called 'linen slaves', the doffers and weavers, reelers and rovers, spinners and bandtiers who worked in the mills were lucky to reach the age of fifty despite legislation restricting working hours and improving safety. The former duffers and weavers Genevieve met as grandmothers sitting by the open grate were the ones who had survived into old age. The whole process, from the preparation of the flax fibre to the spinning and weaving, put the workers' health at risk, the chief hazard being the dust from the flax that was sucked into the lungs with every breath. In the preparation room, the very fine dust, called pouce by the women, was so dangerous that even the mill managers admitted to an official inquiry that working there was 'a sure death', it was only a matter of time.

The younger women and the girls who were half-timers usually worked as doffers in the carding process in which the tow or fibre

too short for making good quality yarn was prepared for spinning. The card, a diabolical machine in the form of a cylinder five
feet in diameter studded with iron pins and revolving at speed, was
used to comb out the fibres, and the doffer's job was to take the full
spindles from the machine. Exhausted by the long hours and overcome by the heat and humidity, the young women sometimes
fainted. If they became entangled in the carding machine as it was
revolving, the injuries were terrible and almost always fatal.

Though accidents were rare, bronchial and respiratory problems, and painful conditions such as onychia, an inflammation of
the toenails caused by standing barefoot all day in tepid and con-
taminated water, were commonplace. The heat and the humidity
were needed to prevent the linen thread breaking and the spray
from the spindles ensured that clothes were constantly wet. The
women worked in bare feet because it made sense. Even in the
rooms that were not inches deep in water, shoes and stockings
would soon have rotted.

The doffer's job was described in a medical officer's report as
the 'dirtiest, most disagreeable as well as the most unwholesome
and most dangerous of all the departments connected with spinning of flax'. If you were a doffer, you were the bottom of the
heap, hence the need to keep your job a secret from any man you
hoped to marry:

> Oh, my name is Rosie Mullan
> I'm a doffer at the mill
> My boyfriend doesn't know it
> And I hope he never will.
> For if he gets to know it
> He would drop me on the spot
> And that would never do
> Because I love him a hell of a lot.

The name 'doffer' eventually became synonymous with the
courage and suffering of all the women and girls who worked in
the mills. The brutal working conditions bred a roughness that
made people wary of crossing the doffers' path and that seemed to

some residents of the Falls who observed the behaviour of Sister
Genevieve's pupils to have been passed on to future generations.
The mill girls may have gone to work 'barefooted, hungry and
with death in their faces' but they returned in a defiant mood,
making long lines across the street with arms linked, singing songs
and shouting abuse at passers-by.

The doffers who were under fourteen, the school leaving age,
attended St. Vincent's as half-timers. They lost their meagre wages
but their parents hoped that an elementary education might
enable them to escape from the mills altogether. For the mothers
there was no escape even when they were pregnant. They worked
until the very verge of confinement because they needed the
money and went back to work immediately after the baby was
born. Old women, acting as 'baby farmers', looked after babies
during the long working day, feeding them tea and whiskey and a
soothing syrup in which the principal ingredient was opium.

When she came to the Falls, Sister Vincent marvelled at the
resilience of the half-timers and at their eagerness to learn but she
could see how poverty and long hours in the mills were taking
their toll. Many of the girls were small and badly developed and
nearly all looked prematurely old with bloodless features and tired
eyes. 'In this part of Ireland,' wrote James Connolly who cam-
paigned for better conditions in the mills, 'the child is old before
it knows what it is to be young.' The half-timers were nevertheless
Sister Vincent's most loyal pupils, supporting the school long after
they had left whether or not the days in the classroom had helped
them avoid a life in the mills.

There is no record of how successful Sister Vincent was in
diverting the half-timers to less hazardous jobs. She had four classrooms for five hundred pupils, roughly half of whom were
attending the school on the same days, so she arranged a system of
boxing and coxing, using the rooms, the corridors and the school
yard, and even so had classes that were seldom less than fifty.
There were six subjects on the timetable. English, arithmetic,
geography, handiwork, music and cookery. In 1912, she added
Irish language. She could not give the half-timers any formal qualification and some of the girls when they left at fourteen went back

to work full-time in the mills as their mothers and grandmothers had done, and their schooldays became just a memory of what might have been.

Sister Vincent was not discouraged. When the system of half-timers was phased out in the early 1920s, she turned St. Vincent's into an 'all-age' primary school for girls aged five to fourteen and pursued the same policy of giving the girls the good basic education they would need to find a job outside the mills. This was the school that Genevieve joined in 1956 and that was the inspiration for her work at St. Louise's. When she was asked in a Radio Ulster interview in 1991, 'When you became head of St. Louise's what was your principal objective?' Genevieve replied simply, 'To carry on the tradition set by St. Vincent's.' The heart of that tradition was Sister Vincent's dream of a better life for the girls of the Falls; its practical expression was Sister Vincent herself. She made her all-age school the most sought-after in the area. There were eleven all-age schools in St. Peter's parish which covered the Falls – an indication of the over-crowding – but St. Vincent's was the one that parents wanted for their daughters.

Sister Vincent's methods were pragmatic. She was not averse to using the class distinction that existed even in the Falls (and in the mills where everyone looked down on the doffers). She went out of her way to attract the daughters of 'the grandees', as she called them, shopkeepers and tradesmen, who considered themselves a cut above the navvies and mill workers and who she thought would have higher expectations of their daughters' schooling. When the school became known on the Road as 'the Eton of the North', it was only partly in mockery of Sister Vincent's recruiting strategy. There was also a grudging admiration for her success in using the grandees to lift the school's reputation.

Sister Vincent was similarly down to earth in her attitude to relations between home and school. She was ahead of her time in recognising that without knowing the home and the family it is almost impossible to understand the child but the close relationship she built with the homes of her pupils was not in response to a theory, it was a natural extension of the sisters' work. The

Daughters of Charity had been invited to the Falls 'to visit the poor in their homes' as well as to educate the half-timers, so that the sisters were welcome in the homes of the schoolchildren in a way that lay teachers and members of other religious orders would not have been. For the Vincentian sisters there was no discontinuity between work in the school and work in the parish, it was the same mission. The sisters not only visited the homes, bringing clothes for the younger children and modest financial help for families on the breadline; they also arranged evening classes for the adults returning from the mills and the factories, and on Sunday mornings went from house to house knocking on doors to wake the families up in time for mass.

Sister Vincent did not have to exhort parents to attend meetings and to support the school, they did so willingly as part of the life of the community and because they were hungry for education on their daughter's behalf. The daughters found Sister Vincent's all-pervading influence had its drawbacks. Pupils do not necessarily share the educator's enthusiasm for a close relationship between home and school – it makes it more difficult to play one off against the other. Playing truant or 'mitching', for example, was hardly worthwhile; if a girl was absent, a sister would be round before mid-morning break to know the reason why.

Useful though the close relationship was, Sister Vincent's discipline did not depend on it. The source of her authority was her total commitment to the pupils' interests. Even the hard girls recognised that she cared for them and for their future and in the long run they were grateful. When she knew she was dying, Sister Vincent asked one of these girls to sit with her, 'a real baddie who had caused all sorts of trouble,' according to Genevieve who told the story. The former pupil and her school principal talked at length about old times during the night before Sister Vincent died.

As a school principal, Sister Vincent probably had more trouble with the priests than with the pupils. St. Vincent's was a church school with a priest as manager holding the purse strings, an arrangement that worked tolerably well in other church schools but was almost always a source of conflict in schools run by the

Daughters of Charity. The hard training and discipline in this company crushed the individuality of some sisters but it also produced some exceptionally strong-minded women who refused to be dictated to by men who knew little or nothing about education. If Sister Vincent's dealings with the clergy were less bruising than Genevieve's it was only because her style was less confrontational than that of her protégée. The tension between the Vincentian sisters who ran the schools and the clergy who owned them and who did not always share the sisters' commitment to the education of the poor, would continue until the Catholic hierarchy decided to replace the single clerical manager with a school committee or governing body on which lay Catholics had an increasingly powerful voice.

As a sister committed to the religious life, Sister Vincent was apolitical. She was prepared to take on the clergy but not to allow the school to be drawn into secular politics. Yet living and working in the Falls, a Catholic ghetto in a Protestant city, a predominantly Irish culture in a fiercely loyal British province, her criticisms of the school system or her decisions on the curriculum had political overtones whether she intended it or not. When she was appointed principal of St. Vincent's in 1908, the whole of the island of Ireland was part of the United Kingdom but long before she retired, Ireland had been partitioned. The birth of Northern Ireland in 1921 had been accompanied by widespread communal violence in which the Catholics of Belfast suffered worst in the number of people killed, driven out of their jobs and forced to seek safety in the Falls. Northern Catholics who had been part of a large majority in Ireland became a religious minority in what they were convinced after the violence of partition was an alien state. Discrimination at the hands of the Protestant majority, particularly in employment, confirmed their sense of not belonging. In this context, keeping a school in the Falls detached from politics was never going to be easy.

Sister Vincent's response to discrimination was to give the Catholic girls the best possible education, including an education in their own heritage. But partition had made the teaching of Irish a controversial political issue. Northern Protestants demanded that the teaching of the Irish language should be banned because its only purpose was 'to ferment antagonism to Great Britain', while the Catholic Gaelic League argued for its retention as 'a political weapon of the first importance against English encroachment'. Sister Vincent refused to see the issue in these terms. Encouraging her pupils to be proud of their Irish heritage, to learn the language and to take part in Irish ceilis or Irish competitions, was not a political statement; but, as Genevieve would later discover during the Troubles, disclaiming a political motive did not protect the sisters from criticism. In the Falls, political neutrality was interpreted as taking sides.

'The sisters certainly pushed us,' wrote a former St. Vincent's girl, 'and every pupil was motivated however great or small her ability. In a working class area this was important. All my class got jobs leaving St. Vincent's.' The best possible education was one that led to employment. St. Vincent's could not measure its success in exams passed or university places gained; its yardstick was the proportion of leavers who got jobs straight from school and preferably outside the linen industry. Typing classes after school helped many of them find clerical work in Catholic offices – others were employed behind the counter of shops in the Falls. A few more able girls were persuaded by Sister Vincent to stay at school until eighteen; by calling them 'monitresses' and giving them duties as teaching assistants, she allowed them to prepare for entry to the Catholic teacher training college.

Although St. Vincent's was owned by the Church it was inspected by the Ministry of Education in Belfast. Inspectors' reports are usually models of restraint and those on St. Vincent's are no exception but the admiration for Sister Vincent's leadership is unmistakable. The inspector's report in 1946 reads: 'Under Sister Vincent's skilful organisation and effective personal supervision commendable results have crowned the work done in this large school over a long period of years . . . the excellent moral tone of the school as a whole bears added tribute to her zeal and efficiency in the discharge of her duties.'

Sister Vincent's achievement in her long tenure of office was to enable the girls from some of the poorest and the most discriminated against families in Northern Ireland to break with the world of the doffers and weavers and to aspire to a job outside the mills, however modest. But she was not satisfied with that. This achievement was the foundation for a greater one. She believed that one day, if not in this generation, then in the next one or the one after that, the girls from the Falls would be the doctors and lawyers, academics and business leaders of Belfast. Her belief, as she explained to Genevieve, was grounded in the extraordinary resilience and willpower of the women of West Belfast. If these women could work long hours in the mills, run a home, bring up a large family and cope with a husband who was unemployed and probably resented not being the breadwinner, there was no limit to what they might achieve if they were given a good education and a chance to compete on equal terms for university entrance and for jobs. Her vision was feminist as well as Vincentian.

Discussion of the struggle for women's rights has tended to ignore or disparage the contribution of those women who chose the religious life. Radical feminists argue that the nuns and sisters, by accepting a subordinate role chosen for them by men, were helping to sustain a patriarchal society; the religious order was just as much of a gilded cage as the ideal of motherhood. But there is an alternative feminist view that however limited and male-serving the role of the nuns and sisters, it provided an outlet and a 'sisterly support system' for women who did not need men and whose abilities might have atrophied in marriage.

Both Sister Vincent and Sister Genevieve could be described as feminists. Their starting point was the teaching of Vincent de Paul but in the context of the Falls, serving the poor and fighting injustice easily translated into equal rights for women and equal opportunities for girls. In relation to education in particular, they shared the fundamental feminist conviction that 'difference of sex is no ground for differential treatment', and their contribution to the fair treatment of the women of West Belfast in education and in jobs was enormous.

Sister Vincent retired as principal of St. Vincent's primary school in 1950 and became superior of Clonard shortly before Genevieve arrived in 1956. It would be difficult to exaggerate the importance of Sister Vincent's friendship and example to Genevieve's career. Genevieve herself acknowledged this when she said that it was Sister Vincent who had persuaded her to remain in Belfast and who had been 'a very strong influence in my life'. When St. Vincent's school closed in 1989, Genevieve paid a tribute to Sister Vincent's memory in the *Irish News*. 'Brave, intrepid, intelligent, sensitive,' she wrote, 'hers was a spirit that never accepted physical or mental limitations. A member of the community of the Daughters of Charity of St. Vincent de Paul, she was steeped in the heroic and unselfish love of her Founder.'

Sister Vincent was a true disciple of Vincent de Paul, as Genevieve wished to be. At some point she recognised in Genevieve the sister who was most likely to carry on her work but there was no immediate prospect of Genevieve being in a position to do so. It was the building of a secondary school for the girls of the Falls that gave Genevieve her chance.

1958–1969

3

'It could not have had a worse start.
Staff were chosen by the chairman
at random'

Three years before Sister Vincent retired, the Northern Ireland Education Act of 1947 paved the way for a radical overhaul of schooling in the province. The full impact of its reforms was not felt for ten years however, because in the aftermath of war there was no money for the new school buildings that would be required. In Catholic areas, where part of the cost would have to be borne by the parishes, the progress of reform was even slower. When Genevieve arrived in the Falls, there was talk of building a new school so that Catholic children could benefit from the reforms, but the hierarchy of the Church seemed to be in no hurry to start.

The main provisions of the Act raised the school leaving age from fourteen to fifteen and established secondary schools for pupils aged eleven to fifteen as a separate tier of education above the primary schools. In the Falls this would mean that the all-age primary schools such as St. Vincent's would become schools for five- to eleven-year-olds and a new school would have to be built for the older girls from all the primary schools in the area. The Church put off building the new school as long as it could, but when the government decided that the new school leaving age would come into force on 1 April 1957, the Church could delay no longer.

The prospect of separate secondary schools for the older pupils was viewed with mixed feelings by the Vincentian sisters working in the Falls. If the schools were a genuine attempt to raise expectations and increase opportunity, they would help to realise Sister Vincent's dream, but if the schools were merely a gesture towards equal opportunity and were specifically designed to re-enforce modest expectations, they would be putting a ceiling on the academic qualifications and jobs to which the secondary school pupils could aspire. It all depended on whether the new secondary schools were going to have the same standing in the community and in the eyes of government as the grammar schools.

In Northern Ireland the grammar school was the gateway to the middle class. Sister Vincent may have dreamed of girls from the Falls becoming doctors and lawyers but the reality was that unless they went to a grammar school they did not have a hope of entering the professions, and the grammar schools before 1947 were restricted to those whose parents could pay the fees and those who could win one of the very few city scholarships. Many people in Northern Ireland, including Sister Vincent, hoped that the post-war reform of education would give every child the same opportunity to rise in the world but the 1947 Act, while theoretically treating all children as equal, in practice treated some children as more equal than others. It abolished grammar school fees and threw open the gateway to the middle class to all boys and girls who could qualify for entry. One of the first Catholic boys to do so was John Hulme who took the Qualifying Examination in the first year. But as the new arrangement for entry to grammar school settled down in the late forties and early fifties, it became clear that opening the gateway for some children meant closing it in the face of others. For the children who did not qualify for entry – between sixty and seventy per cent of the year group – the new secondary schools far from offering a chance to rise in the world, would ensure they remained where they were. The new secondary schools did not have the same standing as the grammar schools, least of all in the eyes of the pupils who attended them. They were seen as second-class schools for second-class pupils who were destined for second-class jobs.

The focus of discontent was the Qualifying Examination. How could an examination taken at eleven tell what jobs boys and girls would be suited for as adults? Even the official history of the Belfast Education Authority admits that 'it was, in essence, little different from the grading of cattle or pigs but with fewer dependable criteria'. The examination consisted of three papers in English language, English composition and arithmetic. The candidates also took an intelligence test but this did not count towards the result. The heavy emphasis on English persuaded some critics that the examination favoured children from literate, middle-class homes but the most consistent criticism was that no examination, however carefully constructed, could accurately predict a child's potential at such a young age.

In Northern Ireland, as elsewhere in the United Kingdom where a similar controversy focused on the so-called 11+ exam, critics of the separation of children at eleven argued that all children should attend the same secondary school which would be 'comprehensive' because it would provide courses for the whole range of ability. In 1953, the Director of Education in Belfast suggested that combining the grammar schools and secondary schools in new comprehensive schools was the best way to overcome the limitation of the Qualifying Examination but the Ministry of Education in Northern Ireland would have none of it. The grammar school lobby was too strong. In England many of the influential positions in society were occupied by the former pupils of the expensive, elite public schools who had no interest in defending the grammar schools, but in Northern Ireland there was no public school tradition and it was the former pupils of the grammar schools who held the power in both the Catholic and the Protestant communities. Any attempt to abolish the Qualifying Examination and the grammar schools in Northern Ireland was doomed to failure.

The Vincentian sisters working in the Falls were among the most implacable and effective opponents of the grammar school lobby and of the separation of children at eleven. In this, the sisters were out of step with the hierarchy of their own church. The Church supported the grammar schools as the key to the advancement of

Roman Catholics in Northern Ireland; in an unequal society, a grammar school education enabled Catholics to challenge discrimination in jobs and in the universities. It was the grammar schools, too, that supplied the Church with its priests, so much so that the boys' grammar school was popularly known as 'the diocesan seminary'. The hierarchy of the Church was not uncomfortable with the hierarchy of schools; the grammar schools would provide the clerical and lay leaders, 'the cream of Catholic society', while the secondary schools would provide an appropriate education for the rank and file.

The Daughters of Charity were coming from a different direction. Vincent de Paul had ruled that in schools run by the sisters the children of well-to-do families could be admitted but only on the condition 'that the poor girls were given preference over the rich and that the latter not look down on the poor'. To the twentieth-century sisters in Belfast, the grammar schools with their middle-class ethos, preferential treatment in terms of resources and snobbish disdain for the secondary schools could hardly have been less in harmony with Vincent de Paul's teaching. The separation of children at eleven into sheep and goats, those deemed worthy of an academic education and those whose apparent lack of intelligence fitted them only for humdrum or labouring jobs, ran counter to everything Sister Vincent had been trying to achieve: it seemed to give official endorsement to an attitude of mind that had condemned the children of the poor to a life in the mills. For fifty years the sisters based at Clonard had worked to give the girls from the Falls the same opportunities as more privileged children but now, instead of equal opportunity, the girls were being offered a secondary education that would result in their opportunities being strictly limited. In theory, a girl from the Falls could qualify for entry to grammar school but in practice very few did; St. Dominic's in the Lower Falls was the only Catholic girls' grammar school and had to cater for girls from all the Catholic districts of the city.

For the sisters, a few grammar school qualifiers only served to emphasise the rejection of the rest. They did not discourage girls from trying to qualify for St. Dominic's, but they refused to accept

that those left behind should have to settle for modest expectations
as far as academic qualifications and jobs were concerned. Their
Vincentian ideals, their long experience in the Falls and their faith
in the potential of the girls who were the granddaughters of the
doffers and weavers, inevitably set them against the dominant educational philosophy of the day in Northern Ireland. Their chance
to prove that they were right came when they were asked to take
charge of the new secondary school in the Falls.

None of the sisters at Clonard, not even Sister Vincent, was
more eager to take up this challenge than Genevieve. When the
new school opened in January 1958, she was thirty-four and had
been in Belfast for exactly two years, during which time Sister
Vincent had convinced her that her mission was to work with the
children of the poor families in the Falls. The fact that the
Catholic hierarchy did not appear to be aware of the educational
needs of these children gave her mission a sharper focus. Over the
next thirty years, Genevieve's unwavering opposition to the separation of children at eleven and to all that implied about privilege
for the few and rejection of the majority had deeper roots in her
background and character. Her Tullamore friend, Bridie Byrne,
makes an interesting observation about Genevieve's schoolgirl
attitudes: 'Mary had no time for very studious girls and she
abhorred snobbery.' It could have been the description of someone
who was born to be out of sympathy with Northern Ireland's
grammar schools. The treatment of the illegitimate children in the
Navan Road during her postulancy and the teaching of Sister
Philomena at Blackrock helped to transform schoolgirl attitudes
into a social conscience. By the time she left the seminary in 1943,
Genevieve was, 'fanatically dedicated to the equality of all human
beings', and wished to devote her religious life to serving the poor
and fighting injustice. Her disappointments as a young sister must
have spurred her ambition but what made her so single-minded
as a school principal was this opportunity to make sense of her
vocation.

Her critics, particularly among the clergy, may have questioned
whether the link between Vincent de Paul's teaching and opposition to the grammar school system was as obvious as Genevieve

seemed to think, but for Genevieve it could not have been clearer. The girls of the Falls were the victims of injustice because they were poor; a disciple of Vincent de Paul was bound to champion their cause.

If Genevieve and the other sisters needed an additional incentive to defy the grammar school lobby and make a success of the new secondary school, it was provided by the Catholic clergy who treated the sisters in an off-hand manner at every stage of the school's development. Although the Bishop of Down and Connor invited the Daughters of Charity to run the school, the sisters were not consulted about the design or layout of the building or about the appointment of the teaching staff. Sister Vincent, as superior in the Falls, was allowed to name the school and to recommend which sisters should fill the posts of principal and vice-principal, but every other aspect of the planning, equipping and staffing of the school was placed in the hands of the manager, a priest who was the administrator of St. Peter's Cathedral in the Lower Falls.

Sister Vincent named the school after Louise de Marillac. It would always be known as St. Louise's, its official titles – St. Louise's Girls' Secondary Intermediate School and St. Louise's Comprehensive College – being too much of a bureaucratic mouthful for popular use. The first principal of St. Louise's would be Sister Ita Polley, the principal of St. Vincent's, with Genevieve as vice-principal. To Sister Vincent, this must have seemed to be the right way round. Sister Ita was experienced; Genevieve was ten years younger, eager to take up the challenge of the new school and the only sister who had taught in a secondary school, albeit as an untrained teacher at St. Joseph's Technical High School in Manchester for only one year.

The two sisters – Ita and Genevieve – turned out to be a 'dream team' and they remained close friends for forty years. Sister Ita had been teaching at St. Vincent's since 1939 and had succeeded Sister Vincent as principal in 1950. A northerner from the village of Dundrum in County Down, she was in many ways the perfect foil for her younger, more volatile colleague. 'They were like a married couple who complemented one another,' a former pupil thought.

The comparisons were not always flattering to Genevieve. When the school celebrated its silver jubilee in 1983, an anonymous contributor to the magazine wrote that Sister Ita was 'without any semblance of self-will or any degree of self-seeking'. 'Ask any present pupil,' the unknown writer continued, 'or any past pupil of St. Louise's to name the person they think best represents the Vincentian qualities of humility and willingness to serve the need of others, and it is more than likely they will nominate Sister Ita.'

Sister Ita *was* self-effacing, but she was strong in a quiet, unassertive way. She was the ideal second-in-command and to a large degree that was the role she played even when she was principal, allowing Genevieve to take the lead in public, taking assemblies and imposing discipline, while she wrestled with the detail and looked after the girls who were unsure of themselves or unhappy or just too mischievous for their own good. There was an element of the tough cop and gentle cop routine in their handling of those who broke the rules and it was the tough cop that most girls remembered. Some of the pupils who were at the school in the early years are surprised to be told that Sister Ita was ever the principal; they thought it had been Genevieve all along.

The Church had acquired a six-acre site at the top of the Falls Road for the new school. Known locally as the Plots, the site was close to the Catholic Milltown cemetery where the Republican Movement's dead were buried and was across the road from the Protestant city cemetery. To the east, the site sloped down to the Bog Meadows, a breeding ground for frogs and between the wars, a favourite hideaway for boys playing truant, like the famous 'mitcher' Flash McBride who used the Bog Meadows to evade the school attendance officer for seven weeks. When St. Louise's opened, the mitchers had gone elsewhere but the frogs soon found their way up the hill to the school buildings and down the backs of the unpopular girls.

The cost of the building explains the Church's reluctance to begin this project and its determination to keep control of every detail in its own hands. The Northern Ireland government would pay the teachers' salaries but would not pay the full capital cost of the buildings and equipment. This was not discrimination against

Catholics but the price the Catholic hierarchy had been prepared to pay at partition to keep Catholic schools independent of local control. The proportion of the capital cost the Church had to find varied over the years; at the time of the building of St. Louise's it was thirty-five per cent. The total cost of building and equipping the new school was £230,000 (the equivalent of £3.2 million today) and of this the people of St. Peter's parish would have to raise £83,000, an immense sum for one of the poorest neighbourhoods in Northern Ireland.

Anxiety about the cost may help to justify the manager's penny-pinching approach – it was his parish that was paying the bills – but it does not explain why he behaved in a way that not only ignored the sisters but guaranteed that the opening of the school would be chaotic. The problem was as much with the system as with the man. Keeping Catholic schools free from local control meant the Church had to appoint a priest to act as the school's chairman or manager (both titles were used). These were the priests with whom Sister Vincent had had so much difficulty. They held the purse strings and knew nothing about education. The latter would not have mattered so much if they had not insisted on taking decisions that should have been taken by the school principal.

The Catholic church in Northern Ireland now recognises that some of these old-style school managers were a disaster because 'they didn't have a baldy about education' yet had executive powers that undermined the authority of the principal. Unfortunately for Ita and Genevieve, the manager of St. Louise's was one of the worst. He did not bother to check exactly how many eleven- to fifteen-year-old girls the school would need to accommodate; it was built for 740 but 850 turned up on the first day. He failed to order most of the furniture and equipment in time for the school's opening. He appointed all but one of the teaching staff without consulting Ita and Genevieve and without interviewing the applicants. He just advertised for teachers in the Belfast newspapers – 'All subjects needed' – and appointed the first thirty women whose applications looked satisfactory, ten of whom were qualified to teach domestic science. Knowing nothing about girls' education, he probably thought that domestic science was the most important subject. It was also the one department whose equipment arrived on time because the subject inspector, Moira McMorrine, had gone to see the manager at the parochial house and refused to leave until the order and delivery date were confirmed.

When the Bishop of Down and Connor opened the school he told the congregation at High Mass that the manager was to be congratulated on his handling of the project. The Bishop, clearly out of touch with what had been happening, assured the parents and pupils present that the manager 'in collaboration with the principal, exercised the greatest care in selecting the staff'. It was the opposite of the truth.

Genevieve was scathing about the manager's performance which, together with the Bishop's bland inaccuracies, confirmed her suspicion that the education of the girls of the Falls was a very low priority for the male, grammar school-educated clergy. In her own written account of the opening of the school she calls the manager 'the chairman':

> There was no preparation made for the opening as the chairman had not a clue about secondary education. It could not have had a worse start. Staff were chosen by the chairman at random and the principal, Sister Ita, heard a week previous to the opening that it was to take place. There were no desks or chairs in the classrooms . . . so the intake of 850 girls (the school was built for 740) came about in the most appalling manner.

Sister Ita, though less impatient than Genevieve with the failings of the clergy and less blunt in her criticism of individuals, still frowns at the thought of the first manager at St. Louise's forty years after the school opened. 'He was one desperate man,' she says.

By Christmas 1957, Ita and Genevieve had met all the staff and the building on the Plots was almost ready for occupation but no date for the opening of the school had been set. Two decisions had been taken about school discipline. Ita insisted that the school

should at least try to control the girls without using corporal punishment; Genevieve insisted that there must be a school uniform.

Corporal punishment was what the girls coming to St. Louise's
were accustomed to; it was used in Catholic schools throughout
Ireland. The principal was in charge of 'the slapper', a flat ruler
two inches wide and two feet long, and administered the punishment which was usually two strokes on the left hand and two on
the right. The experiment of doing without corporal punishment
at St. Louise's was not a success and in the early years the slapper
was sometimes used. But on the question of a school uniform,
Genevieve refused to compromise. The girls at the grammar
school wore uniform, the girls at St. Louise's would have a uniform too. 'One day you will be proud of this uniform,' she told the
girls – and so they would be – but at the beginning it was a battle
to get 800 girls, many of whose parents could not afford all the
items Genevieve prescribed, to look as though they belonged to
the same school.

The only draper on the Falls Road who could handle an order
of this size was Xavier Boyle whose shop was just below Dunlewey
Street, opposite where Sinn Fein's office and the large gable wall
with a mural of Bobby Sands now stand. Genevieve told Xavier
Boyle she wanted a brown and cream uniform, a brown skirt and
a cream blouse, with all the trappings – a brown cardigan, brown
socks and shoes, brown beret and gloves, a brown dexter for the
winter months and a brown blazer with a school crest for those
who could afford it.

The cost of the uniform still rankles and at the time lost
Genevieve the goodwill of some parents. 'We were robbed off the
face of the earth,' a former pupil complained. For the families
who could afford nothing, Sister Vincent asked Xavier Boyle to
send her the bill. Other families paid by instalments or put
together something that was as like the official uniform as possible.
Rose Farrelly was one of nine children living in a small house in
Slate Street, one of the poorest in the Lower Falls. The children
never had new clothes only second-hand from 'Robinson Cleavers'
as the local market was known after the posh shop in the city
centre. 'How I envied the girls in the lovely brown and cream

uniform,' Rose remembers, 'I wore a cream dress with little brown buttons and a brown cardigan, this was the best Mum could do and I was proud of that. In assemblies, Sister Genevieve always plugged the necessity of being in full school uniform and paraded the girls whose parents could obviously afford it. This hurt.'

There were long queues outside Xavier Boyle's drapery store every day of the week before the school opened. Late on the Friday afternoon things got out of hand and Xavier Boyle telephoned Sister Vincent: 'For God's sake send a couple of sisters.' As Genevieve and another sister approached through the fading winter daylight, many of the girls had their first sight of the tall sister whose beautiful but stern features, rattling rosary and high white headdress bobbing up and down they would soon come to respect and fear. The queue fell silent. The folk memory of the sisters as figures of authority in the Falls was still strong and, as most of the girls had been taught by lay staff at their primary schools, they did not know what to expect of this 'butterfly nun' who bore down on them like an avenging angel. Even the bold girls decided to play safe.

On the Saturday evening, the manager telephoned Clonard to tell Ita and Genevieve that the school would open on Monday and to explain what arrangements he had made for the opening ceremony. Ita had known Monday would be the day as the girls had been told to report to their primary schools that morning wearing their St. Louise's uniforms, but she had been told nothing about the programme. The girls, led by their teachers, were to walk in twos in a crocodile up the Falls Road from their primary schools to St. John's Church where the Bishop of Down and Connor would preside at High Mass before the clergy and the congregation moved on to inspect the new school. There would be a lunch in the domestic science suite for the visiting dignitaries to which, the manager pointed out, Ita and Genevieve were not invited.

Monday 8 January 1958 was mild for the time of year but not warm enough to thaw the ice in the gutters. A strong wind blew across the Falls from the north-west as each brown column left its primary school – St. Peter's, St. Joseph's, St. Brendan's, St.

Comgall's, eleven in all – and turned up the easy slope of the Falls Road towards the new school. For the farthest away it was a walk of just over a mile. Ita and Genevieve had been told to wait until the other schools had passed before leading the St. Vincent's girls out of Dunlewey Street.

It may not have had the poise and precise timing of a royal wedding but it must have been a moving sight as each school joined the procession until there were eight hundred girls on the move past the familiar Falls landmarks including the mill buildings, empty now but full of ghosts. 'Is it a nun's funeral?' a bystander asked but the significance of the occasion was not lost on the families who had come to see their girls go by.

The girls filed into St. John's Church in reasonably good order, glad of a chance to sit down but almost at once they had to stand up again when the Bishop's procession entered: two parish priests in cassock and surplice, two deacons with a colourful dalmatic over their alb, holding up the Bishop's cope at the elbow, and Dr Mageean, Bishop of Down and Connor, splendid in his cope and mitre, walking slowly towards the east end of the church measuring the aisle with each movement of his crozier.

'You are getting a beautiful building,' his Lordship told the girls, 'and it will depend on you, on your teachers, on the parents and priests, whether you make that beautiful building a fine school.' They should make the best use of the facilities provided, which had left the parish of St. Peter's with a large debt, so that they could equip themselves 'to meet the battle ahead in this world' and 'become later citizens of the Kingdom of Heaven'.

The semblance of order that the teachers had been able to maintain on the long march from the Lower Falls and that had continued during the service thanks to the solemnity of the occasion, disintegrated rapidly as the girls poured out of the church and down St. James's Street to the school's main entrance. The teachers could only bark like sheepdogs at the edges, trying to steer the flow into the assembly hall. The clergy and the guests followed at a more dignified pace. The plan was for the Bishop to give a Solemn Benediction of the Blessed Sacrament at a specially erected altar in the assembly hall; but as the official party approached the building it was clear from the noise that inside it was bedlam.

Genevieve and some of the more experienced teachers were trying to impose some order on the eight hundred girls who were rushing about like animals released into a new compound. A senior teacher remembers shouting at the top of her voice, 'Stand still! Stop running about' but 'they looked at me as though I had six heads and rushed on again'. It did not help to keep anarchy at bay that the wooden floor was still sticky having been given a final coat of varnish the previous evening so that there were shrieks of laughter as some girls instead of running about pretended they were stuck to the spot.

Genevieve eventually managed to clear a space by the doors at the back of the hall and the official party entered, the Bishop now preceded by a priest holding the censer and by two choir boys as acolytes carrying candles whose appearance drew hissed comments from the depths of the crush. The wafts of incense seemed to have a temporary calming affect and the Bishop, once he had made his way to the altar on the stage, had the sense to keep the Benediction as brief as possible.

When they were safely out of the hall, the guests were guided by the manager to the domestic science suite where they admired the new equipment and enjoyed a good lunch. Meanwhile Ita and Genevieve, having told the girls which form rooms to go to the following morning and then sent them home for the rest of the day, tried to work out how they would accommodate the hundred extra girls and what the staff could teach when there were no desks or chairs or text books. There was a piano and a film projector in the assembly hall so that it should be possible to occupy some of the girls in large groups until the furniture and text books arrived but as they were discussing this they saw a van draw up outside the school. The manager had only hired the piano for the day.

The following morning, Geraldine Murray, straight from college with no teaching experience, asked Ita what she should do with thirty-five twelve-year-olds who had only a jotter and a pencil each. 'Write a big word on the blackboard,' replied Ita calmly, 'and let them make wee words from it.' The first big word that came into Geraldine's head was 'interdenominational'. She wrote it on the blackboard and explained the task. The girls sat cross-legged on the floor, took up their pencils and jotters, and began their secondary education.

4

'I was petrified of this tall, elegant nun in the butterfly headdress'

Genevieve did not become principal of St. Louise's until 1963 but long before then Ita had given her younger colleague responsibility for the day-to-day running of the school. So when Ita fell ill in 1962, Genevieve stepped easily into the role of acting principal. Unlike most headteachers, Genevieve never applied for the job and according to her childhood friend May McFadden, with whom she kept in touch throughout her career, she was nervous about the prospect of being asked to become principal on a permanent basis. But when it was clear that Ita would only be able to return in a supporting role, Sister Vincent recommended Genevieve for the post. Sister Vincent was Genevieve's superior, mentor and friend and had been instrumental in persuading Genevieve to stay in Belfast. If she wanted Genevieve to take over as principal of St. Louise's, Genevieve could not refuse. The accusation of personal ambition later levelled at Genevieve overlooked the fact that it was not self-seeking but the accident of Ita's illness and loyalty to Sister Vincent that propelled her into the top job.

Whether she was vice-principal, acting principal or principal, Genevieve's vision and forceful personality dictated the way the school was run and how it would be remembered by teachers and pupils alike. If she really was nervous about becoming principal that never showed. Helen O'Connor, one of the first intake, writing in 1998 in the fortieth anniversary issue of *The Marillac*, the school magazine, recalled the extraordinary degree to which Genevieve dominated the school from the start:

> Without doubt the single biggest impact on all the girls
> starting at the new school was the vice-principal, Sister
> Genevieve O'Farrell or as she was known 'Sister Gen'. She
> headed up a team of teachers, including Sister Ita, and
> many of these also left their mark on us. But Sister Gen
> dominated the scene. She was everywhere. She was the
> single biggest influence on us all. She annoyed and upset
> many, she chastised us, she frightened many, she
> introduced rules that we thought terrible. But she was a
> great inspiration.

Ambivalence about Genevieve is a theme that runs through the whole of her career. This is partly the normal reaction to a strong personality in a position of authority, particularly when the point of view is that of adolescence. To the young girls, Genevieve must sometimes have been a frightening figure. As she swept down the corridors so tall and regal in her white cornette, with her wooden rosary and her bunch of keys rattling as they swung from her waist, the girls ducked into the nearest classroom, but if there wasn't time, 'then you wished you were a coat of paint on the wall'. 'I was petrified of this tall, elegant nun in the butterfly headdress,' said one of the girls, 'you almost genuflected as she walked down the corridor'.

Genevieve's style was deliberate. Though some called it pride, it must have been a conscious decision to project an image of unassailable authority. The last thing she could afford to be in those early days was friendly and approachable to all. 'Chummy' was the damning nickname the boys at Eton College gave to a new headmaster who tried to be pally with everyone. Etonians are notoriously difficult to impress but it is unlikely that any Eton headmaster had faced such a difficult task as bringing the first intake at St. Louise's under control. Genevieve was aloof because she had to be. Though she had the loyal support of Ita and the other teachers, disciplining the eight hundred girls, some of whom had known little discipline in their primary schools, was her responsibility.

Genevieve had no experience of running a school but she commanded immediate respect not only among the girls from St. Vincent's who knew that she would stand no nonsense but also among the rougher girls from the Lower Falls who had never been taught by a 'nun' before. Her imposing appearance helped, but the true source of her authority was her strong will – the most striking aspect of her personality since childhood. She was her own woman even as a schoolgirl, making her own decisions, and refusing to be dissuaded from joining the Daughters of Charity. As a young sister her strong will or as some of her superiors would have diagnosed it, her wilfulness, was in conflict with the demands of obedience and might have brought her Vincentian career to an end. Now as the authority figure in the new school her determination that things should be ordered as she wished was the principal factor in building the school's reputation.

The key to understanding Genevieve's zeal for discipline is the recognition that, for her, strict discipline was not an end in itself but an essential first step towards giving the girls the chances that the selective schools system denied them. She insisted on discipline because without it her girls would have no future. Every aspect of the girls' lives was to be ordered by rule, even the side of the body on which you carried your books as you walked along the corridor, and just as in the seminary, permission was required for everything, written permission if you wanted to go to the toilet. The teaching staff did not escape the prescriptive style. When their staff room was next to her office, Genevieve put a notice on the board: 'No loud laughter in the staff room.'

Genevieve's emphasis on discipline also reflected what was at stake for her. For Sister Ita and the other teachers the first Catholic girls' secondary school was an exciting adventure but Genevieve was the only one for whom the fortunes of the school were so closely identified with her own mission in life. Only by making a success of serving the poor girls of the Falls could she make sense of her vocation. Whether this was Vincentian idealism or personal ambition or both, it provided a powerful motivation that at times made her impatient and intolerant with anyone who stood in her way or did not share her vision of what the school was aiming to achieve.

While Genevieve's strong will had been evident from child-hood, her volatile temperament seems to have been hidden from her school friends. To May McFadden and Bridie Byrne, Genevieve was the calm, trusted centre of their circle. Those who met her or taught alongside her when she was a young sister make no mention of her being quick-tempered or unpredictable but the references to her being 'pretty wild in the community' at least suggest the possibility that her emotions were closer to the surface than some of her friends and colleagues realised. When she was under pressure at St. Louise's her volatile temperament some-times proved difficult to control. Though she must have feigned anger on many occasions, there were other occasions when she was clearly emotional.

Headmasters and headmistresses who believe passionately in their mission are particularly prone to outbursts of anger when they encounter a pupil who appears to be indifferent or perverse. Thomas Arnold, the paragon of Victorian headmasters, was so obsessed with stamping out untruthfulness among the boys at Rugby that he inflicted eighteen strokes in a fit of temper on a boy he wrongly accused of lying. Genevieve's occasional loss of con-trol, which took the form of angry words but never angry blows, was restrained by comparison. She was neither cruel nor vindictive but there were times when she seems to have forgotten Vincent de Paul's warning that the poor would not always be grateful for the help they were given. Even more than other headteachers she was impatient with pupils who could not be bothered. Girls who were not interested in the opportunity they were being offered or who thought they could get on perfectly well without her help struck at the very heart of her vocation.

It is not unknown for headteachers to clash with individual pupils though being above the fray they usually manage to avoid personal antagonisms. But Genevieve was not always above the fray, certainly not in the early years; both before and after she was appointed principal, she took so much on herself that some clashes of will were inevitable. Girls who refused to fit in to her vision of what St. Louise's was all about or who found themselves over-whelmed by her dominant personality left the school of their own accord. As one former head girl put it, 'with Genevieve, there was no room for an alternative vision'.

If most girls found Genevieve frightening when they were new to the school, the older girls also knew it was sometimes wise to keep out of her way. 'I had always been petrified of Bonaventure,' says the sixteen-year-old heroine of Mary Costello's autobio-graphical novel *Titanic Town, memoirs of a Belfast Girlhood*. Mary Costello joined St. Louise's in 1966 and her fictional portrait of Genevieve as Sister Bonaventure would have rung true to most of Genevieve's pupils:

> Sister Bonaventure was the head nun at St. Catherine's; stern, courageous, intelligent; and, for a nun, unconventional, an odd-bod. She was also the only nun with sex appeal I'd ever met. She was tall and well-made, with a handsome face, high cheekbones and a fine mouth. But she was as hard as yesterday's baps . . . She had me terrified. I was accused of being her pet, but I dreaded her more than most of my classmates. My nerve-endings would contract at the sound of her resonant, Free State voice in the corridors. I would try to make myself scarce.

The real Genevieve knew she must have appeared hard to the girls; the job she had to do could not be done any other way. If a famous public school lapses into anarchy from time to time it makes little difference to its pupils' chances of making their way in the world, but for the Catholic girls from the Falls the school's reputation in the city would be critical. If prospective employers heard that the behaviour of St. Louise's girls compared un-favourably with that of the girls from St. Dominic's, the Catholic girls' grammar school, then stitching shirts or hankies would be the best job the St. Louise's girls could aspire to.

A reputation for good behaviour at St. Louise's must have seemed an impossible dream to those teachers who were encountering the children from the Falls for the first time. Even Genevieve was shocked by the attitude of some of the girls whose behaviour she described as 'undisciplined and extremely wild'. She realised that St. Vincent's primary school with its good order and smattering of grandees' children was not typical of the Falls but she had not been prepared to find in the first intake girls of thirteen and fourteen who could not read and others whose appearance and manners she thought were 'almost primitive'. The most difficult to control were the so-called 'primary nines', fourteen- and fifteen-year-olds who had expected to leave school the previous summer and had been caught by the raising of the school leaving age. But there were wild and disruptive girls in every age group: girls who would not be seen dead wearing a brown beret and gloves; girls effing and blinding on the buses and tattooing their arms with Indian ink; and hard girls who took out their anger on the inexperienced teachers or on the 'posh' girls from St. Vincent's. 'In a class you could really have picked out the St. Vincent's girls,' said Margaret Conlon who was one herself, 'because they wouldn't have cheeked the teacher, but there were other girls from down the Road who were really bold and cheeky and said things back to teachers and we were really shocked.'

The majority of girls came from 'down the Road', from the Lower Falls, the heart of St. Peter's parish. Nostalgia for what the Lower Falls used to be before the Troubles, the high rise flats and the 'emigration' up the Road to Andersonstown and Ballymurphy, tends to dwell on the strong sense of community rather than the hardship and it is the strong sense of community that the former pupils remember. The two-bedroom houses with all the boys in one room and all the girls with Ma and Da in the other, the small primary school nearby with a coal fire, proximity to which was reserved for the teacher's pets, and the narrow streets where everyone watched out for their neighbours' children, this was the only world many girls in the first intake had ever known. So self-contained and introverted was this world that some of the girls had never been to the city centre a quarter of a mile away. A new secondary school with eight hundred girls and over a mile from the Lower Falls, must have been a daunting prospect.

Although some former pupils say that teachers favoured the rich girls there were no rich girls at St. Louise's, only a handful whose families were relatively better off. If a girl in the first intake came from a family with fewer than five children she was probably unusual. Rosie Scott was one of twenty-one children, Helen O'Connor one of sixteen. Families with seven or eight children were not unusual. The principal cause of poverty in West Belfast was unemployment not Catholic fertility rates but some of the poorest girls at St. Louise's came from these very large families. They walked to school unless they could find a lemonade bottle to trade in for three pence, the price of a return bus fare from the Lower Falls and they begged for odd bits of change. 'Any odds?' they would ask sympathetic-looking senior girls.

While some of the most difficult girls came from the poorest homes in the Lower Falls, so did the girls who helped Genevieve put the school on its feet and who became some of its most loyal former pupils. Fifteen-year-old Rose Farrelly, one of the 'Slate Street Kids', was elected the first head of school and was so conscientious in carrying out her duties that the hard girls called at her house one evening to beat her up. (They were driven off by an older brother.) She was proud of her new school and proud to wear its uniform however makeshift her version may have been. Every evening she washed and ironed her one school blouse so that she would look perfect in the morning.

There would always be some difficult and disruptive girls at St. Louise's but the problems caused by the first intake were more acute because the disaffected could exploit the fact that the school was starting from scratch and that some of the teachers were unfamiliar with girls from the Falls and had difficulty understanding what they were saying. In the 1970s, when the Troubles and the expansion of the school to take in St. John's parish (which included the bleak estates of Ballymurphy) produced a new generation of girls who were hard to control, Genevieve's structures for dealing with them were well established. In 1958 it was her willpower alone that prevented the school slipping into anarchy.

The school at first acquired a reputation for roughness that was difficult to shake off. Local inhabitants avoided the bus stops when the 'Brown Bombers' were let out and bus drivers timed their run so that they would be clear of the area before the end of afternoon school. Some of the primary nines who had spent their bus money on cigarettes, walked down the Falls Road arm-in-arm like the doffers returning from the mill defying other pedestrians to stand their ground. Predictably, rumours of pregnancies and bullying circulated confirming some middle-class Catholics in their opinion that girls from the Falls who did not qualify for grammar school were better employed in the mills or the textile factories than in continuing their education.

That was the opinion that Genevieve was determined to change. Her approach to the hard girls was to leave them in no doubt that she could be harder. According to one of these girls, Genevieve's body language on the stage conveyed the unmistakable message: 'I'm not taking any nonsense from any of you. You're here and you'll behave.' The polite exchange that took place at the start of assembly – 'Good morning girls', 'Good morning Sister Genevieve' – was just a genteel way of underlining who was the boss.

Like any other headteacher, Genevieve developed a variety of strategies to impose and keep order. To an unusual degree, she persuaded the senior girls to help put her policies into practice. The girls enforced the rules partly because that is what Genevieve told them to do but principally because she had inspired them with her vision of what sort of school St. Louise's ought to be. Rose Farrelly's naïve head girl repeatedly begging the 'tough nuts' not to let the school down and telling them they should be so proud to be pupils at St. Louise's was not unusual in her identification with Genevieve's aim. Nor was she so naïve. When she had won over two of the toughest primary nines, she was happy to let them 'sort out any other trouble makers for me'. (According to one of Rose's contemporaries, the hard girls offered to perform a similar service for Genevieve: 'Don't worry about her Gen, we'll beat her up.')

By 1962, when Una Donnelly was appointed head girl, Genevieve, the instinctive autocrat, had abandoned the idea of electing the head girl because the popular vote did not always coincide with her wishes. Una was head girl for three terms, and her identification with Genevieve's aims was even more complete than Rose Farrelly's. Rose and Una represented those girls from the Lower Falls who, in the school's early years, were among Genevieve's closest allies: she relied on them more than anyone, with the exception of Sister Ita. Both girls joined the Daughters of Charity of St. Vincent de Paul when they left school though neither stayed in the congregation for long.

Genevieve expected more of her senior girls than most other heads. As well as the normal duties of supervising lunch and policing the bus stops, they were sent to the homes of absentees when the sisters were too busy to go and were expected to return with an explanation of why the girl was not in school. They were also required to act as supervisors and mentors to some of the most disruptive younger girls. The latter were attached to the senior girls for up to two weeks on a one-to-one basis. The so-called 'lodgers' had to follow their host throughout the day and were soon bored and anxious to get back to their own gang even if good behaviour was the price they had to pay. Meanwhile they were subjected to low-key propaganda from the senior girls, who told them what Sister Genevieve was trying to do and how important it was if the girls were to get jobs.

This arrangement was typical of Genevieve's approach. The girls whose behaviour the teachers could not control and for whom routine punishments such as detention proved ineffective were taken out of the classroom but remained in the school. Some were attached to senior girls as 'lodgers'. Others, particularly the difficult 'first years', were attached to Sister Ita. At the changeover of lessons, as the eight hundred girls moved smartly and in silence along the corridors from classroom to classroom, like Grenadier Guards one visitor thought, Sister Ita and the senior girls would have one or more rogues in attendance. Older disruptive girls were sent to Room 21 where they worked all day under the eye of an experienced teacher. Only Genevieve could send a girl to Room 21, known to the girls during the Troubles as Long Kesh, after the prison where many convicted paramilitaries were held.

The policy of containment stretched the school's resources but for Genevieve it fulfilled a practical and an idealistic need. Expulsion would have attracted adverse comment on the Falls grapevine. It would also have been contrary to the spirit of Genevieve's training as a Vincentian sister. The most saintly sister would have found it difficult to recognise her Saviour in the faces of some of the wild girls from the Lower Falls but that ideal would always have been before her. Genevieve was reluctant to give up on even the most disruptive girls if there was a chance to get some qualification, however modest. The girls in Room 21 would have greeted with scorn or hilarity the suggestion that Sister Gen cared for anything other than the school's reputation but whether they recognised it or not, Genevieve the school principal was always Genevieve the disciple of Vincent de Paul.

When whole classes were out of control, Genevieve appeared without being summoned, or so it seemed to the girls. They attributed to her supernatural powers – 'she could hear the grass grow' – which meant it was never safe to assume she was out of range. A popular way to unnerve an inexperienced teacher was for the girl in the corner to bang her desk lid shut setting off a chain reaction up one row and down the other so that the teacher was never quick enough to punish the last offender or warn the next. On one occasion, a girl sitting close to the door thought she had heard Sister Gen's voice. The class and the teacher fell silent, listening for the firm, unmistakable footsteps in the corridor, the swish of the heavy habit and the rattle of the wooden rosary. The girls kept their fingers crossed but when the door opened and they saw the red flush of Sister Gen's neck they knew they were done for and sprang to their feet as though the speed of their movement might deflect her wrath. It was not being kept in after school they feared but Genevieve's disapproval.

Occasionally, Genevieve's descent on a class revealed more than just her response to the routine demands of the school day. A class of fourteen-year-olds asked their teacher to tell them the facts of life. This was long before it was taken for granted that sex education had a place on the curriculum and the embarrassed teacher said she would have to seek guidance in prayer. Instead she sought guidance from Genevieve. The bush telegraph alerted the girls to the fact that Genevieve had left her office and was heading their way. 'I believe you want to know the facts of life,' she said in a matter-of-fact voice as she entered their classroom but they were not deceived. 'The facts of life!' She threw the book she was carrying onto the teacher's desk. 'I'll tell you the facts of life. Your mothers take in washing to pay for your school uniform. Your fathers are unemployed and so were their fathers before them. Those are the only facts of life you need to know.'

When the storm had passed the girls discussed whether Genevieve had been really angry or just pretending. Some girls thought that Genevieve had had an unhappy love affair – why else would an attractive woman have buried herself in such a hard order? – and that this was why she was sensitive on the subject of sex. She was said to have been angry when she found a girl writing verses for St. Valentine's Day and she placed the Whiterock Road out of bounds when she was told that girls were meeting boys from St. Thomas's secondary school there on the way home. Even more revealing, the girls thought, were her attempts to censor scenes of passionate kissing in the films that were shown in the assembly hall. If she attended the films herself, she would stride forward and place herself in front of the screen so that it was almost impossible to see what was happening as the frames flickered across her face and headdress. If she could not attend, she instructed the projectionist, who was the first male member of staff, to hold a card in front of the lens during the offending scenes.

It is tempting to assume that men and women who have taken a vow of chastity find it difficult to deal with young people's interest in sex, but those who worked closely with Genevieve over many years insist that she was open-minded and well-adjusted on the subject of sex and that she was as far removed as possible from the image of the nun whose chastity has only been achieved at great psychological cost. Though her training had been strict, it had not left her emotionally scarred.

If someone who has taken a vow of chastity can be said to have a healthy and normal attitude to sex, then this was true of

Genevieve. Her reaction to the girls' interest in sex in the early years was typical of school authorities at the time. It is easy to forget that before the revolution in public attitudes in the late sixties, sex was a taboo subject in all but the most progressive schools and pupils who asked about the facts of life were regarded as troublemakers. For Genevieve the disciplinarian there were also practical considerations. She disliked the shouts and whistles that the kissing scenes invariably provoked and she viewed assignations with St. Thomas's boys on the Whiterock Road as bad for the school's reputation.

Because the Daughters of Charity lived in the world it could be harder for them than for cloistered nuns to sustain the absolute purity of thought and action that their vow of chastity required, which is why Vincent de Paul gave them practical advice on the subject. In the seminary, the sisters had been taught to practise both exterior and interior mortification: exterior mortification that rejected any pleasure in the senses, and interior mortification that rejected the pleasures of the imagination, of curiosity and of memory. All these pleasures a Vincentian sister had 'generously forsaken for God'. But if mortification was intended to produce individuals who could live in the world while being detached from it, in Genevieve's case it does not appear to have been entirely successful. Behind her authoritarian mask was a warm, outgoing personality who loved being with people and who did not shy away from physical contact. Over and over again, her former pupils emphasised how uninhibited she was about putting her arm around a girl's shoulder; she was by all accounts 'a great toucher' and 'a great hugger'.

Nor did she shy away from the company of men. There was no suggestion from the many people who drew attention to this aspect of her character that her fondness for men applied to individuals; she just enjoyed male company and was skilful at handling men when she thought it was in the school's interests for her to do so. She used her undoubted charm to win men to her cause, whether they were employers who could give the girls jobs, inspectors who could give the school a good report or British politicians who could give St. Louise's an edge over its rivals. 'She was all woman,' recalled Margaret Crawford, one of the first intake, 'and she used everything God had given her to best advantage.' That may make Genevieve sound like one of Chaucer's female religious on the road to Canterbury but, despite what may have been said of the young sister, the mature Genevieve was shrewd and calculating and clearly saw nothing wrong with using her charm as well as her single-mindedness to obtain what she wanted for girls.

The girls soon developed a strategy for dealing with Genevieve when she believed they had done something wrong. There were two schools of thought. One argued that it was best to be submissive. 'If you grovelled you were OK,' one woman explained. Girls who favoured this approach never met Genevieve's gaze and developed the art of bursting into tears convincingly. The other school argued that it was safer to stand up to Genevieve, to look her in the eye and to state your case. 'If you were in the right, stand up to her,' said Dolores Shields who now works for the BBC in Belfast, 'but if you were in the wrong, don't even start.' Catherine McErlean, another girl who joined the Daughters of Charity, tried this approach and it worked. Genevieve wrongly accused her of copying another girl's work but when Catherine proved that she could not possibly have done, Genevieve apologised with good grace. But it took courage to stand up to Genevieve and open defiance was so rare it stuck in the minds of those who witnessed it for years after. 'Pull your skirt down,' Genevieve ordered a fourteen-year-old, one of the headbangers from the roughest part of the Lower Falls. The girl put her hand to her mouth, pulled out her chewing gum almost to arm's length and then drew it back again. 'What was that you said, Sister?' The other girls were amazed but Genevieve just repeated the order, saw that it was obeyed and moved on. She knew perfectly well that there was no danger of the girl's insolence setting a trend.

Some of those who stood up to Genevieve as senior girls said that the experience made them stronger and empowered them as women. 'If you mastered her, you could master anybody,' was a typical comment. But the majority of girls did not decide to stand up to Genevieve or to risk provoking her by being disruptive or lazy. They got on with their lives, normal schoolchildren, loving school one moment, hating it the next, inevitably influenced by Genevieve's strong personality but on the whole keeping out of her way. They may have been frightened of her – many had been warned in advance by older sisters, 'Don't cross her, don't mess with her' – but they benefited from her strict regime, not least because it reduced bullying and provided a secure environment especially during the Troubles.

Genevieve's determination to build the school's reputation on good behaviour of the girls led her to place school uniform at the top of her disciplinary agenda. The debate about the merits and demerits of school uniform, so characteristically British and so puzzling to foreigners, did not interest Genevieve. She had no doubts. Having all the girls wearing the same uniform would develop unity and pride, and would throw down the gauntlet to the girls' grammar school whose wine-red uniform had hitherto distinguished the elite from the rest in the Falls. Those who accused her of snobbery missed the point; it was social justice not social pretension that motivated her. Unlike many of the secondary and comprehensive schools in England, which went out of their way to jettison all the characteristics of a grammar school, including uniform, Genevieve decided to take the grammar schools on at their own game. If their pupils were noted for their good manners and smart appearance, her girls would do better.

At the beginning and end of each school day there were teachers at the door to check the girls' uniform. Senior girls saw that berets and gloves were still being worn when the Brown Bombers got on the bus and girls walking home had to be alert to the possibility that Ita and Genevieve might be patrolling in their car. 'Don't take your beret off until you walk through your own front door,' was Genevieve's rule and for beret read blazer or gloves or dexter. There were snap inspections in the school when berets and gloves were recycled many times to cover the deficiencies and there was the occasional public criticism at assembly. 'Come up on to the stage, Deidre, where we can all see you. Deidre thinks she's too good to wear her school beret . . .'

Modern school principals would find it hard to imagine themselves acting in this way or involving themselves in the enforcement of the uniform code to the extent that Genevieve did. They would be afraid of making fools of themselves. Genevieve got away with a performance that sometimes looked as if it was part of a comedy film about a girls' school partly because she was feared and respected, but also because, although she left the girls in no doubt that she was serious, she did not take herself too seriously. She knew that as she drove up and down the Falls Road, honking her horn or wagging her finger at any girl who had taken off her beret she was close to self-parody. If a girl wrong-footed her she had the sense to laugh, as when she drew up at the bus stop to reprimand Margaret Connolly for not wearing her blazer and Margaret stepped forward saying, 'Are you offering me a lift, Sister?' It was a game and not a game. The girls could laugh at the stories of Genevieve patrolling in the car while recognising that it would be unwise to be caught themselves.

At the school's first prize distribution ceremony in July 1958, Ita reported that 'the uniform has now become very popular and is worn by every girl in the school'. It was an optimistic interpretation of what was happening. Some girls hated having to wear a beret and gloves and being the butt of the ribald mockery of the boys on the way home. As soon as Genevieve's cruising car had disappeared they pulled off as many items as they dared and lit a cigarette like soldiers relaxing after a parade. But Genevieve had established that at St. Louise's uniform mattered. In this she had the enthusiastic support of the first head girl. 'St. Dominic's, the grammar school, was the opposition, mostly middle class or well-to-do girls,' Rose Farrelly wrote, still passionate for Genevieve's cause forty years on. 'I wanted St. Louise's girls to be equally well thought of by the people of the Falls. St. Louise's girls should walk down the Falls with heads held high, just like the girls from St. Dominic's.'

Genevieve was right to make good discipline her priority. Listening to her talk about her job in retirement, it was clear that good discipline remained her priority throughout her career at St. Louise's, and that she thought too many headteachers had lost

sight of the simple truth that if discipline fails, then the school is
bound to fail its pupils. Her autocratic regime of the early years
does not seem to have been based on any particular model. When
she was asked whether there was any other school that she
admired, she replied, 'Harrow'. Perhaps she was joking. Harrow
was one of the most traditional and socially exclusive of English
public schools. On the other hand, perhaps not. Unlike many
headteachers who work with disadvantaged children, she had no
ideological objection to recognising that there were aspects of
English public schools that she would like to reproduce at St.
Louise's, notably a reputation (not always deserved) for good
discipline.

The contrast between Harrow and St. Louise's helps to explain
why Genevieve made the establishment of good discipline such a
personal crusade. If she had visited Harrow in the sixties, she
would probably have found the headmaster, Dr R.L. James, reading *The Times* in his study and drinking tea. James was a hands-off,
low-key headmaster who nevertheless presided over a successful
and well-disciplined school. Having inherited a traditional structure of housemasters and monitors and a detailed handbook of
how things were done called *Existing Customs*, he was able to
detach himself from the everyday enforcement of discipline.
Genevieve inherited nothing. From the first day, she had to dictate
what was and was not acceptable behaviour and to involve herself
at every stage in the disciplinary process. Her hands-on approach
was a risk because it provided so many opportunities for her
authority to be challenged. A headteacher's authority contains an
element of bluff; when towards the end of her career she was
reminded of this fact, she roared with laughter – it was inconceiv-
able then that anyone would dare to call her bluff. But there must
have been occasions in the early days when she only just got away
with her dictatorial style.

What saved Genevieve's autocratic regime from being merely
repressive was her vision of what her girls could achieve in a disciplined environment and her commitment to even the least
co-operative of them. It was typical of her idiosyncratic approach
to the latter that she sometimes sentenced them to sit in silence on

a chair in her office so that people coming to see her were disconcerted to find assorted rogues in attendance who were described by Genevieve as 'my friends'.

It would take more than good discipline and a smart uniform to encourage St. Louise's girls to walk down the Falls with their heads held high. Despite the defiance of the bold girls and the eager pride in the new school exemplified by Rose Farrelly, the girls in the first intake had little self-confidence. The one thing they all had in common was that they were the rejects from a school system that barely disguised its low opinion of their ability and prospects. If Genevieve's strategy was to succeed she had to inspire all the girls to believe in themselves and that would be a harder task than bringing them to heel.

5

'Shoulders back. Heads up. Be proud of your school'

'This isn't a second-class school for second-class people. You are as good, if not better, than the girls in any other school in town.' Genevieve would pause to let the message sink in. The eight hundred girls stood in rows facing the stage, the younger girls at the front, the older girls at the back with a teacher at the end of the row. 'Don't think those people wearing red uniforms down the Road are any better than you.' Time after time, Genevieve drove the message home. It was a risk because pupils soon tire of the sound of the headteacher's hobbyhorse but Genevieve was a skilled communicator who knew how and when to vary the emphasis so that sometimes it had a feminist edge, the implicit message being that 'women can make it', and at others a note of unashamed jingoism. 'Never forget who you are. Shoulders back. Heads up. Be proud of your school. St. Louise's is the best.'

The assembly for the whole school every morning was a religious and secular occasion which promoted unity and pride and re-enforced Genevieve's already powerful charismatic hold on the minds of the young. The girls marched in by forms with their prefect in charge and waited in silence for the sounds of Genevieve's approach. When she entered the hall there was an unmistakable change in the atmosphere as fear, awe and anticipation accompanied the wings of her high white headdress advancing through the ranks like a regimental colour or the centrepiece of a religious procession. Hymn, prayer, homily, followed by congratulations, criticisms and comment – there was nothing original about the formula but Genevieve's personality could make a routine assembly an inspiring occasion.

The source of an individual's power to inspire others is elusive. To say, as many people do, that Genevieve was charismatic is not an answer, just a restatement of the question. Where did her charisma come from? Her looks, her bearing and the mystique that surrounded the sisters were useful assets but the more likely source of her ability to inspire so many girls and teachers was the conviction with which she believed in her mission and her skill in translating conviction into words. Howard Gardner in his study of leadership, *Leading Minds*, identifies linguistic intelligence as one of the marks of future leaders: 'They do not merely have a promising story; they can tell it persuasively.' Former pupils and teachers bear witness to Genevieve's ability to 'tell it persuasively' yet by all accounts she was not a natural or even a confident public speaker. As a schoolgirl, her shyness had led her to prefer a non-speaking role. 'Byrne, won't you do the talking,' she would say to her friend Bridie Byrne. As an adult, she seldom spoke off the cuff, writing notes even for the short homily at morning assembly. Her talks to meetings and conferences were always typed out verbatim and rehearsed with her closest friends. But when she started speaking in public, it was as though the handwritten notes and the typescript did not exist. She spoke directly to her audience with fluency and unmistakable conviction. It was not the gift of the gab, which the pupils in particular would have seen through, but the gift of finding the right 'voice' with which to communicate the strength of her own convictions. When she told the girls they were as good as the girls in any other school it was not just rhetoric, it was what she believed. If she had not managed to convince the girls of this, her attempts to boost their confidence would have been patronising and ineffective.

Because Genevieve's belief in the equality of all human beings was rooted in her Christian faith and her Vincentian training, it was not open to discussion or compromise. She thought that an

education system that treated her girls as second class was anti-
Christian and she said so, provoking the hostility of the grammar
school lobby and of the Catholic hierarchy. She did not shrink
from the confrontation, on the contrary she rather enjoyed it, and
the image of the religious sister battling with the powers that be
on behalf of her pupils enhanced her charisma. She may never
have said at assembly, 'Together we can take on the world', but
that was the subtext, particularly when she was talking to them as
girls and not just as pupils. Sister Vincent's belief in the great
potential of the women of West Belfast had given Genevieve's
dedication to equality a feminist bias. The school's ideals as
defined by Genevieve were 'Equality of opportunity for all girls
and an utter abhorrence of the selective system, which has done so
much to dechristianise modern thinking'. But while she was determined that her girls should fulfil their potential, Genevieve was
realistic about the range of ability in the school. Her version of the
parable of the talents was that all the girls at St. Louise's had talents of which in most cases they were unaware and which would
be wasted if she did not challenge the girls' lack of self-belief.
They were not all capable of going to university or even of following an academic course in school but they were all capable of
something better than an unskilled job. She believed in them and
that is what came across when she stood on the stage and told
them, 'You're as good as anybody else'.

Building the girls' confidence could not be done by persuasion
alone; the school had to deliver qualifications and jobs. Only
when the possibility of obtaining jobs outside the few remaining
mills and the factories became a reality would the girls begin to
believe that they were not failures after all. Genevieve knew this
and made sure that every aspect of the school's life, not just what
was taught in class but the extra-curricular activities, the discipline, the leadership expected of the senior girls, even the
Vincentian ethos expressed in the numerous Catholic societies
she established, contributed to this end. Genevieve believed that
St. Louise's would produce girls who were so well qualified in
their confident, courteous and articulate manner as well as in the
examinations they had passed, that employers who never would

have hired a secondary school girl from the Falls, would be forced to think again.

There was, however, a major stumbling block. Genevieve's ambitions for her girls went beyond what had been intended by those who had designed the selective school system, those who had an almost Calvinistic belief in what a child was predestined to achieve. To these educationalists, the suggestion that the St. Louise's girls should enter for public examinations just like their peers in the grammar school seemed both wrong-headed and subversive. What was this Vincent de Paul sister thinking about? The external examinations that the grammar school pupils took at sixteen and eighteen, the so-called Ordinary and Advanced Levels, were too difficult for girls who had already shown that they had no academic bent.

To Genevieve, this was just another example of injustice. She would enter her girls for public examinations whether the authorities liked it or not even if she had to enter them as private candidates. When she discovered that her girls were also barred from taking the Junior Commercial Certificate because St. Louise's was not a commercial school, she started a search for organisations such as the Royal Society of Arts in London that awarded recognised qualifications in commercial subjects.

Genevieve refused to accept a system that discriminated against her girls and she set out to prove that it was wrong. She *was* subversive because she was not afraid to overturn the norms. She was also uncompromising. Those who were responsible for running Northern Ireland's school system, the province's Ministry of Education, the Belfast Education Committee (later the Belfast Education and Library Board) and in the case of Roman Catholic schools, the Diocesan Education Committee, soon learnt that in Sister Genevieve they were dealing with a school principal who would not take 'No' for an answer, who believed that the end justified the means when it came to getting what she wanted for her girls and who refused to take into account the bigger picture and the effect of her tactics on other schools. Access to public examinations was only the first of many battles she fought with one or other of these authorities over the next thirty years.

By 1963, five years after the school opened, Genevieve could say that every girl at St. Louise's had a chance to leave school with a qualification that would be accepted in the job market. The qualifications were the targets she thought every girl needed and their requirements dictated the curriculum and the way the classes were organised. Though Genevieve was opposed to selecting girls for different schools according to their ability she had no hesitation in using this yardstick to place them in different classes where they would be working towards different qualifications. She had no time for the policy, soon to become ideologically correct in England, of teaching children in mixed ability classes so that the able and the less able were seen to be treated as equals. As far as she was concerned, the girls at St. Louise's *were* treated as equals because they all had the same opportunity to obtain the qualification that was within their grasp. The academically inclined minority studied for the Ordinary Level examination while the majority either combined a limited Ordinary Level course with commercial subjects such as book-keeping for which the Royal Society of Arts awarded certificates or concentrated on domestic subjects such as cookery, laundry and dressmaking, and on the less demanding commercial qualifications such as the Pitman Certificates in shorthand and typing.

By placing the emphasis on leaving school with a paper qualification at all costs, whether it was nine passes at Ordinary Level or 'one hundred words per minute Pitman script', Genevieve was taking a narrow view of education: education for education's sake was a luxury the poor could not afford. In the context of West Belfast, jobs were bound to be the priority, and not any job but one better than their mothers and grandmothers had been forced to take. For most of the girls who went to St. Louise's in the early years, a good secretarial job was the fulfilment of a dream; their certificates in typing and book-keeping meant they were the first girls in their families to have the choice of not working in the mills or the textile factories.

While Genevieve's aim was qualifications for all, she badly needed some academic success and was prepared to pay for it. When Anne McGreevy, one of the brightest of the first intake had to leave to get a job and bring money into the home, Genevieve offered to use the Daughters of Charity funds to pay the equivalent of her wages. What Genevieve said to Anne was: 'I know there are problems at home; I'm prepared to pay you to stay at school.' Anne's mother declined the offer but in other cases Genevieve, with Sister Vincent's support, deployed the congregation's money successfully to keep able girls in the school.

Money could not remove a more serious threat to the school's academic credibility. It was in theory possible for girls to transfer to the grammar school at the age of thirteen if they could show they were up to standard by passing the Junior Grammar Certificate. In practice, the Ministry of Education was reluctant to accept St. Louise's girls as candidates because if the girls passed it would show up the deficiencies in the Qualifying Exam they had failed at eleven. Genevieve was torn between her desire to see the 11+ exam discredited and her anxiety not to lose her most able girls. She decided that she could not stand in the way of the girls' chances, however much she feared that if they were successful a haemorrhage of talent to St. Dominic's grammar school would become an annual occurrence. She entered the girls for the exam without the Ministry's permission and paid the entry fees herself. Thirty girls took the exam in the summer of 1960 and all passed. The Ministry was embarrassed but could not refuse the parents' request for a transfer to the grammar school. In the event, only half the girls opted to take up the grammar school place but it was still a serious blow to St. Louise's.

Fortunately for Genevieve, grammar school snobbery played into her hands. St. Dominic's insisted that the girls from St. Louise's should re-sit the Junior Grammar Certificate at the end of their first year as though confirmation was needed that the girls from the back streets really were grammar school material. This mistake, so typical of the grammar school mentality at the time, meant that the girls were a year behind those who had stayed at St. Louise's and it put an end once and for all to parental requests for their daughters to transfer. From 1961 onwards, the most able girls not only remained at St. Louise's but in increasing numbers stayed on after the school leaving age thus enabling Genevieve to create that most distinctive characteristic of any school with academic ambitions, the sixth form. The first Advanced Level courses started in 1962 and within two years so many girls were staying on that temporary classrooms had to be erected on the site.

The development of a sixth form was a triumph in an area where many families needed the income of girls old enough to leave school and in a school system that assumed that only grammar school pupils would want to continue their studies beyond the statutory leaving age. At St. Louise's, the sixth form was open to any girl who wanted to stay. They were not all expected to take an Advanced Level. Some stayed to take more Ordinary Levels while others combined academic and commercial courses. As long as they had a qualification to aim for, they were welcome.

'It has been the experience of teachers that by giving any class a goal to aim at, disciplinary problems have been automatically solved,' Genevieve told parents in 1961. 'This is a point that cannot be too strongly stressed. At present one hears so much about free activity and *laissez faire* in secondary schools but the teachers in these schools would agree that this policy from the disciplinary and moral points of view is disastrous.' She may have been an idealist in what she hoped to achieve at St. Louise's but she was a realist in how she proposed to achieve it. 'Free activity and *laissez faire*' were not only alien to someone trained in the discipline of the Daughters of Charity, they would – Genevieve believed – prevent her girls from obtaining the qualifications they needed. Structured lessons, good discipline and clearly identified goals in the form of examinations to be passed and certificates to be gained – that was the way to lift the girls from the Falls out of poverty not the application of some educational theory about letting children discover knowledge for themselves.

Liberal educationalists whose advocacy of child-centred education was just beginning to capture the imagination of teachers in the rest of the United Kingdom would have been horrified by Genevieve's severely practical and unsentimental approach, and by the methods she used to motivate her pupils. The method the girls feared most was known as Reading of Remarks. For this public review of each girl's work and attitude, which critics

thought had something of the atmosphere of a show trial behind
the Iron Curtain, three classes were seated in the assembly hall,
with Genevieve and the class teachers sitting facing them on the
stage. On the table in front of Genevieve were the report sheets on
which teachers had recorded their opinions as well as factual information such as the number of times the girl had been late for
school. When Genevieve called out a name, the girl stood among
her peers to be questioned, congratulated, criticised and, if necessary, sentenced. Even if the report was satisfactory, it was an
ordeal. If the teachers had remarked on your lack of effort or your
unco-operative attitude, the cardinal sins in Genevieve's eyes, you
received a public dressing down you would never forget. Some
girls were sentenced on the spot to move to a lower form or, in the
case of bad behaviour, to a spell in Room 21.

No one has funny stories to tell about Reading of Remarks. It
was a serious business and it continued throughout a girl's school
career so that an eighteen-year-old taking Advanced Level had to
undergo the same public review of her performance. At least every
girl in the school knew that Sister Gen had read her report carefully and taken a genuine interest in how she was getting on, but
as a method of motivating pupils Reading of Remarks had its limitations. The public nature of the occasion persuaded some
teachers to water down their criticisms. On the surviving Reading
of Remarks sheets there is a suspiciously high proportion of ticks
for 'satisfactory'. As they grew older the girls developed ways of
handling Genevieve at Reading of Remarks. 'Do you want a lie or
the truth?' Anne Donegan asked when Genevieve demanded an
explanation for her failure in mock Advanced Level exams. The
truth was that Anne had done very little work and she said so.
Impressed by Anne's nerve as much as by her frankness, Genevieve
settled for a mild rebuke.

Genevieve's robust approach to motivating her pupils and her
desire to create a strong academic stream ran the risk of discour-
aging the less able girls, which was precisely what she wanted to
avoid. One of her most perceptive senior colleagues thought that
'her burning belief in the dignity of each individual girl' prevented
those in the lower forms being undervalued but, not surprisingly,

some former pupils think Genevieve favoured the academic girls. No school can claim with certainty that it has solved the problem of how to make the less gifted pupils feel as valued as the stars, however stardom is defined. Genevieve's acute awareness of the injustice all the girls suffered at the hands of the selective school system would have made her keen not to reproduce the same separation into sheep and goats in her own school. She went out of her way on public occasions to assert that 'one hundred words per minute Pitman script' was no less an achievement than an Advanced Level pass. But her good intentions could be undermined by her own decisions. Each year group was divided into seven classes to be labelled alphabetically A to G but Genevieve insisted that the highest class, which contained the academic girls, should be labelled G and the lowest class labelled B. The attempt to disguise the hierarchy by eccentric labelling fooled no one, but Genevieve genuinely wished all girls to be treated with equal respect whatever their ability.

The qualifications for which the girls were working would with any luck earn them an interview but could not guarantee them a job. Some of the girls would present well at interview but the majority would be too inexperienced or too rough to make a good impression. As the time for an interview approached, Genevieve conducted a practice interview herself, insisting that the girl came to school smartly dressed in her own clothes and carrying a handbag but the process of giving the girl self-confidence, poise and the ability to put her own case had started long before. Some of the methods Genevieve used – the debating, the public speaking, the senior girls taking assembly and the annual musical that involved as many girls as possible – were typical in most schools but she introduced some no-nonsense methods of her own. Whereas other headteachers might hope that pupils will pick up the rudiments of polite behaviour from the example of adults and from what the school is seen to disapprove of, Genevieve thought that good manners were too important to the girls' future and to the school's reputation to be left to chance. A list of 'courtesy points' was published and every week the girls had to learn one of the points by heart. At its longest, the list contained over sixty courtesy points ranging from 'Be ready to give up your seat to an elderly or handicapped person on the bus' to 'The prongs of the fork should always face down when eating', from practical advice about correct speech and personal appearance to this echo of Polonius, 'If you get something on loan from someone, make sure you return it without having to be asked'.

At morning assembly every Friday Genevieve asked girls at random to recite the courtesy point for the week and failure to do so correctly earned a public rebuke and a trip to Genevieve's office. Some of the girls pinned the week's courtesy point to the back of the girl in front just in case. As with the rules on uniform, it was a game and not a game and no doubt some girls discarded the courtesy points as promptly as they took off their blazer and beret as soon as Genevieve's back was turned. But by placing good manners in such a prominent position on the school's agenda, Genevieve was teaching the girls what their own priorities ought to be and giving them the opportunity to acquire a qualification that might be just as valuable as an exam certificate when it came to a job interview.

She was as sensitive to criticism of the girls' behaviour outside the school as any headteacher, perhaps more so because the people of the Falls had initially been inclined to expect the worst of the Brown Bombers and because prospective employers had enough bad reasons to discriminate against her Catholic girls without adding a good one. Even sectarian insults had to be ignored. 'If they spit at you and call you Fenians,' she told the netball team before an away fixture against a Protestant girls' school, 'you must not retaliate.' It was asking a lot of fifteen- and sixteen-year-olds, some of whom came from strongly Republican families but even during the Troubles, Genevieve seems to have persuaded the girls that their first loyalty on such occasions was to the good name of the school.

Genevieve took on so much herself and was such a powerful presence in the life of the girls (it was said that they could always tell when she was in the school whether they had seen her or not), that she tends to dominate their memories to the exclusion of Sister Ita and the other members of staff. As she takes the controls and struggles to lift the school off the ground like the pilot of one of those ramshackle early aeroplanes, Genevieve appears to be flying solo but she had thirty-two colleagues in the staffroom on whose loyalty and competence she depended for the day-to-day implementation of her policies. When the school opened, all the teachers were women. Most were strangers to one another and to the Falls, many were young and had little or no experience of teaching. Apart from Sister Ita, it is unlikely that any of them at first shared Genevieve's vision of what the school was aiming to achieve; they had been appointed to teach domestic science or general subjects not to fight injustice. On the other hand, they would not have applied to join the first Catholic secondary school for girls, which no one expected to be an easy ride, if they had not possessed something of the pioneering spirit. Genevieve was determined to harness their youth and energy to her mission so that they could become part of a team with a clear sense of direction.

Ita's willingness to let Genevieve take the lead in establishing the school's priorities was both generous and far-sighted. In any other school it could have been a formula for disaster. Head-teachers are bound to delegate but they will not hand over the effective running of the school to a junior colleague for fear of undermining their own authority. Ita's unconcern for her own status was remarkable but it was not weakness. She had known Genevieve for two years both as a teacher at St. Vincent's primary school and as a sister in the Daughters of Charity House in Clonard, and she was well aware of Genevieve's reputation within the Vincentian community. Though Genevieve was said to be flamboyant, volatile, wilful and ambitious, all faults in a Vincent de Paul sister, what Ita saw in Genevieve was a woman with a mission whose drive and idealism were just what was needed to launch the new school. It was an act of shrewd humility to give Genevieve her head.

For three years until Ita's illness was diagnosed in 1961 and she left to undergo an operation, the two sisters were inseparable. Each morning they walked together from Clonard to the Falls Road to catch the bus. If the bus was crowded, the passengers sprang up to offer the sisters their seats because 'in those days we still respected cloth'. When Sister Vincent bought them a small car, Genevieve usually did the driving and recited her favourite psalms as she and Ita kept a watchful eye on the girls waiting at the bus stops or straggling along the pavements. Inside the school building, though Genevieve was the front-woman and the trouble-shooter, they were more frequently seen together than apart so that the staff and the pupils realised that St. Louise's was being run by a partnership not by an overmighty subject and a weak monarch.

In relation to the staff and the pupils, Ita's principal role was a pastoral one. If a teacher needed reassurance she went to Ita; if she needed a decision or a problem solved she went to Genevieve. The pupils made the same distinction: if you wanted a bit of a laugh or a bit of a cry you went to see Ita but an interview with Genevieve was almost always about serious business. For the lonely and unhappy girls and particularly for those whose home life was a struggle for survival, Ita played the traditional pastoral role tempering the wind to the shorn lamb. Genevieve was not blind to the appalling conditions in which some girls had to live but she deliberately did not make any allowances. The girl who hid in the coal shed overnight to escape the violence of her drunken father knew that Genevieve expected her to be properly dressed in her school uniform in the morning but she also knew that if she arrived looking a mess Ita would be there to take her on one side and tidy her up before assembly. In 1983, when Ita had retired from the teaching staff, Genevieve paid this tribute to her friend's pastoral gift. 'Sister Ita's forte has always been the young-sters who found school life hard; she has picked up, counselled and helped hundreds of pupils to settle down and make a success of their lives, girls who otherwise might have become the dropouts of society.'

No potential dropout owed more to Sister Ita than Genevieve herself. In her childhood and youth, Genevieve had adored her mother to whom, as the youngest child and only girl, she was very close; as a seminary sister she had worshipped Sister Philomena from afar, and when she arrived in Belfast her admiration for Sister

Vincent Wallace had almost certainly saved her from dropping out
of the Daughters of Charity altogether. Her relationship with Ita
was different. Ita was a friend, the older sister Genevieve had
never had who was proud not envious of her younger sister's many
gifts and who was always there to talk over the problems, to coun-
sel patience and, from time to time, to assert her authority. 'I was
wishing Genevieve had been made principal,' Ita says of those
early years, but Sister Vincent had made the right choice. The
three years during which Genevieve's zeal was tempered by Ita's
quiet authority helped Genevieve to develop a style of leadership
that despite the allegations of pride, ruthlessness and ambition
always retained sufficient humility to listen to the criticism of
those closest to her.

In practical, everyday terms Ita saved Genevieve a great deal of
trouble. Both before and after they had exchanged titles, she not
only looked after the shorn lambs, she personally persuaded many
of the truants to return to school and she used her extensive
knowledge of the homes from which the girls came to brief
Genevieve. When Joe Hendren, as a young doctor in the Falls,
went to see Genevieve about one of his patients who had three
daughters in the school, he was astonished by Genevieve's detailed
knowledge of the girls and their family, but the chances are that Ita
had provided the information shortly before his arrival. It mattered not at all to Ita that it was Genevieve who gained the
reputation for possessing almost encyclopaedic knowledge of the
pupils and their backgrounds.

If Ita had a weakness as principal it was her reluctance to stand
up to the manager who, having done so little to get the school off
to a good start, now regarded it as his role to ensure that costs
were kept to a minimum. He would appear uninvited in the school
in the winter months and go from classroom to classroom closing
windows so that the heating was not wasted. Ita maintained diplomatic relations (which Genevieve would not have done) and
described him in her first annual report as 'a valuable friend'.

When Ita returned after her operation, she renewed her partnership with Genevieve and her pastoral role. She retired as a
teacher and as vice-principal in 1977 but continued to be a presence

in the school as secretary of the school committee (as the new style governing body was called) until 1988 when she finally left St. Louise's at the same time as Genevieve.

The other experienced teacher who played an important part in the creation of St. Louise's was Maire McFadden, a native of Belfast and a university graduate. Although she held no formal position other than housemistress until she succeeded Ita as vice-principal in 1977, Maire was Genevieve's natural ally from the start. She was convinced that establishing good discipline was the priority and she was highly critical of a school system in which winning a place at grammar school depended on the number of places available, with the result that many talented girls were rejected. She accepted that the aim of the curriculum at St. Louise's was to deliver qualifications for jobs but as a graduate she was as keen as Genevieve to give the talented rejects the chance of going to university. She combined, therefore, the traditional grammar school concern for academic standards and good order with a determination to demonstrate that selection at the age of eleven was fundamentally flawed.

Ita, Genevieve and Maire McFadden worked closely together but their triumvirate, like the school itself, was driven by one woman's clear vision of where they were going. For the younger teachers, some of whom were on probation and subject to regular visits from the school inspectors, Genevieve's certainty was a godsend. Few things make it more difficult for an inexperienced teacher to settle down in a new school than a headteacher who is vague or hesitant about what she expects. Genevieve made her expectations explicit. Every detail of a teacher's duties was spelt out, either at staff meetings or in the written instructions that soon covered every aspect of the school from fire drill to the exact form of prayer with which form teachers were expected to start the first lesson of the day. To the latter, Genevieve appended a characteristically practical note: 'In addition to being a spiritual exercise, it settles the class.'

Genevieve also made explicit the attitude she expected all teachers to adopt. Commitment was the key: commitment to the aims of the school ('to her ambition' critics said), commitment to the

Catholic and Vincentian ethos, commitment to the girls and their
hopes for the future. Those for whom teaching was just a job like
any other were of no use to Genevieve and she was sharply dis-
missive of women who, in her opinion, were only teaching to pay
for the family holiday. 'Everyone here is an enthusiast,' she told
visitors and those who were not enthusiastic soon left; there was a
buzz in the staffroom, a sense of urgency and a willingness to
tackle problems rather than moan about them.

Despite the commitment and the enthusiasm, former teachers
like former pupils are ambivalent about Genevieve. The admiration, even love, she inspired is tempered by the recollection of her
domineering and autocratic style. 'Teachers are sheep and must
be led,' she said on one occasion and in the early years staff meetings were opportunities for her to issue instructions not for
teachers to express opinions. Mary O'Reilly, who joined the staff
in 1959 as head of music recalls that in those early days it required
considerable courage to say anything at a staff meeting and
that disagreement with Genevieve was unthinkable. Whenever
Genevieve entered the staffroom, some teachers automatically
stood up. 'We're adults for Christ's sake!' one young teacher
protested when Genevieve had gone but her colleagues would
have found it difficult to act in any other way. One teacher
remembers a moment of panic when she was caught in heavy
traffic on the Falls Road and knew that Genevieve sometimes
checked each teacher's arrival, standing at the door with a pocket
watch held out in front of her.

The teachers, like the girls, had to decide whether to stand up
to Genevieve or, in a phrase used frequently by former members
of staff, 'allow her to walk all over you'. Though standing up to
Genevieve was easier for an adult, it still called for a strong nerve.
Frank Horisk who joined the staff in 1960 at the age of twenty-
three, the first male and the first scientist to be appointed,
thought that if he did not stand up to Genevieve at the start he
might never be able to do so. His resolution was soon put to the
test. When he pointed out to the science inspector that it was
dangerous to have thirty-six girls in a laboratory designed for
twenty-four Genevieve was furious. 'No one is going to tell me

how to run my school,' she told the inspector, who had passed on Horisk's comments. But Frank Horisk insisted that to allow teenage girls to do scientific experiments in an overcrowded laboratory risked an accident for which the school would be responsible. Genevieve's moods were said to be unpredictable but her anger was almost always provoked by what she perceived as a negative attitude or a threat to her authority. Her return to reasonableness could almost always be guaranteed by a refusal to be browbeaten. Frank Horisk found that he had earned her respect. She agreed to a reduction in the size of the science class and gave him additional responsibilities, including censoring the films in her absence.

Genevieve's autocratic manner did not prevent her winning the loyalty of her staff. Her unshakeable self-belief was bound to be attractive to teachers setting out on the uncharted waters of secondary education for Catholic girls, so was her willingness to support her staff when they encountered difficulties. 'For that you forgave her a lot,' said one of the early teachers recalling how Genevieve had taken her side against the inspector. Those who were not prepared to tolerate her dictatorial regime or who found her idea of education too narrowly focused on qualifications and jobs, left to pursue their careers elsewhere, so that by a form of natural selection the staff at St. Louise's increasingly identified with Genevieve's mission. They were not yes-men and yes-women, however, far from it. Genevieve went out of her way to fill the vacancies with ambitious young teachers who saw St. Louise's as an exciting new venture where they would have more opportunities to make their mark than in established schools. It was one of the paradoxes of Genevieve's regime that she encouraged enterprise and innovation while keeping all the reins of government in her own hands. She wanted St. Louise's to have the reputation of being a go-ahead school even though her own attitude to almost every aspect of education was traditional, but the innovation had to be consistent with her vision of what the school was trying to achieve. Innovations that she thought were encouraging an alternative vision, such as the adult community school in the seventies and eighties, were eventually suppressed.

She expected her staff to work long hours – 'Does that school never close?' the neighbours grumbled – and to take on any number of extra duties without payment. By 1961, there were a thousand girls at St. Louise's but only thirty-eight teachers, a far less favourable pupil:teacher ratio than the grammar schools enjoyed, yet Genevieve wanted her girls to have the same opportunities both in and out of class. Every member of her staff had a pastoral as well as a teaching role. For the purpose of encouraging the competitive instinct in work, behaviour, sport and charitable endeavour, the girls were divided into four houses named after shrines and titles of Our Lady – Lourdes, Fatima, Loreto and Immaculata. Every teacher was attached to one of these houses and most were form teachers as well whose various administrative and pastoral duties included 'setting the correct tone for the rest of the day'.

Genevieve led by example. She arrived early and left late. On Saturday morning she took an extra class for girls in the academic stream. For those who had a Saturday job (or said that they had), she taught the same lesson after school on Monday evening. Her subject was French. According to her former pupils, she was a superb teacher of the old school, relying on irregular verbs learned by rote but enlivening her traditional methods with her infectious love of France and its culture. France was the country of Vincent de Paul and Louise de Marillac and, despite her ambivalence towards the French regime in the seminary, Genevieve was a Francophile. Her school trips abroad, to Lourdes or to Rome, always included a stay in Paris, her favourite city, so that after they had paid their respects to the bodies of St. Louise de Marillac and St. Catherine Laboure in the church of the mother house of the Daughters of Charity in the Rue du Bac, the girls who had never been outside the warren of West Belfast could walk down the Champs Elysées.

Genevieve wanted every girl to learn another language despite the fact that some girls had hardly mastered English. Her ideas on what should be taught were dictated by two aims that were sometimes incompatible: her desire to see that every girl left school with a paper qualification and her determination that St. Louise's should offer as rich a curriculum as the grammar school down the Road. The choice of languages in the early years was French, Irish and Latin. She wanted the girls to have the opportunity to learn Irish, which she called 'our national language', because it was the key to their distinctive culture but Latin was there to keep up with the grammar school and once it had lost its prestigious status in British education, it was dropped.

Genevieve's high hopes for the girls of the Falls were as uncompromising as Sister Vincent's had been, but in the first ten years of the school's life more modest and realistic goals were needed if the parents were to be convinced that a school such as St. Louise's had some practical value. She had to sell education to the people of West Belfast and for all the well-attended parents' evenings, the musical shows and the prize distribution ceremonies, it was Genevieve's boast that no girl left to go straight on to the dole that won parents over.

She could not 'save' all the girls in the first intakes from the mills and factories of the textile trade because for girls who left school at fifteen, doffing, weaving and stitching and unskilled work in a laundry, a café or a shop was all that was on offer. The girls' problem was not their lack of a qualification but their age. The way to escape these humdrum jobs was to remain at school after the leaving age because the better jobs in offices became available at seventeen or eighteen. Some parents saw the point and encouraged their daughters to stay on but Genevieve had difficulty persuading others. A girl who stayed on cost the family a 'fee' in lost income and fathers in particular thought that learning to stitch in a textile factory was more useful to a girl who would soon be married and have a family of her own than working as a secretary in an office. Margaret Crawford, who was thirteen when her mother died and who as a schoolgirl had to help her unemployed father bring up her four younger siblings, went straight from school into a shirt factory even though she had learnt shorthand and typing at St. Louise's because the family needed her wages and her father insisted that stitching shirts was a better job for a girl.

Even in the 1980s there were fathers in the Falls who disliked Genevieve's underlying feminism and believed that the only 'career' for a girl was to marry and have a large family, an attitude that the Roman Catholic church did little to discourage. In the 1960s, Genevieve found that most parental opposition to girls staying on was overcome once parents saw the seventeen- and eighteen-year-olds landing clerical and secretarial jobs in the Civil Service, banks, hospitals, legal offices and commercial firms, so that throughout this decade the number of girls going straight into unskilled jobs declined. It was not until the late seventies, however, that 'shop assistant' became an unusual destination for leavers and 'stitching' disappeared altogether.

By 1964, so many girls were staying at school after the age of fifteen that eight temporary classrooms had to be provided, but very few of these girls were studying for Advanced Level exams. For the great majority, the sixth form was a place to take Ordinary Level exams and commercial qualifications. It was also an employment agency. Genevieve reckoned that if her strategy for lifting the girls' expectations was to work, the school would have to offer more than routine careers advice. So she made the rounds of the banks and offices herself, charming the managers who had probably been none too keen to be interviewed by a nun, and asking them what qualities and qualifications they were looking for. She became so skilled at matching the girl to the job, that employers soon started telephoning her whenever they had a vacancy. 'Most of us got our jobs through the school,' wrote Mary Crossey who had been placed by Genevieve in the Civil Service office in Belfast.

In terms of her school career and the job she got when she left, a characteristic St. Louise's girl of the 1960s would have been Mary McGorman. Mary was from Divis Street in the heart of the Lower Falls. Her mother died when Mary was only three and her introduction to education was sitting beside her older sister at St. Comgall's primary school because there was no one to look after her at home. At St. Louise's, she worked her way up into the academic stream and persuaded her father to let her stay on in the sixth form where she passed five Ordinary Level exams and qualified in shorthand and typing. Genevieve fixed her up with an interview for a clerical job in a bank and briefed Mary on what to say and what to wear. Mary got the job, as did hundreds of other girls who benefited from Genevieve's networking. In the more affluent and sophisticated parts of the United Kingdom, Mary's achievement would have seemed modest enough, but it was a first step away from the poverty in which the families of the Falls had lived for generations.

Two groups of girls in this period were not typical: those who aspired to higher education and those who had religious vocation. The few girls who passed Advanced Level exams went to Catholic teacher training colleges, such as St. Mary's in the Falls Road and Sedgley Park College in Manchester, rather than to university. The regular flow of Genevieve's pupils to universities in Northern Ireland and on the mainland did not begin until the seventies.

In the school's first decade, there were more religious vocations than university candidates. Though the school's records are incomplete, it appears that there were at least two or three girls every year who joined a religious order or congregation on leaving school. They were regarded with awe and perhaps a little envy by their contemporaries. 'Some of the lucky ones who have had religious vocations are taking religious vows in convents all over the world,' wrote a young former pupil in the school magazine. 'The majority of course, like myself, have gone into jobs in Belfast.'

For Genevieve, a girl's vocation was a success of a different order from the school's growing reputation for good discipline and providing girls with qualifications and jobs. The call to the religious life was not within her sphere of influence but she could take pride in the vocations nevertheless because they reflected favourably on the spiritual life of the school. 'Another of our past pupils, Eileen Drain, joined the Marianites of the Holy Cross in September,' she reported to parents in 1962, 'making a total of three from St. Louise's in that same Order.'

Because in the story of the school's early years Genevieve is the strong-willed, feminist autocrat driving her chariot against the prejudice and injustice that she believed stood between her girls and equality of opportunity, it is easy to forget that she, too, had received the gift of a vocation. Whatever secular battles she had to fight, she was no less determined that St. Louise's should be, in her own words, 'a school where religion is seen as a corner-stone of life'. When she told the staff that 'the Vincentian character of our school sets it apart from other schools', she was not, despite her well-developed competitive instinct, thinking of the advantage this might give St. Louise's over its rivals. She really did want the example of Vincent de Paul and Louise de Marillac to influence every aspect of the life of the school and to mean as much to her girls as it meant to her.

6

'She had a holy impatience with the Church'

In 1964, while Genevieve was getting ready for a Prize Night at the school, she received the news from her father in Tullamore that her mother had died. The news was a great shock to Genevieve because her mother had not been ill, but she went ahead with the Prize Night nevertheless, praising the girls' achievements and giving no hint of her own sadness. In the morning, she drove to Tullamore. Although in theory there was merit in not attending their parents' funeral because it showed how completely they had forsaken their previous lives, most sisters rejected that extreme form of self-denial. 'To be a true Daughter of Charity,' said Vincent de Paul, 'you must leave father and mother and everything of this world,' and it was still the case when Genevieve joined the company that sisters did not visit their homes for the first five years and very seldom, if ever, thereafter. But Genevieve found this attitude to the family 'totally incomprehensible'. With Sister Vincent's blessing she had kept in touch with her parents and was deeply affected by her mother's death and by that of her father in the following year.

Genevieve was a strong woman but she needed the routine of the religious life to help her come to terms with the loss of loved ones and with the everyday pressures of the job. She lived in the company's house in Clonard with eight or ten other sisters, most of whom worked in the surrounding parish, and thanks to Sister Vincent's enlightened regime the atmosphere in the house was friendly and purposeful. By accident or design, the Sister Provincial in Mill Hill had placed Genevieve with a superior who recognised that some of the company's rules were traditional but not essential or, as modern sisters would say, 'time based, not value based'.

Genevieve usually got up at 5.30 a.m. Vincent de Paul's '4 o'clock precisely' made sense when the sisters went to bed at 9.00 p.m. but not when Genevieve was working late. Her room was small with a simple wooden bed, a crucifix on the wall and a bedside table on which were a copy of the New Testament, a glass container with holy water and a small figure of Our Lady of Perpetual Succour. It was an austere room, the only concession to luxury being a wash-hand basin. In the morning, when she had washed and dressed she joined the other sisters in the chapel for an hour of meditation and prayer. At seven, she walked across the road to mass in the Redemptorists' Church, a huge, high ceiling building that was part of the red-brick monastery complex of the Redemptorist Fathers which stood on the borderline between the Protestant Shankill and the Catholic Falls.

After breakfast, Genevieve drove to school saying aloud favourite psalms and prayers. Those who travelled with her regularly recall that her prayers often included the words: 'Lord help us to use the talents you have so generously given us.' At the end of the school day, she returned to Clonard for the community service in the chapel. However late she was retiring to her room, she invariably read a chapter of the New Testament before turning out the light.

It is easy to record the daily routine but much more difficult to capture the true nature of Genevieve's spiritual life. The account given here is based on the insights of those sisters and priests who knew Genevieve best and on the fragmentary evidence of her own writing, including the prayers and thoughts she jotted down in notebooks and on scraps of paper.

The word most frequently used to describe Genevieve's spiritual life is 'prayerful'. To those who knew her as a woman who had chosen the religious life not just as a headmistress, she was 'a simple, prayerful sister'. Simple is not a word that sits easily with Genevieve's complex character but prayer was bound to be at the heart of a Vincentian sister's spirituality; exposed to worldliness and its temptations, 'constant union with God' was essential. The problem for the sisters was how to find time for prayer when they were often engaged in demanding work from dawn to dusk. 'Oh, never mind, my dear daughters,' Vincent de Paul told them, 'keep yourselves in the presence of God and direct to Him the sighs and desires of your hearts.' It is hard to imagine Genevieve directing to God the sighs and desires of her heart as she strides purposefully down the corridors of the school day. She needed the peace she could only find in the sisters' house in Clonard, especially in the early morning. 'For me the morning hour of mental prayer sets the tone for all that follows,' she wrote, 'only by steeping myself in Christ's outlook and attitudes can I have anything to give to others. There is no problem or tragedy in life that does not find its counterpart in the New Testament. The mornings I miss that hour always hail a disjointed and disorganised day.' As the pressures of living in West Belfast intensified and the streets of Clonard became anything but peaceful, she increasingly chose to make her annual retreat in those cloistered and enclosed orders she had rejected in her youth where she knew she would find a community dedicated to a life of prayer.

The young parish priest of Corpus Christi in Ballymurphy who was for a time chaplain at St. Louise's thought that Genevieve's commitment to prayer was of the same single-minded nature as her commitment to the girls of the Falls. The two commitments were interdependent. The prayerful sister who read a chapter of the New Testament every night was as much a part of Genevieve's mission as the inspiring and domineering headmistress. What linked the spiritual life and the temporal job was the character of her vocation. As a Vincent de Paul sister she read her New Testament with the eyes of the poor so that every page of the gospel confirmed God's great love for those on the margins of society. Once she had convinced herself that the girls from the poor Catholic families fell into that category, the identification between the prayerful sister and the school principal was complete.

There was nothing in the traditions of the Daughters of Charity that precluded Genevieve from exercising secular authority or occupying such a prominent position nor was she the only sister to do so. Sister Joan Dwyer, a near contemporary who confirmed that 'no one would stay in the community unless she was a praying person', was for many years the successful head of a large girls' comprehensive school in a deprived area in County Durham. Sister Vincent had ruled her all-age primary school for forty-two years. Whether it was the 'hard order' that attracted strong-minded women or the training in the seminary that produced them, there was no shortage of sisters to take on the job of provincial or superior or headmistress, so that while most sisters worked out their Vincentian charism to the full in total obscurity, others accepted a leadership role and became to a greater or lesser degree public figures.

As a Vincentian sister, Genevieve wanted the school to reflect the spirit of Vincent de Paul's teaching. A large number of religious occasions built into the timetable established the Catholic nature of the school but the Vincentian ethos depended more on the various societies dedicated to the service of others and on the example of the sisters themselves. There were only three sisters on the staff – Sister Genevieve, Sister Ita and Sister Mary, a gentle and kindly sister who taught typing and organised the girls' trips abroad – but it was they who created the school's ethos and decided its priorities.

A characteristic society for the senior girls was the Marillac Association. On the face of it, the girls who became Marillacs undertook the same sort of community service that was becoming fashionable in other schools; they visited, befriended and did chores for elderly women living in the Falls. But this was not community service as it developed elsewhere, an alternative to compulsory sport and a useful addition to the university application form; it was a religious commitment the girls were expected to fulfil in the Vincentian spirit and to continue after they left school. 'The spirit of the Marillac,' Genevieve instructed them, 'is one of joyful charity, of always being ready to serve, of undertaking happily, humble, even unpleasant tasks for the old person.' Before they set out each week to visit their old people, the Marillacs, who always went in pairs, said a prayer together: 'Lord I am going to visit one whom Thou dost call Thy other self. Grant that the offering I bring her and the affection with which I give it may be acceptable to her. Grant that the moments spent with her, endeavouring to do her good, may bring forth fruits of Eternal Life for both of us.'

The Marillac Association was one piece of the complex pattern of religious occasions and sodalities the sisters established. Within three years of the school's opening, three Marian sodalities had been started: the Children of Mary for the older girls, the Aspirants for the next in line and the Holy Angels for the first years. In school, the members of these sodalities wore round their necks distinctively coloured ribbons with a copy of St. Catherine's Miraculous Medal, so that they became a recognisable religious elite noted for their loyalty to Genevieve's vision of what the school ought to be. Alert as ever to the connection between religious commitment and good discipline, Genevieve told parents that 'these girls wearing their blue and green ribbons round the school have set a very high standard of behaviour and integrity for others'.

Even if the majority of girls did not find their way into the ranks of the Children of Mary or of the other sodalities, such as the Crusaders of the Blessed Sacrament, that sprang up over the years, they could not escape the influence of the powerful ethos Genevieve had created. Quite apart from the routine of assembly and religious instruction, Genevieve found so many feast days to celebrate that the record of the school year reads like a religious calendar. Hardly a week goes by without a special mass or a retreat. The highlights of the year were the celebration of the feast of St. Louise, the school's patroness, in March and the crowning of the statue of Our Lady at the beginning of May. Every Thursday, afternoon school finished early so that the girls could attend the Novena in honour of Our Lady of Perpetual Succour at the Redemptorist Church in Clonard and even visits to the cinema could be turned to spiritual advantage. 'The Feast of Our Lady of Lourdes was celebrated with a visit to the Imperial Cinema,' a dutiful head girl noted in the official diary, 'where we enjoyed *The Song of Bernadette* and resolved to follow in her footsteps.'

The impact on the girls of this crowded religious schedule is difficult to assess. Nothing remotely resembling protest occurred, even in the late sixties when school pupils across the Irish Sea were refusing to sing in chapel or to bow their heads in prayer. The girls came from Catholic families in an overwhelmingly Catholic area (before the Troubles there were still some Protestant families living in the Falls) and would not have found the proliferation of celebrations and sodalities at all odd. They took their Catholicism seriously. When in 1963, the head girl and house captains initiated the saying of the rosary in the assembly hall in the lunch hour, the hall was filled every day.

The former Children of Mary insist that the religious atmosphere was serious but not precious; they took away from St. Louise's a love of ritual and a Vincentian desire to give their faith practical expression not excessive piety. 'Faith without works is void,' Genevieve had often reminded them and when they left, those who had a religious vocation chose to join congregations such as the Daughters of Charity and the Presentation Sisters that allowed them to be active in the world. Their dispatches from the front were printed in the school magazine. 'Please God I will see many more years of service to these wonderful people,' wrote Sister Mary Basil alias Muriel Turley, once captain of the netball team, who was teaching English to Muslim children in the Presentation convent school in Pakistan.

For most of the girls at St. Louise's Genevieve was a feminist rather than a religious role model; she showed them what women could achieve in this world. But as an attractive, dynamic and still relatively young sister she was bound to influence some girls to follow her into her congregation. 'I was obsessed with pleasing the nuns initially, especially Sister Genevieve and was in seventh heaven when she praised me,' wrote a girl who became a Vincentian sister. 'I can't honestly remember who suggested I enter the Daughters of Charity, it was as if it was inevitable.' Such youthful enthusiasm did not always last but the girls from St. Louise's who dropped out of the religious life were the exception; five of Genevieve's former pupils are currently Vincentian sisters and all but one have been in the community for many years.

Genevieve's own relationship with the traditions of the Vincentian community was made easier in the mid-sixties by the Second Vatican Council inaugurated by Pope John XXIII and in particular by the papal decree *Perfectae Caritatis* on the Renewal of the Christian Life. The decree urged religious orders and congregations to adapt 'to the changed conditions of our time'. While remaining true to the inspiration of their founders, they were encouraged to modernise their operation: their manner of prayer, life and work should be in harmony with the present day; the religious habit too should be appropriate to the times; superiors should listen willingly to their 'subjects' and the latter should bring their own powers of intellect to bear on the instructions they received. In the spirit of the 1960s, uniformity was out and individuality was in.

This suited Genevieve well though she could hardly claim that since her arrival in Belfast her individuality had been cramped or her talents wasted. The Renewal of the Christian Life was for her, as for many other nuns and sisters, a liberating experience. 'What a complete turnabout!' she wrote, 'sisters are now encouraged to remain loyal to their own particular spirit and to live out the message of the gospel in their own lives, to develop their own personality and not be afraid to be different. Above all, the talents and gifts of sisters are appreciated. Indeed the voices heard loudest in the championing of human rights and social justice are often those of the sisters.'

The encouragement to Catholics to champion human rights and social justice stemmed from the new conception of the role of the Church that the liberals had persuaded the Vatican Council to accept. Before the Council, the Catholic church saw itself as an embattled fortress in a hostile and sinful world. The command structure was necessarily hierarchical, the discipline necessarily

strict; what was required of the laity, the foot-soldiers, was obedience. Religious sisters, such as the Daughters of Charity, might
work to alleviate suffering but their eyes should be fixed on a
crown of glory in the next world not on the need to reform this
one.

The conception of the Church that emerged from Vatican Two
was radically different. The Church was no longer a fortress, it was
a pilgrim people, in other words a body of equals, priests and lay
people together, seeking to transform this world into the Kingdom
of God. Not surprisingly, some priests found it hard to adjust to a
Church in which their superior status was not taken for granted
and to an agenda that seemed to them to have more to do with
left-wing politics than Christian theology.

Genevieve had no such difficulty. As a Vincentian sister she
had to be apolitical but her sympathies were with the ideals of the
political Left. Her commitment to the poor had been the key to
her vocation and it will be remembered that she left the seminary
'fanatically dedicated to the equality of all human beings'. She
also wrote of her seminary training 'that it was then that it dawned
on me how akin the Christian-Vincentian and Marxist philoso-
phies were – the protest against social injustices, the concern for
the weaker members of society and a desire for a fairer distribution
of wealth.'

Finding similarities between Christianity and Marxism was so
much a characteristic of the fall-out from Vatican Two that it is
surprising to find Genevieve saying she had come to that conclusion a quarter of a century earlier. It is unlikely that she studied
Marxism with the Mercy nuns and even more unlikely that she
read *The Communist Manifesto* as a seminary sister. Perhaps she was
projecting back onto her time in the seminary the excitement she
experienced in the sixties when Christians and Marxists seemed to
be talking the same language. Whenever her left-wing sympathies
developed, they remained almost exclusively focused on education.
The effect of Vatican Two was to make her more outspoken in her
attacks on the selective school system and more inclined to identify her mission at St. Louise's with the wider movement in the
Church in support of demands for greater social justice.

Nothing in the life of the Roman Catholic church after Vatican Two was so bedevilled by misunderstandings and disputes as activities associated with the concept of social justice. The most controversial activities were inspired by what became known as liberation theology which in its most radical form in Latin America justified the use of violence if there was no other way to overcome a 'structural injustice' such as the concentration of power and land in the hands of a few.

Genevieve did not condone violence, on the contrary, during the Troubles she publicly condemned it, whoever was responsible, but some aspects of liberation theology struck a chord with her, especially the emphasis on the subversive role of education in liberating the poor from a mood of passive despair. 'The girls did not speak as oppressed Catholics,' a senior official in the Northern Ireland Office commented after visiting the school. Few compliments would have pleased Genevieve more. The ideas of liberation theology also seemed to endorse her opposition to the school system in Northern Ireland; the separation of pupils into first-class sheep and second-class goats at the age of eleven was an example of a structural injustice that as a Christian she was called on to overcome. The fact that many Christians in Northern Ireland, including those who were most influential in both the Catholic and Protestant traditions, supported the selective school system, only served to strengthen her sense of being against the established power structure or, as she preferred to put it, of being 'a sign of contradiction'.

Genevieve used this phrase again and again to define her relationship to those who held power. She was proud to be a sign of contradiction to the education establishment, to the Catholic hierarchy and, during the Troubles, to the Republican leadership in West Belfast. There were times when she appeared to relish being controversial and unpopular. There is no question that she was motivated by her Christian faith and by her Vincentian reading of the life of Christ, but the sincerity of her motives did not preclude enjoying her reputation as someone who was always against the government. In that role she saw herself as part of the Vincentian tradition. 'I may be a sign of contradiction to many,' she wrote, 'but then in the seventeenth century St. Vincent de Paul and St. Louise de Marillac were signs of contradiction to a society orientated towards privilege and social advancement.' No wonder the priests found her difficult to stomach. If her attacks on them as stick-in-the-muds did not make enemies, what they interpreted as her pride certainly did.

Inside the school, Genevieve's radical sympathies were reflected in the content of her homilies at morning assembly. To the girls she was a sign of contradiction in a different sense; she was an autocratic headmistress who preached against the abuse of power. The notes she made for a senior assembly are worth quoting verbatim because they show how far she had absorbed the ideas and vocabulary of liberation theology:

> Poverty is an evil. Powerlessness is an evil. Try to make a difference to the world. Not here waiting for the next world. Poverty is unnecessary. The way Jesus chose to condemn the power structure that led to his death. They did away with him because he was dangerous. He pointed out injustices and that could have repercussions. Must make people aware how they are being exploited. Must understand the situation and tell others. Must be a threat to establishment. St. John the Baptist. Jesus did not compromise with truth. Mark writes about man Jesus. His fidelity to truth and justice was His virtue. Main thrust of Bible is that if people are powerless there is something wrong.

For Genevieve and for her senior girls the natural outlet for these ideas was not left-wing politics but the civil rights movement that had started in Dungannon in 1963 as the Campaign for Social Justice and had developed by 1967 into the non-sectarian but predominantly Catholic Northern Ireland Civil Rights Association. The powerlessness of the Catholic minority was what the movement was all about. Genevieve made no secret of her support for civil rights. She had lived in the North long enough to know how the structural injustices operated. A voting system for the

Northern Ireland Parliament that was loaded in the Protestants' favour and local electoral boundaries gerrymandered to ensure Protestant control meant that discrimination against Catholics in housing and employment was allowed to continue unchecked.

Denied any effective power to challenge discrimination, the civil rights movement took to the streets. But Genevieve did not join them. She supported their aims but she was making her contribution to social justice in Northern Ireland in the field of education. But some of her more politically minded pupils did march and in one case at least peaceful support of civil rights was a prelude to active involvement in the armed struggle.

Liberation theology was not the only outcome of Vatican Two that worried conservatives in the Church. Women in religious orders and congregations seized the opportunity to throw off – literally in the case of their religious habit – the lifestyle and priorities that had previously defined their role. The ease with which these women adapted to the new mind-set of the Church – free, more open, less hierarchical – disconcerted conservative clergy who saw it as secularisation inspired by disobedience and women's lib. Few women in the religious life in Ireland can have personified this development more provocatively than Sister Genevieve. She was everything the conservative priests feared the nuns and sisters might become: assertive, independent, feminist.

If they expected her to behave in a deferential manner or to play the servant, they were disappointed. At one-to-one meetings with senior members of the hierarchy, she left them to pour their own coffee while she berated them for their reluctance to condemn selective schooling.

One of those with whom she disagreed strongly on this subject was the Bishop of Down and Connor, Cahal Daly. The soft-spoken prince of the Church cannot have enjoyed being challenged by a feminist sister who had no time for the subtleties of pragmatism but today Cardinal Cahal Daly is generous in his praise of Genevieve's leadership of St. Louise's, especially during the Troubles. Other churchmen with whom she clashed are less forgiving: they think her style was unnecessarily confrontational and that her dislike of having to defer to men clouded her judgement.

A priest who conducted retreats that Genevieve attended said of her that 'she had a holy impatience with the Church'. It moved too slowly for her and not only on the question of ending selection in Catholic schools. The fact that despite Vatican Two the Catholic church remained an extreme example of an organisation where mediocre men could be promoted to management positions while more able women were confined to supporting roles did nothing to moderate her impatience. When in retirement she told a radio interviewer that 'women are by far the superior race', it sounded less like a feminist statement than an expression of frustration with having to put up for so long with the most glaring structural injustice of all – the male monopoly of power in the Church. She did not advocate the ordination of women though she did point out publicly how remote the prospect of women priests was in a Church that was still arguing about young girls serving at the altar. 'It will be a long time,' she added with studied understatement, 'before we can expect to see a woman in a responsible position in the Vatican.'

Such comments did nothing to reassure conservative clergy but in the field of Catholic education Genevieve's difficulties with priests were not unusual. Billy Steele, who was head of a boys' secondary school on the Antrim Road, described the Church as 'a stumbling block' rather than a help. The clergy on his governing body opposed his attempts to introduce academic courses and to develop a sixth form because they feared he would attract pupils away from St. Malachy's College, the nearby grammar school which provided many of the candidates for ordination. The Church's apparent lack of interest in the fate of children who did not qualify for the grammar school provoked both Billy Steele's and Genevieve's conflict with the clergy but in Genevieve's case, the conflict was more personalised because she was an outspoken sister. Michael Murphy who became principal of St. Peter's Boys' Secondary School in 1968 and who as a new Catholic principal in West Belfast turned to Genevieve for advice, quickly spotted what it was that made some priests so hostile to her. 'She saw the priests as a weight about her ankles,' he recalled, 'and I don't think she would have used great diplomacy, I have to say that.' Brother

Dominic who was principal of La Salle Boys' School in nearby Andersonstown admired Genevieve's determination to overcome any obstacle: 'She was driven exclusively to get the best for the girls in her school and would not let the priests on her Board or the Church stand in her way.'

Genevieve had no intention of playing the essentially male game of the art of the possible. She knew what she wanted for the school and could not see why any further discussion was needed. Monsignor Colm McCaughan, who was closely involved with the development of Catholic schools in Belfast in this period and who is one of the few people able to give a dispassionate account of Genevieve's work and personality, believes that 'a lot of Genevieve's problems with the clergy were of her own making'. He puts this down not to her feminism but to her unwillingness to consider anyone else's point of view; she was so convinced that she was right that discussion was difficult, even impossible. 'If you did not agree with her, *exeunt omnes.*'

Every school principal wishes to be seen to be decisive if only because there is no more damaging criticism than to be called indecisive. But Genevieve's certainty that she was right went far beyond what was required to see off her critics. One friend described her as 'Margaret Thatcher with a spiritual dimension', and there is no doubt that despite the differences in political and religious outlook, Thatcher was someone Genevieve admired and used in her speeches as an example of a strong woman who had the courage of her convictions. 'Margaret Thatcher arouses mixed feeling,' she said on one occasion, 'but one thing is certain she has never lacked courage in proclaiming *her* message and adhering to *her* standards. Can we do less in a Catholic school?'

Genevieve admired in Thatcher qualities she knew that she herself possessed but it is in her own field of education that the more interesting comparisons can be made, particularly with the early pioneers of girls' education who needed the courage of their convictions to overcome society's scepticism. Dorothea Beale, the principal of Cheltenham Ladies' College for nearly fifty years in the nineteenth century had many qualities in common with Genevieve, though the Ladies' College in Cheltenham could

hardly have been more different from St. Louise's in the Falls
Road. They were both headmistresses driven by a belief in their
divinely inspired mission, certain that they were right and, typically of such people, stimulated by opposition. The words used by
Beale's biographer to describe her personality, 'a fusion of the
practical and the spiritual', could equally well be applied to
Genevieve and much of the notice written by a former pupil in *The
Times* after Beale's death could have been written by one of the
girls who had been at St. Louise's with Genevieve, especially this
sentence: 'Though she never sought, or perhaps enjoyed, popu-
larity in the ordinary sense of the word, many who had feared her
in their schooldays, grew afterwards to love her as well as to
admire her.'

The differences are no less revealing. Dorothea Beale was the
more intellectual figure, Genevieve the more passionate. As a
child, Dorothea had played schools in her imagination with herself
as headmistress, whereas teaching had been the last thing
Genevieve had wanted to do. Most interesting is the contrast in
their attitude to fun. Dorothea Beale was always in earnest, noting
in her diary the time she had wasted in 'idle thoughts' and 'unnecessary rest'. 'She had little understanding of, or sympathy with
any form of frivolity,' her former pupil wrote in *The Times*. In
contrast, Helen O'Connor once saw Genevieve jump on a bus in
the days when the ankle-length habit and winged headdress were
still worn and, grasping the bar on the bus platform with both
hands, swing round full circle before the bus started moving.
There are other memories and glimpses – Genevieve playing
rounders barefoot on the beach at Portstewart or sitting at a pavement café in Paris – that help to lighten the portrait, adding a few
relaxed, good humoured lines to what would otherwise be stern
features, suggesting what her friends knew well even if her pupils
did not, that although Genevieve was a driven woman she still
could be fun to be with.

For many of the priests who crossed Genevieve's path she was
neither a simple, prayerful sister nor fun to be with. She was a
sister with attitude. They reacted to her in the same way as she
reacted to disobedient or unco-operative girls who had 'an attitude

problem'. The priest who had to deal with Genevieve on an almost daily basis was the school manager. Until 1968, the diocese persisted with the arrangement whereby a single clerical manager exercised the authority that would normally be exercised by the school's governing body. Other priests who were the legal owners and proprietors of the school acted as a Board of Trustees. In 1968, the single manager was replaced by a school committee with a priest as chairman and lay members as well as clergy.

Genevieve welcomed this change but she realised that much would depend as it does in any school on how well she got on with the chairman. The omens were not good. The priest appointed as chairman of the new school committee, a post he held for ten years, was Father Padraig Murphy, the administrator of St. Peter's pro-Cathedral in the Lower Falls, a priest of the old school who smoked fifty cigarettes a day, was only comfortable in the company of other priests and believed in authority and obedience. A forceful character with a tall, imposing presence, he is still remembered in the Falls when people talk about the power the Roman Catholic church used to have. When Father Murphy went into the pulpit to tell the people that they should move into the new high-rise Divis Flats and not listen to Gerry Adams and other young Sinn Fein activists who dismissed the building as 'a multi-storey car park disguised as a block of flats', the people did as they were told. This was the man with whom Genevieve would have to work during the most difficult years of her career.

In 1968, Genevieve was forty-five. Michael Murphy, her neighbouring headmaster who visited her for the first time in that year, described her a little patronisingly as 'an attractive young lady principal'. She had proved the pessimists wrong by establishing St. Louise's as a school where the toughest girls toed the line and all the girls were given a chance of a qualification and a job. Her dream that the girls from the poorest families should have the same opportunity of entering university and the professions as girls from the more affluent parts of the city remained unfulfilled, but she had good reason to be optimistic about the future. It was not just the tide of religious opinion that was running her way. While the Second Vatican Council was reforming the Roman

Catholic church, a new Labour government in London was preparing to dismantle the selective school system on the mainland. In language that Genevieve would have approved, the prime minister, Harold Wilson, assured delegates to the party conference in 1967 of his government's 'determination to end the vicious system under which the education future of a child can be determined by an arbitrary and unscientific test at the incredible age of eleven'. Although Labour's policy of replacing the selective system with comprehensive schools that would take children of all abilities would not apply to Northern Ireland, Genevieve understandably saw it as further confirmation that her opposition to selection was right and the Catholic church's reluctance to move ahead of public opinion on this issue was wrong.

What Genevieve did not foresee was that the context in which she would have to pursue her dream was about to change dramatically. The decision to double the size of the school was totally unexpected because the original plan had been to accommodate the additional pupils in a new school. The outbreak of communal violence, marking the start of the latest phase of the Troubles, was also unexpected, however much in retrospect it might appear to have been signalled well in advance by the rising tension over civil rights. In 1968, civil rights marches were increasingly associated with what were euphemistically described as disturbances, notably in Derry on 5 October when the marchers who included women and children were baton-charged by the Royal Ulster Constabulary. Events such as this made people fear for the future but did not reveal the future's hand. If Genevieve had been told that the Falls was soon to become a war zone and that her school was about to embark on twenty-five years of living with anarchy and sudden death, she would have found that hard to believe.

1969–1988
The Troubles

7

'You were walking a tightrope between the paramilitaries and the army'

In the long drawn out conflict from August 1969, when the Northern Ireland government lost control of the streets and asked the British government to send in the army, until the IRA cease-fire of August 1994, all sectors of society suffered but it was overwhelmingly the working-class people in the inner city ghettos, such as the Falls and the Shankill in Belfast, who did the fighting and the dying. Inevitably schools in the ghettos were more directly affected by the Troubles than schools in middle-class areas where pupils might only learn what had happened the previous night less than a mile away from where they lived by watching the news on television. Middle-class schools were not untouched by the disruptions and tragedies of these years but unlike the schools in the Falls and the Shankill they were not in the front line. Pupils who were in the front line had to learn quickly how to distinguish between the war going on around them and the danger they could not ignore. 'Any trouble up your way last night, sonny?' Billy Steele asked one of his pupils from the Catholic New Lodge district. 'No,' the boy replied, 'there was a lot of shooting but no trouble.'

St. Louise's and its pupils were in the front line. The guerrilla war between the IRA and the British army was fought on the streets where the pupils lived and where they travelled to and from school. The school itself occupied a sensitive position. A short way up the Falls Road were the Milltown Cemetery where the IRA buried its dead (and where the gravediggers were Genevieve's spies primed to report girls who hid there when they were playing truant) and the heavily fortified Andersonstown Police Station, which the British army used as a local base. Even closer to the school was another British army base at Macrory Park on the Whiterock Road. The Troubles, like the French Revolution, had its journées, dramatic events that seemed in retrospect to have been turning points in the story, and thanks to the proximity of the Milltown Cemetery some of these, notably the funerals of the IRA hunger strikers, took place on the school's doorstep.

The girls who attended St. Louise's during the Troubles came from areas – The Falls, Ballymurphy, Turf Lodge and Andersonstown – that were regarded as Republican strongholds by the police and the army, but there is no way of knowing exactly how many girls came from Republican families, not least because 'Republican family' is difficult to define. Given the nature of the extended family networks in West Belfast, girls whose immediate family had no connection with the Republican movement might nevertheless have a relative in the IRA. Even when a girl's immediate family was Republican, that term could embrace the whole spectrum of opinion from those who supported Republican strategy and voted Sinn Fein but who had no involvement with the paramilitaries, to families who had been committed to the armed struggle for generations. There were also families whose support for Republicanism rose and fell with events; girls who were at the school during the hunger strikes, for example, had the impression that many of their contemporaries were at that period pro-Republican and uninhibited about saying so.

A family's long-standing Republican sympathies were not necessarily passed on to the younger generation. The Shannons, whose three daughters attended St. Louise's in the early eighties, were a traditional Republican family. Father, grandfather and uncle were interned in 1971. Liam Shannon, the girls' father, had no connection with the IRA but he was held for three years and was one of the 'hooded men' whose interrogation resulted in Britain being found guilty of inhuman and degrading treatment by the European Commission of Human Rights. When his daughters started at St. Louise's it was assumed by their contemporaries that they would be active Republicans but Liam Shannon and his wife put no pressures on their daughters to share their Republican views and insisted that the girls' education came before everything else. Despite the turbulence of the early eighties, the girls were not allowed to miss a single day's school. They went on marches 'because everyone did' but their only involvement with Republican activities was to play in a Republican band.

Despite the difficulties of definition, it is safe to say that the girls whose immediate families would have called themselves Republican were in a minority at St. Louise's. Most of the families Genevieve had to deal with during the Troubles would have called themselves Nationalist not Republican and would have voted for the Social Democratic and Labour Party (SDLP), which was founded in 1970, not for Sinn Fein.

When a family's history of Republicanism was common knowledge, the daughters were usually anxious to keep a low profile in the school. Marie-Terese Hannaway was dismayed when Genevieve introduced her to a teacher as Alfie Hannaway's grand daughter, Alfie being well known in the Falls as a prominent Republican. There was a good reason for these girls not to talk about their families. Both the RUC's special branch and the British army saw schools in Republican areas as potential sources of intelligence, a fact that was not lost on the Republicans themselves. Early in the Troubles, before Internment was introduced in 1971, someone (presumably the IRA) broke into St. Louise's at night and burned the school's records which would have contained the addresses and other information about families in whom special branch was interested.

Known Republicans among the parents were, with few exceptions, loyal supporters of Genevieve's policy of business as usual during the Troubles. It is true that when she accepted a British honour some were highly critical, but for the most part Republican parents were scrupulously correct in their dealings with the school and seem to have gone out of their way not to criticise Genevieve. The more committed they were to the Republican cause the more determined they appear to have been not to allow the Troubles to interfere with their daughter's chances of a good education. Maire McFadden, Genevieve's deputy, said girls from active Republican families 'were probably our best attenders' during the Troubles, an opinion echoed by Brother Dominic at La Salle Boys' School who said that active Republicans were good parents, 'assiduous in making sure that their children did not miss school'. But the burden of ensuring that the children's education was not harmed fell on the mothers. When father was in prison or on the run, his part in his children's upbringing was minimal, though some fathers did their best to keep in touch. Joe Cahill, an IRA veteran from the forties and fifties who became commander of the Provisional IRA's Belfast Brigade in the early seventies, was on the run for much of the time that his daughters were at St. Louise's. They went to see him in the holidays when they could, taking their school reports for him to read, but it was their mother who had to stand in line on parents' evenings. According to Patricia Cahill, when her father was on the run he only commented on the good things in their reports, never on the bad.

Genevieve respected the Cahills for their determination to see that their daughters had as normal an education as possible. With other leading Republican families she was on familiar terms because they were her neighbours in Clonard. The Hannaways who sent their daughters to St. Louise's and lived near Genevieve had an impressive Republican pedigree that had stretched back several generations to Michael Hannaway who joined the Irish Republican Brotherhood before the First World War. Michael Hannaway's great-grandson is Gerry Adams, who became president of Sinn Fein in 1983.

Genevieve's respect for and friendship with some Republican families did not compromise her opposition to the IRA. She unequivocally rejected its use of violence. But the Troubles did force her to reconsider her attitude to Irish unity which was the Republican's goal. The attitude she brought to Northern Ireland had been formed in her childhood and youth. For her parents'

generation memories of the painful birth of the Irish Free State
were still fresh and Irish unity was not uppermost in their minds.
Proud of their newly won independence and of the special position
it guaranteed for their Roman Catholic church, the people of the
South gave little thought to their co-religionists in the North who
were still under Protestant and British rule. As young Mary
O'Farrell, Genevieve absorbed this indifference to what was happening north of the border and developed a typically romantic
view of the new Ireland. W.B. Yeats was her favourite poet and
Padraig Pearse, the schoolteacher and poet who had led the Easter
Rising, was her hero in much the same way as Bobby Sands was a
hero to many of her pupils of a later generation; and just as her
pupils admired Sands' courage and idealism without implying support for the IRA, so Genevieve admired Pearse without condoning
his use of violence or his curious notion that 'bloodshed is a
cleansing and sanctifying thing'.

In 1991, Genevieve tried to explain why, as a southern Catholic,
she had arrived in Belfast with little or no idea of the position of
the Catholic minority in the North:

> We were the super-Catholics of the world. The past was
> more important to us than the present and we thrived on
> hatred. Everybody seemed prepared to die for Ireland, not
> to live or work for it. So there we were, smug, self-satisfied
> Catholics with little knowledge of the minefield on our
> doorstep. And into this minefield I was thrown.

The thirteen years she had spent in Belfast before the Troubles
started had opened her eyes to the discrimination suffered by
Northern Catholics and had brought her into contact for the first
time with their perspective on Irish unity. For many Northern
Catholics, a united Ireland was the only sure way to end discrimination and to secure their civil rights. It seemed to them that the
British State was unable or unwilling to prevent the Protestant
majority in the province from practising blatant discrimination in
housing and employment that would never have been tolerated in
any other part of the United Kingdom. Genevieve understood

and sympathised with the aspirations of the Northern Catholics but as a Christian she was opposed to those among them who favoured the use of violence to achieve Irish unity. To this extent she was an Irish Nationalist. She was publicly apolitical but the sisters were allowed to vote and her friends think she voted for the nationalist SDLP or possibly for the Alliance Party, founded in 1970, as a non-sectarian grouping in Northern Ireland politics. 'There is all the difference in the world between being an Irish Nationalist and a member of the IRA,' she told an audience in 1989, 'the former favour a United Irish Republic through peaceful methods, the latter a United Ireland brought about by violence and force, whether the majority want it or not.' Such public criticisms of the IRA do not appear to have affected her relations with Republican families; it was her willingness to play ball with the British not her rejection of violence that annoyed them.

In the school, Genevieve's Irish nationalism was tempered by practical considerations. She thought and spoke of her girls as Irish – 'open, frank Irish girls' she called them – but she knew that they would have to make their way in a British province. She wanted them to be proud of their Irish heritage not held back by it. 'Our national language has its special place on the curriculum,' she assured parents, but that was only for the younger girls. The older girls had to concentrate on obtaining British qualifications. Her approach was similar to that of the Alliance Party, which argued that there was 'no inconsistency between being culturally Irish and legally British'. Needless to say, that compromise was anathema to Republicans and even some non-Republican parents expressed the fear that 'our children will be brought up as young Brits'.

Genevieve's even-handed approach to the school's cultural activities produced some curious juxtapositions; one moment the girls were winning prizes for reciting Irish verse in one of the numerous Irish festivals in the area, the next they were singing Gilbert and Sullivan on the stage in the assembly hall. Padraig Pearse's poem 'Mise Eire', a favourite with festival organisers, and the chorus in praise of being an Englishman from 'HMS Pinafore' (the school's production in 1975) were strange bedfellows. Before the Troubles few parents would have worried about this cultural ambiguity but looking back now some former pupils can hardly believe Genevieve got away with it. '"The Mikado", for Christ's sake, in the Falls!'

With British soldiers patrolling the streets and British politicians responsible under Direct Rule, which was introduced in 1972, for the government of Northern Ireland, the question of whether Genevieve was in the Irish camp or the British camp became an issue. Even so, it was more a political than a cultural issue. Parents continued to flock to the Gilbert and Sullivan operas put on by the school despite the fact that some now regarded the British as the enemy with whom they were at war and Genevieve's public occasions continued to have the flavour of an English grammar school. 'I might almost be in middle England,' observed an official from the Belfast Education and Library Board who was attending one of Genevieve's prize nights during the Troubles. But as anti-British feeling intensified, more parents questioned whether the school was Nationalist enough. When Genevieve decided to associate with British politicians who now ran education in the province in order to get what she wanted for her school, she was accused of being a 'West Brit' and insensitive to the feeling of the local community.

For Genevieve and her neighbours in the Lower Falls the Troubles began on the night of 14 August 1969. It was nearing the end of the summer holidays and Genevieve had recently returned from Scotland to prepare for the new term. On 12 August there had been fierce fighting between the police and the Catholic residents of the Bogside in Derry following a Protestant Apprentice Boys' parade. The next day the trouble had spread to Belfast when Catholics deliberately provoked the police in order to take the pressure off their fellow Catholics in Derry. Catholic attacks on the police in Belfast in turn provoked Protestant anger along the Orange-Green line that separated the Catholic Falls and Ardoyne from the Protestant Shankill. Without wishing to oversimplify or trivialise states of mind at this critical juncture, it could be said that the Protestants wanted to teach the Catholics a lesson not only for provoking the police who were overwhelmingly Protestant but more generally for daring to demand their civil rights, and that the Catholics wanted to show the Protestants that they had had enough of discrimination and were not going to take it any more.

On the warm, humid evening of 14 August, Protestant and Catholic crowds faced one another on the streets connecting the Shankill and the Falls. The Catholics thought the Protestants were massing to invade the Falls; the Protestants thought they were about to be attacked by Catholics acting as a screen for the IRA. In fact, the IRA was totally unprepared to defend the Falls; defence of Catholic areas had never been part of their strategy, so that when the Protestants' invasion began, only a handful of IRA veterans with old weapons joined local people in trying to deter the mob. When the IRA opened fire, the police, who appeared to Catholics to be doing nothing to discourage the invaders, returned fire with heavy calibre Browning machine guns. One of their bullets killed a nine-year-old Catholic boy asleep in his bed in the Divis Flats.

The night sky was soon lit up with flames from Catholic houses burning in the streets between Clonard, where Genevieve and the other sisters were living, and the Shankill Road. The Protestants had come well prepared with petrol bombs and as they went from house to house driving out the inhabitants if they had not already fled, they tossed the bottles filled with petrol and sugar into the ground-floor windows. Bombay Street at the end of Clonard Gardens was burnt out. Over the two days and nights of fighting in the Lower Falls, seven people were killed, five Catholic and two Protestant, and hundreds of Catholic families were forced to flee their homes, leaving their possessions to the looters or the flames. The fact that the Daughters of Charity house had not been damaged did not reflect the mob's sensitivities or the effectiveness of Catholic defence; the house was just too far into the maze of Catholic streets.

Many if not all the Catholic families driven from their homes in this Northern Ireland version of ethnic cleansing would have been known to the Vincentian sisters; these streets were their parish. Genevieve had spent the night of 14 August ferrying families to safety in her car, an action that won the admiration of Alfie

Hannaway. She decided to open St. Louise's as a temporary relief centre for the refugees. Other schools a safe distance from the Shankill Road, such as Holy Child Primary in Andersonstown, and many Catholic homes also provided food and shelter. When the events of August 1969 passed into Republican legend, however, the role played by Genevieve and St. Louise's was not mentioned; those who had come to the aid of the refugees turned out to have been almost exclusively prominent Republicans.

Genevieve ran her relief centre with customary efficiency. Girls who had left school the previous term were telephoned to come and help. They collected mattresses for the families to sleep on the floor of the classrooms and the assembly hall and helped refugees fill in the forms that were used to pool information so that families separated in the scramble to escape could be re-united. Genevieve's leadership created a sense of order in shattered lives. Some refugees feared the Protestants would reach them even here; others worried about how they were going to pay for what they had lost. 'It's all on the HP, Sister,' one woman told Genevieve, 'what am I going to do?' Not surprisingly, many of those who fled from the Lower Falls never returned, preferring to remain in Andersonstown or Ballymurphy or to cross the border into the Irish Republic. By chance, a sixteen-year-old girl who wanted to enter the sixth form at St. Louise's chose 15 August to visit the school and see the principal. She walked up the Falls Road 'amid burning buildings and barricades, mesmerised by what I saw', to find Genevieve directing operations for the refugee families but happy to discuss the Advanced Level subjects the girl wished to study.

The fighting and destruction in the Falls on 14 and 15 August convinced Harold Wilson's Labour government that the British army should be deployed on the streets of Northern Ireland and that troop re-enforcements should be sent immediately to the province. The people of the Falls at first welcomed the soldiers as protection against any further Protestant attacks; to the dismay of veteran IRA men such as Joe Cahill, housewives in the Falls were soon offering British soldiers cups of tea. The residents of the Falls also looked to their own defence. Barricades were thrown up

and a Central Citizens Defence Committee was established
including Catholic politicians, church leaders and the IRA. One of
the church leaders who was prepared to sit down with the IRA at
this time of crisis was Father Padraig Murphy, the new chairman
of the school committee at St. Louise's. Father Murphy, like
Genevieve, had played a prominent role in helping families in the
aftermath of the Protestant invasion and this shared experience
made it easier for these two strong-willed people to respect one
another and work together as school principal and chairman of the
governors.

The trauma of those August days and nights fuelled fears of
another Protestant pogrom for years to come but by the time the
school term was due to start the refugees had moved on.
Genevieve's priorities now were to ensure that the girls would be
able to travel to and from school safely and to make life in the
school as normal as possible however abnormal life became on the
streets outside. These would remain her priorities throughout
the Troubles, but she would soon add another when she recognised the danger of her girls being drawn into the world of the
paramilitaries.

At first, this danger did not seem to be very great. The IRA's
failure to provide an effective defence of the Falls in August had
provoked anger and contempt among the very people it should
have been able to look to for support. Slogans on the walls suggested that IRA should stand for 'Irish Ran Away'. The failure
also exposed a fundamental disagreement in the Republican
movement between the politicians and the militarists, between
those who believed that political involvement was the way forward and those who believed that participation in political
institutions would imply recognition of the partition of Ireland
and that the IRA should keep to its traditional role of 'physical
force' to drive out the British. When the split occurred in
December 1969, those who favoured physical force and absten-
tion from political involvement walked out to form the
Provisional IRA. Those who remained, the Official IRA, rejected
'abstentionism' but did not reject the use of violence. Although
the Provisionals quickly became the dominant faction in Belfast

and Derry, the Officials conducted operations against the British army in the early Seventies. Rose Curry and Patricia McKay (née Kelly), who are thought to have been the only two of Genevieve's former pupils to be killed 'on active service', were members of the Official IRA. Rose Curry was eighteen when she was killed in 1971 by the premature explosion of a 5 lb bomb on which she was working with another member of the Official IRA in the kitchen of a house in the Lower Falls. According to the *United Irishmen*, the Official IRA's publication, these two volunteers were the first fatalities suffered by the Officials in the Troubles. Patricia McKay was twenty when she was shot dead in a gun battle with the army in Belfast in 1972. In the same engagement a British soldier aged eighteen was also killed. It appears that all the other girls from St. Louise's who joined the IRA were members of the Provisionals.

For Genevieve, the problem of keeping the girls focused on their education was most acute in the early 1970s and early 1980s. The introduction of Internment in 1971, Operation Motorman in 1972 when British troops forced their way into the no-go areas of Belfast and Derry and the deaths and funerals of the IRA hunger strikers in 1981, were times of great tension in West Belfast and difficulty for the school. But there were no easy times. Periods of comparative calm were not periods when life returned to normal. The increasingly hostile stance of the British army, the activities of IRA punishment squads, the threat of Protestant loyalist terror gangs, the boom in crime especially by car thieves or 'hoods', even the slogans and icons on the gable walls, all helped to create a sense of permanent abnormality.

Genevieve's sternest critics acknowledge that she was remarkably successful in minimising the impact of the Troubles on the school so that there at least the girls could experience normality. It is less easy to be sure how successful she was in her other stated aim of indoctrinating the girls against uncritical acceptance of political propaganda (by which she meant Republican propaganda) and against joining any political organisation (by which she meant the IRA or the Fianna Eireann, the youth wing of the Republican movement) before they were eighteen, indoctrination which she hoped would keep them out of the orbit of the paramilitaries for

good. But given the areas from which the girls came and notwithstanding the fact that girls were less likely than boys to be drawn
into paramilitary activity, the number of girls who joined the IRA
appears to have been surprisingly small.

When Genevieve was asked by BBC Radio Ulster in 1991
what it was like to be headmistress in the Falls during the
Troubles, she replied: 'Running a school in the late sixties and
seventies in hindsight seems to have been a tremendous adventure
but very, very tough. You were walking a tightrope between the
paramilitaries and the army.' The constant reality of the Troubles
for Genevieve was not a sectarian war between Protestant and
Catholic but a guerrilla war between the Provisional IRA and the
British army. Loyalist assassins were a real threat to the people of
the Falls and some of her girls' fathers were murdered in horrify-
ing circumstances, but the problems she had to deal with on an
almost daily basis were the result of the activities of the Provos
and the army.

It was during the Troubles that many of the most distinctive
and admirable aspects of Genevieve's personality found full expression: her talent for leadership, her courage and resilience, her
single-mindedness and her compassion. Her resilience in particular stands out because the early years of the Troubles coincided
with the expansion of the school from 1,000 to 2,400 pupils. She
was wrestling with complex problems of how to accommodate
and integrate the new arrivals while trying to prevent the guerrilla
war disrupting the life of the school. In public, she seemed
indomitable; in private, her impatience with the Troubles sometimes showed. In August 1972 she wrote to her young secretary
from Perth where she had gone for a short holiday: 'I love
Scotland and one day I hope to come back here to teach. It's so
completely different from Belfast. No talk of trouble, explosions
etc. I really am sick of all that. Maybe one has to be a native to be
able to live with it.'

The Troubles also re-enforced Genevieve's dislike of being subject to an authority she did not respect. The new power-brokers in
the Falls were the British army and the IRA and Genevieve made
it clear from the start that she had no intention of being dictated

to by either of them. Despite being in a war zone, she would not tolerate any interference in how she ran the school, so that soldiers who thought they could search the premises without her permission or Republicans who expected her to close the school for an IRA funeral were no more successful than the priests in imposing their authority. Her attitude was essentially practical – there was room for only one authority in the school and that was hers – but it would not have escaped her notice that the army and the IRA were, like the Catholic church, male dominated organisations that relegated women to a supporting role. Her willingness to stand up to these organisations earned her the title of 'the best man on the Falls Road', a description she did not object to and that critics of her high profile suggest she probably invented herself.

It was typical of Genevieve that in these difficult times she should have used her religious habit to advantage. Young second lieutenants not long out of Sandhurst were disinclined to argue when a tall blue nun appeared at their side and told them they would have to move their patrol well away from the school gates. Her habit also offered a measure of protection when she criticised the IRA's methods of controlling West Belfast. 'As a nun, I have the advantage of being able to be more outspoken since I have no family who may suffer as a result,' she explained. 'Fear is the weapon used to control people in our Catholic ghetto. As a religious with total commitment I am in a position to rise above this fear as no lay person could.' It still required courage to defy the IRA, not least because unlike the majority of teachers at St. Louise's, Genevieve and the other sisters lived inside the ghetto. According to a Republican source her life was threatened on one occasion not for criticising the IRA but for accepting a British honour. If this story is true, the threat must have been made by a 'freelance', as it is most unlikely that the Provisional IRA leadership would have sanctioned such a step.

Genevieve insisted that her courage and resilience owed everything to the disciplines of the Vincentian life she had chosen. 'The basis of all this work,' she said of her stewardship of the school during the Troubles, 'and the origin of the inner strength needed, is prayer. Giving at least an hour to mental prayer daily as well as

Mass and the recital of the Divine office is the springboard from which I work.' The Troubles may well have encouraged Genevieve (if she needed encouraging) to return more often to the example of the early sisters. The latter had served on the battlefields, where the white cornettes were easily recognisable to both armies, setting up soup kitchens, tending the wounded from both sides and burying the dead. Walking a tightrope between the paramilitaries and the army in twentieth-century Belfast was in the Vincentian tradition. It also provided the heroic element Genevieve had sought as a young sister but had not expected to find in teaching. When she spoke of 'a tremendous adventure', it was not because she enjoyed the Troubles but because they challenged her vocation in a way she welcomed.

As a Vincentian sister it was easier for her than for lay head-teachers in the ghettos to balance neutrality and compassion, especially when she was praying for those who had been killed. 'Once you're here, no politics,' she told the girls, but there was no question of her ignoring what was happening in the streets. At morning assembly, she prayed for the dead but she disliked evasive generalities such as 'Let us pray for all the victims of violence'. She prayed for British soldiers killed close to the school as well as for 'a first year's daddy who was shot dead last night'. 'English tears are the same as Irish tears,' she insisted, 'Protestant tears are the same as Catholic tears.'

The morning prayers were one of the few occasions on which Genevieve allowed the Troubles to be part of the life of the school. In other respects, she wanted the school to continue as though the Troubles were not going on. The strict discipline, the values and the religious ethos she had already established paid off handsomely when the structure of everyday life outside the school began to fall apart. She refused to lower her expectations. 'We were expected to be in school on time come hell or high water,' Anne Donegan recalled. Other girls remember getting up early when the buses were not running because they feared they would be late. The only time a significant number of girls and teachers did not come to school was in the early summer of 1981 when the first hunger strikers died. Genevieve was as uncompromising as ever on

uniform. Just as barricades and burning buses were no excuse for
being late, the fact that your house had been turned upside down
the night before by the army was no excuse for being incorrectly
dressed. Even when a member of the family had been killed or
injured, the daughter was expected to be back in school as soon as
possible. Roisin Groves thought that when a plastic bullet fired by
the army on Thursday blinded her mother she and her sisters
would at least have Friday off. But their mother sent them to
school.

Genevieve's attitude was not callous. She was sympathetic to all
the girls who were traumatised by the Troubles but, as one of
these girls pointed out, it was a relief that 'she was not sugary-
sweet sympathetic' and that the emphasis was on allowing the
girls to get on with their lives at school without too much fuss.
Genevieve knew that the last thing any of the girls needed,
whether or not they had been hurt by the Troubles, was for her to
go easy on them. By making few concessions to the abnormality of
the times, she provided the girls with an alibi for not being over-
whelmed by family tragedy and a secure environment where they
could be themselves not actors in the long-running drama of the
Troubles. It must always have been the case that some girls were
happy to escape from home to the orderly, predictable life of
school, but during the Troubles the feeling that the school was a
haven they were glad to reach each morning was much more
widespread. A typical comment was that 'the school was a haven
of peace and calm, a totally different world from the world outside'. Some teenage girls in the Catholic ghettos were said to be
taking nerve tablets like smarties, but if that is true, they are
unlikely to have been Genevieve's pupils.

The key to the success of Genevieve's policy was her ability to
convince everyone – the staff, the parents and the girls themselves,
as well as the army and the paramilitaries – that as far as the school
was concerned, the girls' education was more important than anything else. 'Involve the girls totally in their work,' she urged the
staff at the first meeting after the Troubles had started. She also
told those teachers who came from outside the area to go to the
Lower Falls and see what had happened to their pupils' homes.

'This is your school, you are here to be educated,' she told the girls at the start of that September term, 'what is happening outside is really nothing to do with the school. We understand your parents have different views but in here we're only concerned with one thing – you and your education.'

Genevieve feared that the different views, for and against the armed struggle, would divide the school community. Controversial events, such as the shooting by the SAS of three unarmed IRA volunteers in Gibraltar in 1988, did provoke heated argument but the school was never divided into two camps. Girls who approved of the armed struggle and those who were opposed to it were good friends and remain so to this day. Genevieve did not try to stifle argument ('no politics' meant no political propaganda) but she did try to channel the debate into sixth-form studies where different opinions could be refereed by a member of staff. The Troubles were discussed in politics and history classes where the IRA was greatly admired by some girls and equally strongly despised by others. The Gibraltar shooting provoked hostility to the British and some sympathy for the IRA (Mairead Farrell, one of the volunteers killed, had close friends at St. Louise's) but the killing in the same month of two British corporals who inadvertently drove into an IRA funeral in Andersonstown swung most opinion sharply the other way. Speaking to the pupils in an English public school shortly after the latter event, Genevieve said: 'Let me tell you that you could not be more nauseated, disgusted and angered by that event than were girls in our school.' Genevieve was exaggerating a little for her English audience. Not everybody at St. Louise's was disgusted. One of her sixth formers from a Republican family had written a poem celebrating the corporals' deaths.

The staff, too, held different views but they were seldom expressed in the staffroom. As with the girls, particular events could prove divisive. When Carmel Gallagher, the head of history, encouraged the girls to look at the hunger strikers from a historical and more detached perspective, she was accused by some members of staff and some parents of being 'a Brit-lover'. Most teachers were cautious about discussing the latest events in class because they did not know which girls might have relatives involved. An honest expression of opinion could be hurtful. Gerry Kelly's sisters were at St. Louise's when he went on hunger strike in 1973 in an English prison. Kelly, who subsequently escaped from Long Kesh and became one of Sinn Fein's chief negotiators with the British government, had been sentenced to life imprisonment for his part in the Old Bailey bombing. The hunger strike was designed to persuade the British to allow the so-called 'Belfast Ten' to serve their sentences in Northern Ireland. Some girls at St. Louise's, including one of Kelly's sisters, argued in class that the 'Belfast Ten' should be allowed to return but the teacher poured scorn on the idea saying, 'They're murderers – we don't want them back'. What angered the girls whose families were engaged in the armed struggle was not the insensitivity of one teacher but the fact that the school authorities, including Genevieve, appeared to be so hostile to the Republican cause.

The threat to the normal life of the school did not come from arguments among the pupils or the staff but from what was happening on the streets and in the homes. In so far as she could, Genevieve intervened in the anarchy outside in order to keep the school running normally. She never thought that her responsibility began and ended at the school gates. If travel home was difficult because the IRA had hijacked buses and set them alight, she went out onto the Falls Road and flagged down private cars with a line of girls standing behind her like people queuing for a taxi. When the army set up roadblocks on the route home, she marched at the head of a column and demanded that they should be let through. Marjella McCluskey said the girls thought it hilarious that Genevieve should inspect their uniform before they set off and exhort them to 'straighten your backs, hold your heads up, remember you're Irish'. The army sealed the Falls Road after a bomb explosion or a shooting incident, or to carry out a 'lift operation' hoping to catch IRA activists or auxiliaries in the net. Saracens or the one ton armoured vehicles known as 'pigs' were driven across the road, leaving a gap at the centre that could be used by snatch squads and from where the commanding officer had a clear view of what was happening.

Genevieve's pupils going home were not the only people incon-
venienced. Groups of residents on foot, often led by a priest,
demanded to be allowed through. As the army saw little distinction between the local Catholic population and the IRA and
believed that after a shooting incident any one of these 'civilians'
could be carrying ammunition or a part of a weapon, angry con-
frontations were inevitable. In these tense situations, the officer in
command could be forgiven if he viewed with some impatience the
approach of a crocodile of schoolgirls, in brown uniforms and
with their heads held high, marching behind a tall nun who clearly
had no intention of being stopped.

In the early days of the Troubles some British officers affected
a flamboyant or eccentric style, carrying a walking stick or an Irish
shillelagh, and it was with one of these officers that Genevieve
established her right to escort her girls through the roadblocks.
'That man with a stick,' she said to the young teacher walking with
her at the head of the column, 'he must be important. Tell him to
move his vans, my girls are coming through.'

The officer ordered one of the vehicles to be moved and stood
aside as Genevieve and the girls passed through. No doubt
Genevieve enjoyed that moment as much as her girls. According to
those who were led home by Genevieve on subsequent occasions,
the roadblocks 'opened like the Red Sea' when the army saw her
coming.

Although at times the guerrilla war may have seemed like a
game, the girls knew from their own experience how deadly serious it was. It was not unusual for gunmen to time their attack to
coincide with the end of afternoon school so that the pupils pour-
ing out onto the road forced the army to abandon hot pursuit or
risk injuring schoolchildren. At St. Louise's, the girls in the junior
years were released first and made their way up St. James's Road to
the bus stops on the Falls Road. One afternoon, two British soldiers in plain clothes and driving an unmarked Mini were
ambushed at the junction of St. James's Road and the Falls Road.
The gunmen had taken over a shop near the junction. As the first
shots were fired, the girls and their teachers fell to the ground.
One of the soldiers was killed outright, the other was badly

wounded.. The car went out of control and crashed into railings. When they thought it was safe to do so, the girls and teachers got to their feet and continued on their way to the bus stops. Genevieve and a number of her former pupils described this incident and although some of the details they gave differ from the official record, it is presumably the incident that occurred at 4.00 p.m. on 8 October 1979.

Genevieve had to develop a working relationship with the British army because it was the *de facto* police force in the area. The RUC, which was nominally responsible for policing, could not move freely in West Belfast. Her point of contact was the officer commanding the company at Macrory Park whose confidential telephone number was published. On a few occasions she complained to higher authority at army headquarters in Lisburn but the sort of problems she encountered – the frisking of pupils on the way to school, the mocking or abusive behaviour of the soldiers – were best dealt with at local level. Her relationship with the local commander who changed every four months was usually good, although the behaviour of the soldiers on the street did not always match up to the assurances she had been given, an experience shared by other headteachers in Nationalist areas. Much depended on which regiment was involved. In some regiments the soldiers were allowed to behave in a way that swiftly antagonised the local population. 'Rude, abrupt and ignorant,' Genevieve called them. She told the girls not to talk to soldiers but that was hardly necessary; they had no inclination to do so except to trade insults and any older girl who may have been tempted to fraternise was deterred by the threat of being tarred and feathered by the IRA.

The alienation of the British army from the people it had come to protect was unavoidable once the IRA had decided that it was for the Republicans to defend their own people and their own territory. To the IRA the British army was an alien occupying force and therefore a 'legitimate' target for gunmen. Seeing their friends and comrades killed, the soldiers turned against the local population whom they suspected of helping the terrorists. Within a few weeks, the army that had been welcomed with cups of tea was operating in an atmosphere of brooding hatred. The people of West Belfast were persuaded that the army was on the side of the Protestants, the army believed the people of West Belfast supported the IRA. The behaviour of the army, particularly over Internment, ensured that any chance of correcting misconceptions was lost. Girls at St. Louise's whose fathers were dragged away in the night by soldiers who kicked down doors, smashed furniture and tipped the contents of drawers onto the street could not be expected to look on the British army as their protectors. In some cases the girls' alienation went further than anger and resentment. Most of the girls from St. Louise's who are known to have joined the IRA did so around the time of Internment in 1971. The sixth former who wrote a poem celebrating the death of the two British corporals in 1988 was drawing on a deep well of hatred that was still there long after Internment had ended in 1975.

Genevieve could see clearly from the attitude of the girls and their families that even those who had no sympathy with the Republican cause bitterly resented the way the British army treated the people of West Belfast. Why, she wondered, did soldiers never learn that wrecking all around them when they searched a house 'puts hatred into a woman's heart'? It is equally clear from what she wrote that Genevieve did not understand the feelings of soldiers who were the targets of bombs and snipers' bullets. She wanted everyone treated with respect in the immediate aftermath of a shooting or an explosion and suggested that soldiers engaged in a follow-up search should stand at the door and say, 'we have just been shot at, can we look through your home?'

One of the army's problems was to know how to deal with boys who threw stones and girls who might be carrying ammunition or a part of a rifle. A sniper never carried a weapon, it was brought to him and taken away afterwards, often by girls because the IRA knew the army disliked searching 'cheeky young girls' even with a woman police officer present. When Genevieve complained that 'after a shooting, the army stops everybody, even girls with prams', it was a curiously naïve comment. Unlike the old Lee Enfield .303

rifle which had to be concealed under an overcoat, more sophisticated rifles could be dismantled and some of the pieces hidden
under a baby in a pram. Did Genevieve know when she complained about the army's behaviour that some of her girls were
acting as IRA auxiliaries in this way? Presumably not, but after the
first few months of the Troubles she must have realised that with
girls coming from fiercely Republican areas, some involvement
that fell short of membership of the IRA was inevitable.

Although Genevieve criticised the army's behaviour, she kept
her most scathing criticisms for the IRA. Walking her tightrope,
she never gave the impression that she thought the army and the
IRA were as bad as one another. The army treated her with a
respect they did not always show to other headteachers in
Nationalist areas. The principal of a Catholic boys' secondary
school on the Creggan estate in Derry was badly injured by a soldier when he tried to calm a confrontation between his boys and
an army patrol. 'Who are you?' the soldier demanded. 'I'm the
principal of the school.' That seems to have been the last straw
for the soldier who hit the principal hard on the head with his
rifle.

In relation to the army, Genevieve was on stronger ground
when she was dealing with the sort of misdemeanours she understood. When a soldier snatched a girl's beret and refused to return
it, she demanded that the patrol should parade outside the school
so that the girl could identify the culprit. The company commander agreed but Genevieve then insisted that the soldier should
make a public apology at the end of morning assembly. While the
soldier was waiting to do so, she encouraged the girls to sing at the
top of their voices, 'Hail Glorious St. Patrick', the anthem of
Catholic Ireland. The girls remember this as one of Genevieve's
triumphs but as a minor incident in a cruel war it is just as interesting as an example of the lengths to which the army was
prepared to go to maintain good relations with the Catholic
community.

Genevieve tried to establish the ground rules with each new
company commander at Macrory Park. As soon as the new man
arrived she telephoned and suggested a meeting. Not only did she

find some regiments more helpful than others but she found the navy, in the form of the Royal Marine Commandos, more helpful than the army. The marines were an elite unit, more carefully selected and more highly trained than the army, and they had had more experience of so-called 'duties in aid of the civil power'.

In 1978, when a company of marines took over the base at Macrory Park, their commanding officer was Captain Ian Binnie who had learnt his counter-insurgency skills in Aden. When Binnie received a telephone call from Genevieve inviting him to a meeting, he accepted straightaway. It was the start of a close, professional relationship that benefited both parties. Binnie still regards Genevieve as 'one of the most incredible women I have ever met'. At their first meeting Genevieve explained that it was her policy to make the school a haven of peace and normality so there could be no patrols in the school grounds during the school day. Binnie replied that he would respect her wishes but could not guarantee that after a shooting incident, marines in hot pursuit would not enter the school. Genevieve had to be satisfied with that, though she expected him to telephone her first.

For the five months that Binnie was stationed at Macrory Park he visited her once a week. The mutual trust that developed enabled them to co-operate to a degree that would have aroused IRA suspicions and would have been criticised by the Nationalist community but Genevieve's sole interest was to protect her girls and her school. One of the principal threats arose from the IRA's constant need to find new hiding places for its weapons. Binnie's men had already found twelve sub-machine guns hidden in the rafters of one school and Genevieve was determined that her school was not going to be used in this way. When she was tipped off that the IRA might be intending to hide weapons in St. Louise's, she telephoned Binnie, using a code name they had agreed, and asked him to send a patrol to keep an eye on the school when the pupils and staff had gone. The presence of the patrol was soon spotted by the 'dickers' or scouts, teenage boys and girls sent ahead by the IRA to see whether the coast was clear, and on these occasions the IRA had to change its plans.

It is not surprising that Genevieve sometimes knew in advance that weapons were on the move. She had known so many families in the Falls for so long, there can have been few secrets that did not reach her sooner or later. Most of them she kept to herself but if the school was at risk she did not hesitate to act on information received.

The IRA posed a greater threat to the normal life of the school than the British army but despite her contact with Republican families, Genevieve had no effective means of communicating directly with the leadership of the Republican movement. What angered her most was the atmosphere of fear in which her girls were forced to live when they were away from the school. She publicly attacked the IRA for exercising 'a tyrannical iron control on the inhabitants'. 'There are many prisons in Belfast,' she told a Catholic audience in Liverpool, 'but the most deadly of all is not one with high walls and barbed wire fencing but the prisons of terror and fear with which the paramilitaries rule inside the ghettos and where speaking out is deadly dangerous.' The freedom of expression that was possible inside the school was all the more precious. There is no evidence that girls or teachers who expressed criticism of the IRA inside the school suffered for it outside.

It was vital for Genevieve's policy of normality that the IRA's iron control should not extend to the school and that any attempt by the IRA to influence school policy should be seen to be resisted. The IRA's most direct challenge to her authority came in 1981 when it tried to enforce the closure of schools on the occasion of the funeral of one of the hunger strikers.

There had been many IRA funerals at the Milltown Cemetery in the early 1970s and the timing of the requiem mass at one of the churches on the Falls Road sometimes meant that the funeral cortege was passing the gates of St. Louise's towards the end of afternoon school. 'Hold the bell!' was an order that pupils and teachers became accustomed to and knew how to interpret. But the funerals of the hunger strikers took place in a different context. More than at any other time before or since, the Catholic population of Northern Ireland felt that it was united. 'We were a nation,' said Jennie

Shannon who was at St. Louise's at the time. Regardless of whether or not people supported the armed struggle, they respected and were moved by the courage and sacrifice of the hunger strikers.

The Republican movement wanted everyone to be seen to be part of this unity and on the days of the funerals put out the word that children should not go to school. Genevieve was opposed to that. She would decide the priorities – not the IRA – and in her view, the girls' education came first. On the morning of one of the funerals, two men walked down the slope from the Falls Road to the entrance to the school and Genevieve went out to meet them. The men were not wearing dark glasses or any paramilitary trappings but they brought a paramilitary message. The girls were being forced to remain in school and should be released so that the school could close as a mark of respect to the hunger striker who was being buried that day.

Aidan Hamill, one of the senior members of staff who went out to support Genevieve, thinks the argument went on for twenty-five minutes. Genevieve said the girls were not being kept in school against their will. Their parents could have kept them at home on that day but since they had sent the girls to school it was her duty to educate them. She recognised the injustices the people of West Belfast had suffered for generations and she was fighting these injustices her own way. Some members of the school were able to watch this confrontation from the windows of the classrooms overlooking the entrance. As the arguments went back and forth, a number of senior girls went out to stand beside Genevieve in a gesture of solidarity. When the men saw that Genevieve was not going to budge, they had no choice but to leave. No threat was issued, nor was there any comeback. A number of leading Republicans had daughters or sisters in the school at the time.

Unlike the carpeting of the soldier who snatched the girl's beret, this was an important victory for Genevieve. She had shown that as far as the school was concerned she was in control. She was not the only headteacher in a working-class district having to resist pressure from the paramilitaries. In 1974, Jim McBride, who ran a Protestant secondary school in Fane Street, received a visit from two members of the Ulster Defence Association, the largest loyalist paramilitary group. They demanded to see a young teacher who had dared to speak out against the Ulster Workers' Strike. Fortunately, McBride recognised them as former pupils. He gave them a smoke and asked if they remembered who was in charge of the school. 'You are, sir.' Like Genevieve, he knew that if he allowed the paramilitaries to dictate to him, his authority would be undermined.

Visits from the paramilitaries were not always so easily dealt with. Two men came to see Billy Steele in his Catholic secondary school on the Antrim Road. One sat silently with his right hand thrust into his overcoat pocket like a gangster in a Hollywood film, while the other accused Steele of allowing his school to be used as a recruiting agency for the British army. Steele explained patiently that if a boy wished to join the British army, one of the few employment opportunities open to young Catholic men, it was his duty as a headmaster to help him. 'There are six of your boys going for interview in England on Sunday night,' the spokesman continued unimpressed, 'if one of them puts a foot on the boat, you'll not have a school on Monday morning. We'll blow it to bits.'

The problem for people who received visits from men apparently representing the paramilitaries was to know exactly whom they were dealing with. The anarchy in the ghettos gave freelances and criminals the opportunity to take the law into their own hands. The revolver in the pocket, 'our great psychological sexual symbol of the past' as the Irish writer Sean O'Faolain described it, could be bluff. Some threats had to be taken seriously. A warning from the IRA to leave Ireland in forty-eight hours or be 'put in a box' was not bluff; when Genevieve received an appeal for help from the mother of a man who had had such a warning, she arranged for him to leave Northern Ireland that night and to be found temporary accommodation at one of the community's houses in London. But the authenticity of a threat from two anonymous men to blow up your school if you allowed pupils to join the British army was more difficult to assess. Billy Steele consulted the parents and decided to take the risk. His boys went to England for interview and his school was not blown to bits.

Genevieve never claimed that the problems she faced during the Troubles were unique. She recognised that boys in the Catholic and Protestant ghettos, especially those at secondary schools, who had little self-esteem and who expected to follow their fathers onto the dole, were more vulnerable to the pressure of the paramilitaries than girls. 'The early 1970s were traumatic and terrible years on the Falls Road,' she wrote. 'It was almost impossible for boys to survive. They were the obvious targets for the army and the RUC who in turn were constantly attacked and stoned by young people acting under orders. Almost every boy joined the Provisionals.'

What gave Genevieve's problems their special character was the school's position on the Falls Road. Other schools had children from Republican families and pupils who were involved with the paramilitaries; while some of Genevieve's girls carried concealed weapons for the IRA, some of Billy Steele's boys were using the school's facilities to make timing devices for IRA bombs. But the Falls Road and the Milltown Cemetery put St. Louise's at the heart of the Troubles. The Falls Road was both a killing ground and a theatre, one of the most dangerous parts of the city and a stage on which many of the most dramatic events unfolded. To have kept the Troubles at bay and created a haven of peace and normality for the girls would have been an achievement in any of the working-class ghettos; to have done so on the Falls Road was remarkable.

Not even Genevieve, however, could hope to keep the school operating normally on the day that Bobby Sands died in the early summer of 1981. The death of the man who was to become one of the icons of the Republican movement could not be 'kept at bay'. It challenged her expectation that her girls would come to school regardless of what was happening on the streets and her argument that the IRA did not represent the people of West Belfast. To a large degree, Sands temporarily united Nationalists and Republicans. Although Genevieve insisted that 'the IRA are not the successors of Padraig Pearse or any 1916 leaders', Bobby Sands

was a hero to many of her girls in the same way as Padraig Pearse
had been to her own generation.

Sands joined the Provisional IRA in 1973 at the age of eighteen.
In that year he was sentenced to four years in prison for possessing
illegal arms and in 1976 to fourteen years for his part in the fire-
bombing of a furniture company. Between the sentences he married
and had a son. On 1 March 1981, he started his hunger strike as the
leader of a group of Republican prisoners who were demanding
political status. At first the hunger strike had limited public support
but Sands' election as the Westminster MP for Fermanagh-South
Tyrone attracted the attention of the world's media. His determination not to end his strike unless the British government conceded all
the prisoners' demands and Margaret Thatcher's equally determined refusal not to give in to what she regarded as blackmail,
ensured that this struggle of wills would have only one outcome. At
the beginning of May, Sands sank into a coma.

Monday 4 May was the day on which many pupils at St.
Louise's were due to start public exams. It was also the day on
which a BBC unit started filming in the school to make a docu-
mentary for the *Forty Minutes* programme, so that some of the
events of the next forty-eight hours were captured on film. The
school was now too big to have one morning assembly. To the
girls in the middle school who were about to take their exams,
Genevieve's message was simple: whatever is happening outside,
be single-minded in your approach to your exams. But to the
senior girls in the sixth form, she took a different line:

> We can't be indifferent to Bobby Sands. Now let's forget
> politics. We're here for education; I've always said that to
> you. Well, you're young adults and in this adult gathering
> we know this man is suffering. We know his family is
> suffering. We know there are others suffering. I've said to
> you in the past, tears are the same wherever they come
> from. So many of you too have been touched. So now we
> say together a very slow Hail Mary and we have uppermost
> in our minds Bobby Sands. We also have uppermost the
> families of the bereaved. Hail Mary, full of grace . . .

That evening when it was known that Sands' death was immi-
nent, there was an eerie silence in West Belfast. On the Falls Road,
people gathered and prayed while others went quietly about the
business of preparing petrol bombs. In the wings, the army in riot
gear and the RUC waited beside their Saracen armoured cars and
Landrovers. Genevieve's pupils went to bed though anticipation
made it difficult to sleep.

Bobby Sands died at 1.17 a.m. on 5 May. In Andersonstown,
thirteen-year-old Karen McKenna had decided to sleep with her
blinds open. She was awakened by the sound of a sheet of corru-
gated iron being dragged along the pavement to rouse people
from their beds. Almost at once it seemed, the Saracens and the
soldiers arrived. In her austere bedroom, Genevieve was woken by
the sound of bin lids banging on the streets of Clonard. She got up
and dressed knowing there would be no more sleep that night.
The Shannon sisters, too, were woken by the sound of the bin lids
and wanted to go outside but their father, Liam Shannon, refused
to let them. In Whiterock, Patricia Cahill and her sisters were
woken by their mother with the news that Bobby Sands was dead.
They dressed and went outside where the crowds were banging
their bin lids, blowing whistles and throwing stones as the army
tried to clear away the burning cars and the barricades. At 7.30,
their mother called them in. It was time to change into uniform
and get ready for school.

Genevieve drove to school early with Sister Ita and Sister Declan
Kelly who had joined the teaching staff in 1979. The barricades had
been removed but the streets were littered with debris of the
night's rioting and black flags hung from buildings on the Falls
Road. Uppermost in Genevieve's mind was whether girls who
were taking exams would come in to school. Some exam candidates who lived outside West Belfast did walk in the three miles,
but other candidates who lived nearer decided to stay at home
out of respect for Bobby Sands. The Shannon sisters were sent to
school as usual, so were the Cahills, but many of their contemporaries stayed away. For once, the impact of the Troubles was
stronger than Genevieve's expectations of the girls. Genevieve
telephoned one of the examination boards in London to ask

whether the exam could be postponed until the following day, but despite extensive television coverage the board could not understand what the problem was. She decided to hold an assembly and to send the girls home early. 'Bobby Sands has appeared before his God,' she told the girls, 'he has appeared before a Just Judge and no doubt he has received his judgement. We pray that he is already at peace and enjoying Eternal Life.' Privately, her compassion outweighed her desire to remain neutral. 'I am infinitely sad about Bobby Sands,' she said, 'and so are the girls.'

Many senior girls, particularly those who lived in West Belfast, were profoundly affected by the hunger strikes and remember that summer term as a time of 'raw tension' in the school. They were supposed to be working for their Advanced Level exams but the sixth-form common room overlooked the Milltown Cemetery where hunger strikers' funerals took place, while outside the school gates, the Falls Road was frequently the scene of marches and riots. The desire to take part could be overwhelming. A woman, who was one of these sixth formers, said: 'Don't label us Republican. We just wanted to join marches to express our frustration with what was happening.' At some point, about sixty sixth formers walked out of the school, whether with permission or in defiance of Genevieve is a matter of dispute. One girl, whose brother was a Republican prisoner in the H-Blocks, now says that she led a walkout but another girl, whose sister was a Republican prisoner in Armagh, says that the girls had permission from the head of sixth form to attend a meeting on the hunger strikers at Queen's University. Both agree that all but a very few of the girls involved had had relatives killed or imprisoned. Genevieve took no action as a result of the 'walkout'. That summer term of raw tension was the one time when she was unable to insist on business as usual.

She did not want any bad publicity however. When the death of one of the hunger strikers occurred shortly before the end of afternoon school and some of the girls who lived close by joined in the banging of bin lids on the pavement while still in their school uniform, Genevieve asked them to go home and change. During the hunger strikes the world's media was never far from the Falls Road and a picture of St. Louise's pupils taking part in the protest would not have been good for the school's reputation.

8

'Would you please pray for a first year's daddy who was shot dead last night'

No girls benefited more from Genevieve's determination to make the school a haven of peace and normality than those whose family lives had been disrupted or destroyed by the Troubles. According to Genevieve, 'lots of girls at St. Louise's had fathers and brothers who were killed or imprisoned'. They would have included members of the IRA who were killed on operations or imprisoned, often for very long periods, fathers who were murdered by loyalists, family members who were interned during the years 1971–75, fathers who were on the run and fathers who were not paramilitaries but who were sent to prison for crimes arising out of the Troubles. The latter included a man with two daughters at St. Louise's who had been so angry at the sectarian killing of young Catholics in his district that he had gone out and murdered the first Protestant he could find.

For some girls the disruption of family life was brief but dramatic. A senior girl questioned by Genevieve because she was late for school, explained that she and her family had only just been released. The whole family had been held at gunpoint in one room since the previous evening by gunmen who were intent on ambushing an army patrol. In the morning, when no patrol had passed, the gunmen took the family car and warned that any attempt to contact the police would have serious consequences.

'And now, if you'll excuse me, Sister, I am late for orchestra practice.'

The British army was also a source of disruption to family life.
Girls' homes were 'turned over' during the night and girls from
Republican backgrounds or who just happened to live in a
Republican area, were taken in for questioning. Dolours Ferguson,
who was fifteen, was at home in Clonard doing her shorthand
homework when she was 'lifted' by the army. Still wearing her St.
Louise's uniform, she was taken in an open jeep to the battalion
headquarters in a disused mill and questioned for two hours. Do
you know this man? When did you last see that man? When
Dolours went to school the following morning, she received a
summons to report to Sister Genevieve. 'That,' says Dolours, 'was
a bigger shock than being lifted by the army.' Genevieve had heard
from the parish priest what had happened and put in a formal
complaint. Two days later, the army apologised but according to
Dolours, in the early seventies, a number of St. Louise's girls were
lifted by the army and taken in for questioning.

The urban guerrilla war could be particularly disruptive in the
Lower Falls. Anne Donegan, going home to Balkan Street from
St. Louise's, was caught in a gun fight between the IRA and the
army and dived into the nearest house where she found the occu-
pant, an elderly lady, sheltering under the kitchen table. Not long
after, the Donegans' house was destroyed when an IRA bomb
intended for an army patrol exploded prematurely two doors away.
The family moved to Whiterock but for Anne and her sisters the
immediate problem was that their school uniforms were under
the rubble. Their father, Joseph, was unemployed, so the uniforms
would not be easily replaced. Genevieve asked the Donegan girls
to wait outside assembly while she appealed for items of uniform
to be donated to the family. 'It was,' Anne recalls, 'terribly embar-
rassing.'

Fathers on the run tried to minimise the disruption but they
saw their children less than men who had been imprisoned and
however much they may have wished to make contact, they had
to put their own security first. When Joe Cahill returned to
Belfast for his father's funeral, he was so heavily disguised that his

daughters would not have recognised him if they had passed him in the street. One IRA volunteer must have decided that it was better to keep the family together; on the day he escaped from the Maze prison in 1983, his daughter left St. Louise's and did not return.

When a father was imprisoned the disruption of family life could be so long drawn out that his children came to regard it as permanent. 'When are you coming home?' one young girl would ask her father when she was taken to visit him in prison, but by the time she was eleven and starting at St. Louise's she had stopped asking. Her father, an IRA volunteer, was serving two life sentences for murder. Young IRA men who had married and conceived a child shortly before they were arrested and sentenced to long terms of imprisonment were not only strangers to their children; in some cases they were strangers to their grandchildren too because they were still in prison when the daughters they had never really known gave birth to their own children in their late teens.

'Brendan's' daughter was born after he had been sent to prison for life at the age of eighteen. Eleven years later, when his daughter started at St. Louise's, she proudly wore her school uniform to visit him in prison but although he followed every step of her school career and wrote to Genevieve about his parental anxieties, he recognised that he and his daughter were not close. For all his fatherly concern, he could never bridge the gap caused by his absence since her birth.

Some marriages broke down under the strain of the long separation, increasing the likelihood of father fading into the background. Wives who had accepted their husband's decision to join the paramilitaries began to resent being left for so long with sole responsibility for bringing up the children. Prison visits, far from keeping the relationship alive, focused the wife's frustration on what she saw as an unfair division of labour. While her husband only had to walk a short way to the prison visits area, she had an hour's journey with the children in a minibus and was kept waiting by prison security staff who often treated her little better than a criminal.

If the marriage broke down, it was not unknown for the mother's family to take the opportunity of turning the children against their father. In a case that particularly worried Genevieve, the father in prison had no visitors. His wife was dead and his daughter, who was at St. Louise's, refused to visit him. She had gone to live with an aunt and uncle on her mother's side and called them mummy and daddy. Genevieve could have ignored the father's isolation but she decided that, like any other parent, he had a right to be kept in touch with his daughter's progress so she arranged for a rota of teachers to visit him in prison throughout his daughter's schooldays.

The effect on the girl at school of the father's imprisonment was bound to vary from family to family and from crime to crime. It cannot have been easy, for example, for the daughter at St. Louise's to come to terms with the fact that her father, an IRA volunteer, was serving life for killing a six-year-old Protestant girl in a botched attempt to murder her father. Some girls were ashamed of their father being in prison regardless of the nature of his crime and hoped that Genevieve would not find out. Others were not at all ashamed of what their father had done but preferred not to talk about it at school. The common denominator was that the girls wanted to get on with their own lives. Reading some of the fathers' letters from prison to Genevieve and meeting some of the girls as adults, it is hard not to come to the conclusion that the fathers missed seeing their daughters grow up more than the daughters missed having their fathers around. At least the daughters had a demanding school life that left them little time to brood.

The busy normality of life at St. Louise's must have enabled many girls to keep the disruption and the killing in some sort of perspective. But Genevieve recognised that there were girls for whom normality was not enough. The Troubles and the rapid expansion of the school in the early seventies encouraged her to develop an elaborate system of pastoral care that involved teacher-counsellors, senior pupils and outside agencies such as welfare officers and psychiatrists. Her confidence in the healing power of normality was not based on a simplistic 'pull yourself together'; the pastoral system created a series of safety nets so that if possible no girl who needed help would go unnoticed. The key to the system was the year counsellor, a member of the teaching staff on a reduced timetable who took over a year group when they entered the school and stayed with them for five years. As the year group could be as large as four hundred, Genevieve was asking a lot of the year counsellors who were expected to know the girls and their parents and to keep Genevieve informed about girls who were experiencing particular difficulties.

The power of normality to heal and the skill of the year counsellors were severely tested by the sectarian murders of the eighties. In a talk she gave in Edinburgh in 1987, Genevieve indicated that at least twenty fathers of girls at St. Louise's had been murdered during the Troubles. Four fathers are known to have been the victims of sectarian killings in the eighties; three were killed because they were Roman Catholics, one because he was a Protestant married to a Catholic. In the latter case, the daughter, who was fourteen, answered the doorbell at home and was confronted by a group of men wearing balaclavas. When she screamed, her father came into the hall and was shot dead in front of her.

Although Genevieve referred to this tragedy on more than one occasion, she did not say whether the girl ever recovered from her experience and, if so, to what extent returning to normal school life and having access to the school's system of pastoral care might have helped. But there is enough evidence from the other sectarian murders to suggest that Genevieve's confidence in her approach was not misplaced.

Few sectarian killings were more shocking to public opinion than that of Joseph Donegan, the father of the girls who had been so embarrassed when Genevieve appealed for items of uniform on their behalf. The Donegans had seven children, five daughters who all went to St. Louise's and two sons. When the father was killed, Jean, the youngest daughter, was fifteen and still at the school.

Joseph Donegan had no connection with the paramilitaries. On the night of 23 October 1982, returning home after a drink with a friend, he hailed a black taxi on the Falls Road assuming it belonged to the Falls Taxi Association. When he opened the door, he saw that the taxi already had one passenger which was not unusual as the Falls taxis picked up and set down several fares on one journey. Two days later Joseph Donegan's body was found in an alley in the Shankill. He had been so badly beaten and tortured that he could only be identified by a bracelet and wristwatch that his family had given him on his birthday. His teeth had been pulled out with pliers and his features had been obliterated by repeated blows with a garden spade.

The man in the taxi had been Lenny Murphy, the leader of the Shankill Butchers, the most notorious loyalist murder gang. Murphy had hijacked the taxi with the intention of kidnapping a Catholic and holding him hostage against the release of Thomas Cochrane, a sergeant in the Ulster Defence Regiment who had been kidnapped by the IRA. But as soon as Donegan got into the taxi Murphy attacked him with such ferocity that from the start Donegan was destined to be a dead man not a hostage.

The impact of this killing on Donegan's family may be imagined. Anne Donegan, who had left St. Louise's and was a journalist on the *Irish News*, made a public appeal to the IRA to release Sergeant Cochrane so that his wife would not have to suffer as her mother was suffering but the IRA made the Cochrane family wait almost a week before dumping his body on the border. He had been beaten and shot.

'My daddy came home on the Friday,' Jean Donegan recalls and on that day, when the body was returned to the family, Genevieve visited the house to pay her respects and bring a wreath from the school. Jean's year counsellor and two girls from Jean's form came with Genevieve. It was the beginning of the process that would enable Jean to return to school immediately after the Halloween Break that started that day. Jean's mother agreed that the sooner Jean could return to school the better and Jean herself knew that it was 'no good sitting at home dwelling on things'. 'I can remember the first day back, walking into the school with my friends. I did not forget my daddy, but getting back into the school routine was the best thing for me.' In school, the year counsellor kept an eye on Jean and reported to Genevieve.

Genevieve's way of enabling the school community to identify
with the bereaved family was usually low-key, a simple prayer for
the dead man and for his family at morning assembly. That had
been her practice before the Troubles when a member of a girl's
family died. But the timing of Joseph Donegan's death meant that
both he and Sergeant Cochrane could be remembered at a special
mass. November was the Month of the Holy Souls. Masses were
celebrated in school with each year group for the repose of the
souls of those who had died or been killed in the previous year.
The school's policy was to support the girl *and* the family so Jean's
mother and sisters attended the mass and Jean joined the procession of girls who had been bereaved. For Jean, this public grieving
was an important step on the long journey to come to terms with
her father's death.

'Marion' was eleven and in her first year at St. Louise's when
her father was murdered by the Ulster Volunteer Force (UVF), a
loyalist paramilitary group based in the Shankill. It was probably
on this occasion that Genevieve was handed a note as she went in
to morning assembly. 'Please pray for a first year's daddy who was
shot dead last night.' 'Marion' had been brought to school each
morning by her father, a taxi driver; her mother had died a few
years before so her father had been her world. Returning to
school, 'Marion' showed no emotion; she was a model pupil and
with the encouragement of the relatives with whom she was staying, took part in every possible school activity. Genevieve paid for
her to join the school's trip to the continent and on the bus,
'Marion', who had a beautiful voice, led the singing of an Irish
ballad, *The Fields of Athenry*. But when the school party returned to
Northern Ireland and the other girls started talking excitedly
about going home, 'Marion' for the first time broke down and
sobbed. It was several months after her father's death.

The problem for Genevieve and the year counsellors was to
know whether to let the grieving come in its own time. Children
need to grieve but should they be encouraged to do so? Genevieve
clearly believed that in most cases the low-key approach was right
and that a swift return to the normality of school life did not suppress grief in a way that was harmful. Ellen O'Connor supports

this view. When her father was murdered by the UVF in June 1987, she was eleven and due to start at St. Louise's that September. She had seen her father's killers from the window of the house and had heard her mother's screams. When shortly after the shooting, her mother had a breakdown and the children had to move to their elderly grandparents' house in the Lower Falls, Ellen felt guilty because she could not grieve for her father. She says she had to pretend to cry and just did not understand the significance of what had happened.

At her grandparents' house, Ellen was visited by Genevieve and Sister Declan who assured her that St. Louise's was 'a great place' and that when she arrived in September she would be happy despite what had happened. And so she was. Ellen believes that it was, paradoxically, the fact that school life left so little time to think about anything else that enabled her to grieve for her father, and she is grateful to the school for treating her normally with just a word of encouragement from Sister Declan now and then. Her responsibility for her three younger siblings must have helped too; as a young pupil at St. Louise's she had to attend parents' evenings at the primary school to ask the teachers how her younger sisters were getting on. Ellen is now a primary school teacher herself.

These sectarian murders raised in an acute form the problem that Genevieve had faced since the beginning of the Troubles: how to deal with violent death. In the early seventies, when killing was an everyday occurrence especially in West Belfast where most of the girls lived, Genevieve confronted the violence and the implications of sudden death in her homilies and prayers at morning assembly. She could not avoid the subject altogether however much she wanted to keep the Troubles out of the school and she must have hoped that by talking about it in the context of a Christian assembly, she was making it easier for the girls to put death and violence out of their minds for the rest of the day.

Some of the notebooks in which Genevieve wrote down her thoughts before assembly have survived and these include the period 1972–74, the most violent years of the Troubles. The entries are not dated, however, so it is only possible to guess at

what prompted her one morning to write, 'Lord, save us in this
dark hour in Belfast, save our homes, our families or we will
perish', or what, on another day, made her feel the need to reassure the girls that 'as you stumble along the Falls Road in the
midst of shootings, death, suffering and tears, Mary your Mother
is near'.

Like many other headteachers, Genevieve left her notes for
assembly until the last minute; they are scribbled down in a characteristically wayward hand. In the early seventies, her notes also
have another sort of immediacy: she is trying to express in words
her reaction as a religious sister to the news of more killing. She is
obviously not prepared to deal with violent death in the sort of
ready-made religious language that would distance herself and her
listeners from the reality. On the other hand, she wants to com-
plement the reality of death with what was for her the equal reality
of God's mercy and Eternal Life.

Funerals parade up the Road every day. Make us realise
that these brown boxes contain people who walked our
streets and have now appeared before God to give an
account of their lives. Have pity on them Lord.

She seldom allowed violent death to monopolise an assembly. It
was typical of her style that reflections on recent violent deaths
should be part of the same assembly as an attack on arbitrary punishments and reminders to the girls on how to behave. These are
her notes for an assembly on one Friday in 1973:

This week a lot of horrible things have happened in our
city. Men have been shot down in cold blood. Irish and
English. Wives, mothers and children have cried bitter
tears. Suffering is the same everywhere. An English child
who has lost her daddy feels it just the same as an Irish
child. What does Christ think of us, his followers in
Belfast? If you do not forgive others, your Father in
Heaven will not forgive you. Mary, you are in Heaven. Ask
your Son to take to Heaven all who died this week.

She then takes a swipe at arbitrary 'justice':

> We saw how Christ was condemned to death unjustly. We
> understand this. We know how many people have been
> condemned by mock courts or by no courts at all in our
> city.

Finally, she returns to the familiar themes of her Courtesy Points:

> Behave as if you believed you were worthy of respect.
> Don't put a cheap price on yourself by shouting and
> smoking in public, by joining crowds. Remember to give
> up your seat on the bus for adults.

The assembly ends with a robust exit hymn. Genevieve likes a
good sing and the Battle Hymn of the Republic, 'Mine eyes have
seen the glory of the coming of the Lord', sends the girls out of
assembly on a positive note.

Morning assembly was one of the keys to Genevieve's success in
making the school a haven of normality. She was trying to control
the way in which the events of the Troubles were perceived by her
pupils. As the school expanded in the seventies, the whole school
assembly disappeared but Genevieve made sure that she took each
year group assembly once a week, adapting her message to the different audiences. She also relied increasingly on senior girls,
allowing them to take assembly which she attended but did not vet
in advance. The senior girls did not talk about violent death but in
talking about the need for forgiveness they sometimes went farther
than Genevieve. Genevieve herself recorded that on more than
one occasion, the senior girls insisted that it was not enough to
forgive; they had to forget as well and of the two, forgetting would
prove the more difficult.

Although the early 1970s were the most violent years in
Belfast, the longer the Troubles went on the more the girls had
other reasons to value the normality of life at school. 'The great
tragedy of the Troubles in Belfast,' Genevieve wrote in 1983, 'is
the breakdown of family life in the Catholic ghettos.' The strong

family ties of the past were weakened by the urban guerrilla war
and by the destruction of tight-knit communities as some families
fled the inner-city and the threat of loyalist incursion, while
others were rehoused in high-rise flats. The Divis Flats that
Father Padraig Murphy had all but ordered his flock to move
into became a byword for squalor and crime. The old communities may have been extremely poor but they possessed dignity,
cohesion and resilience; in the new communities the dominant
mood was despair. Some of the young sought to escape the all-
pervading hopelessness of their lives by joy-riding, a euphemism
for car theft and dangerous driving. The fact that joy-riders or
hoods operated so freely, making life intolerable for everybody
else, underlined the extent to which the cohesion of the Catholic
community in West Belfast had been fragmented. For a long
time, the RUC seemed unable or unwilling to arrest the hoods
and the IRA was reluctant to act as a community police force as
this would be 'a diversion from the war against the British'. The
British army did not regard it as their responsibility to deal with
joy-riders unless they were perceived as a threat. One of
Genevieve's pupils, Doreen McGuiness, was sixteen when she
was shot dead by the army in the early hours of New Year's Day,
1980. She was the passenger in a stolen car that was driven at
speed through an army roadblock on the Whiterock Road. 'It
wasn't just the Troubles,' said Mary O'Hara, who started at St.
Louise's the following year, 'but the whole anarchic, hopeless,
vicious world of the ghetto that made the school seem such a
haven of normality.'

Until the sisters moved away from the Lower Falls in 1983,
they, too, experienced the anarchic, hopeless, vicious world of the
ghetto. It had been fundamental to Vincent de Paul's project that
the early sisters should live among the poor they were trying to
serve so that Genevieve and the other sisters who taught in the
school had a dual, overlapping pastoral role that embraced the
families who lived in the Falls as well as the pupils who went to the
school. Thus when Internment was introduced in 1971, Sister Ita,
who was Genevieve's deputy at St. Louise's, still found time to
visit all the families whose men had been taken into custody.

Captain Ian Binnie recalls an incident in 1978 which suggests how in this overlapping pastoral role, Genevieve was trusted with some of the family's most sensitive secrets. Binnie's army base at Macrory Park overlooked the city cemetery on the other side of the Whiterock Road. One night a sentry spotted figures moving among the graves but marines sent to investigate found only a plot of newly turned earth and a bunch of flowers. Binnie decided to consult Genevieve before ordering his men to check this new grave for hidden weapons, but when he called on her in the morning he was surprised by her response. She tried to dissuade him from taking the matter any further. 'Trust me,' she said, 'I can assure you that there are no weapons in that grave.'

For once, Binnie felt that he could not take Genevieve's word for it and he ordered his men to start digging. They found a foetus that had been recently buried. Further down, they found four more foetuses, but no weapons.

There is no evidence that the mothers were Genevieve's pupils. Some may have been, but with family life breaking down and many men serving long prison sentences, schoolgirls were not the only ones who might wish to terminate a pregnancy. As a Catholic sister, Genevieve would never have condoned abortion but her compassion for those in trouble would have encouraged families to trust her as someone who was more likely to understand than to condemn. Women who were at the school during this period say that her attitude to pregnancy was above all practical. If a girl was pregnant, she went home to have her baby (which was looked after by her mother) and then returned to school without fuss to continue working for her qualifications.

Whatever the true explanation for the contents of the grave, the fate of the unborn children was a part of 'the great tragedy of the Troubles' that worried Genevieve as much as, if not more than, the violence on the streets. Republicans argue that Captain Binnie's story gives a distorted view of the way the Nationalist community behaved during the Troubles and they point out that the British used such stories as black propaganda to sow mistrust in Republican ranks, but the story was not publicised at the time and there would seem to be little point in Binnie spreading disinformation twenty-two years later. Genevieve's role certainly rings true. She knew so much about the families in the Falls that it is entirely credible that she should have known about the unofficial grave and that she should have wished to prevent the security forces uncovering its secret.

On one subject, however, she was not as well informed as she would like to have been, largely because the families themselves were kept in the dark. It was often too late and only when they had been arrested or killed, that she knew for certain which of her pupils and former pupils had decided to play an active part in the armed struggle.

9

'I realise your frustration but please don't get involved'

Genevieve's policy during the Troubles had two aims: to keep the school running as normally as possible and to deter the girls from any involvement in the conflict, whether that meant joining a crowd out of curiosity or carrying a concealed weapon out of conviction. She wanted to prevent the girls being used, as she put it, 'as pawns in a ruthless political game'. As the Troubles developed she decided to go a step further and encourage the girls to reject sectarianism as well as political propaganda. Openness to Protestants and Protestantism, which had not been a feature of her teaching before the Troubles, now became part of her strategy to liberate the girls from the ghetto mentality on which the paramilitaries thrived.

She set out to train the girls to resist the paramilitaries by the same methods she used to train them in good manners. Just as she had a list of Courtesy Points, so during the Troubles she had a list headed 'Slogans'. The IRA had its slogans and so did she. 'Don't ever be part of a mob,' she told the girls, 'it is useless and degrading'; 'Wait until you are eighteen before you join any political organisation'; 'Have the courage to say "No"'; 'Think for yourself'.

At a local level, Genevieve and the IRA were in competition. The IRA claimed to stand up for second-class Catholics, the ones

who were left behind in the ghetto when the grammar school educated Catholics moved away. Genevieve encouraged the girls to
stand up for themselves.

> We shamelessly indoctrinated them . . . in thinking first
> before acting and in the necessity of always acting as
> individuals never as a mob. We as teachers decided that we
> were pretty worthless if we could not take on the so-called
> protectors of young people, those who tried to get them,
> especially the poorest and less able among them, involved
> in organisations while too young to understand. We
> realised that if we succeeded in getting them past the
> fourth year, the impressionable age, they would never be
> used by others as they would have found their own voices
> and know how to use them. This we did week in, week out
> at assemblies.

Indoctrination did not rely on slogans alone. Genevieve used her
authority as a headmistress and as a Vincentian sister to argue for
the Christian values that she had always tried to teach. She insisted
that 'a Christian school has to instil the principle that behaviour
has to be in accordance with beliefs, that for Catholics it is not
enough to go to Mass on Sunday and to go out stone throwing and
rioting on Monday'. She also appealed to the girls' ambition and
feminism. Education was their passport to freedom – freedom
from the ghetto, from poverty, from discrimination against them
as women and Catholics – so they should not let anyone or anything distract them from the single-minded pursuit of their
qualifications. Above all, she was herself a role model of an independent-minded woman who was not afraid to stand up to the
paramilitaries.

Most of the parents strongly supported Genevieve's policy. Like
a later generation of parents who looked to the schools to keep
their children away from the drug culture because they felt pow-
erless to do so themselves, the St. Louise's parents of the seventies,
trapped inside the ghetto where fear reigned, looked to Genevieve
to keep their daughters away from the paramilitaries. Over ninety

per cent of parents attended parents' evenings during the Troubles, many more than the average English school could expect. One parents' evening was interrupted by a massive bomb explosion at Andersonstown police station which shook the assembly hall and covered Genevieve and the other teachers on the platform with a layer of dust. When the Falls Road was impassable to cars, the parents still came to concerts and plays, and when the anarchy on the streets threatened to spill over into the school, parents stood guard at the gates with broomstick handles.

Genevieve must have realised that her policy of indoctrination would not be hundred per cent successful but how much she knew about the activities of girls who ignored her advice is unclear. Brenda, who was a Republican when she was sixteen and still at the school, thinks Genevieve must have guessed that there was a danger of this happening because she took Brenda on one side and told her: 'You're a rebel, Brenda, I wish you were a rebel without a cause.' Genevieve told her own schoolfriend, May McFadden, that she usually knew when her girls had been involved in throwing stones at the army because they were paid to do so and some of the poorest girls came to school with cash in hand. Living in Clonard and knowing many of the families well, she must also have been aware that her girls were attending Republican parades and rallies at the weekend, though she may not have known which girls were just following the crowd and which had made a commitment to the Republican movement by joining the Fianna.

Na Fianna Eireann, the Republican movement's youth organisation, was founded in 1909 to counter the influence of the British Boy Scouts. Unlike the Boy Scouts, it had an explicitly political purpose which was 'to train the youth of Ireland to fight Ireland's fight when they are older'. In Northern Ireland, it was an illegal organisation but that did not stop it holding parades in Republican territory. Cumann na gCailini was the girls' branch and until it merged with Fianna Eireann in 1977, this was the organisation Genevieve's pupils would have joined. Members of the Fianna, both girls and boys, not only attended parades but acted as dickers, carrying out low-level surveillance tasks such as keeping a lookout for strangers in the area and noting the registration numbers of unmarked cars leaving British army bases.

If the girls thought that the Fianna would be a welcome contrast to Genevieve's strict regime, they were mistaken. The Fianna was just as keen on uniform, and its clothes list and rules could have been written by Genevieve herself. The girls were required to wear a green beret with a Fianna badge, orange neckerchief, beige shirt, white lanyard, green jumper (in the winter only), black skirt or trousers and black socks. No earrings, rings, watches or jewellery could be worn and smoking, eating and drinking in uniform were forbidden. 'Smart appearance, discipline and good conduct in public,' the members were told 'will help to win new recruits.'

Girls and boys were eligible to join the Fianna between the ages of five and eighteen but in practice if Genevieve's pupils joined they did so between the ages of thirteen and fifteen. Genevieve was probably right in thinking that if the school could deter the girls from joining at 'the impressionable age', the chances were that they would not join at all. After 1977, the Fianna became more secretive and more closely geared to membership of the IRA but before that date there was no automatic progression from one organisation to the other. The introduction of Internment in 1971, however, meant there was a shortage of men so that it was not unknown for girls in the Fianna to be recruited into the IRA as young as sixteen, one reason for Genevieve's persistent attempts to discourage girls from joining any organisation until they were eighteen.

'Bernadette' joined the Fianna when she was fourteen. She joined the IRA when she was sixteen. The first group of Genevieve's pupils to join the IRA were at their most impressionable and idealistic age when they witnessed Catholic families driven from their homes by Protestant mobs, their fathers and brothers interned without trial and their streets invaded by an army that, whatever its original mission, soon came to be regarded as an enemy occupying power. These young people hardly needed an ideological rationale for joining the resistance. As one woman who joined the Provisional IRA in the early seventies told

Republican News in 1982, 'like many volunteers who joined the organisation then, ninety per cent of my commitment was purely a gut reaction response to British occupation'. For 'Bernadette' there was also the excitement. Far from being traumatised by the Troubles, she recalls that 'our whole lives were one big buzz'.

Bored by surveillance duties, 'Bernadette' graduated to carrying weapons, part of a modern rifle, such as the American M16, in her underwear or an old .303 Lee Enfield under her overcoat. She worked with two women who were in the IRA and one night was summoned to a house and sworn in herself. It is probable that she initially joined Cumann na mBan, the women's IRA which was responsible for intelligence gathering, communications and transporting weapons. Until Cumann na mBan and the Provisionals merged in 1977, women who joined the movement could remain in the women's IRA or, if they wanted to participate more fully in operations, join the Provisionals. 'Bernadette' was insistent that if she had been killed she would have counted as an IRA volunteer.

Eight of Genevieve's pupils are known to have joined the IRA in the early seventies, either in their last year at school (which in most cases meant when they were sixteen) or soon after leaving. There may have been others whose membership of the organisation has not come to light. Apart from Rose Curry and Patricia McKay who joined the Official IRA, they were members of Cumann na mBan or the Provisionals or both. At school they did not acknowledge one another or talk about their involvement to other girls. Neither the school nor, in some cases, the parents knew for certain that the girls were members of the IRA until they were killed or arrested and sentenced.

'Bernadette' was lifted by the army several times but there was never sufficient evidence to charge her, which is surprising because as an operative she clearly had her limitations. Carrying live rounds one evening (as usual she had told her mother she was going to the youth club), she realised too late that the rounds were falling out of her dufflecoat pocket. Members of an army patrol passing on their way to Andersonstown turned to look at the young girl out after dark but failed to notice that she had left a trail of bullets on the pavement. It was perhaps just as well that

'Bernadette' ceased to be active in the IRA when she reached eighteen.

While 'Bernadette' may have been looking for excitement, other girls from St. Louise's who joined the IRA were uncompromisingly at war with the British army and the political status quo. When Patricia McKay was killed, the *United Irishmen* described her as 'a serious, dedicated revolutionary'. Before joining the Official IRA, she had been on the staff of a girls' Fianna Battalion and at the time of her death she was the adjutant of a slua – a Fianna unit – in the Divis Flats.

Brenda Murphy was a no less dedicated revolutionary. As a young girl at St. Louise's in the late sixties, she was already politically minded, reading avidly about the civil rights movement in the United States and taking as her role model Angela Davis, the militant black activist. When she was only thirteen she joined the civil rights march in Derry on 5 October 1968 where she witnessed the police baton charge of a crowd that contained women and children. It was the turning point in her young life. If injustices could not be overcome by peaceful protest, then 'I realised that violence was the only way'. Although she felt the same anger and frustration as her contemporaries at Internment and the British 'occupation' of Catholic areas, her motivation was more revolutionary than Republican. The 'structural injustices' of Northern Ireland State justified the use of violence. There was no history of Republicanism in the family; her father, grandfather and uncle had served in the British army.

Brenda joined the Republican movement when she was sixteen and starting her final year at St. Louise's. By her own account, she was always in trouble at school and had little academic motivation but she was neither lazy nor stupid; her mind and her energies were directed elsewhere. Like many other headteachers, Genevieve was inclined to believe that pupils who did not conform were immature and that, in the context of the Troubles, teenagers who joined the IRA did not really know what they were doing. 'I am convinced that these young teenagers of the early seventies who got involved in things beyond their understanding were victims of ruthless paramilitary leaders,' she wrote twenty years later, 'and were only fodder for that dreadful sinister organisation.' She even used the argument as a stick to beat the grammar school lobby; the selective system played into the hands of the paramilitaries by creating a pool of resentful, rejected youngsters. 'Our prisons are peopled by victims of our selective system at 11+,' she wrote, 'and in this context I talk about political prisoners, the IRA, all alumni of Catholic schools.'

Boys and girls in the ghettos *were* cynically exploited by both Republican and Loyalist paramilitaries who recognised that young people without hope could be persuaded to take risks in order to earn the respect they had never been given at school. But it was not true that the IRA's recruits came only from the ranks of the low-achievers and the 11+ failures. Some of the most prominent women volunteers such a Mairead Farrell and the Price sisters, Dolour and Marion, were high-flyers from the Catholic grammar schools. Nor was it true that teenage recruits were always victims of 'ruthless paramilitary leaders'. Brenda was not a victim. She knew exactly why she was joining the Republican movement and she accepted the risks. Nor were the IRA leaders in Belfast the sinister, mafia-style godfathers of Genevieve's imagination, they were young men only a few years older than Brenda herself. Many years later Genevieve visited in prison a former Loyalist paramilitary who had been recruited into the UVF at a young age and who was serving thirteen years for murder. When it was suggested to him that the godfathers of his ghetto had exploited him, he responded angrily that that was an insult to his intelligence. Like Brenda Murphy, he took full responsibility for his actions.

In 1972, Brenda Murphy was carrying a Lee Enfield rifle under her coat between Ballymurphy and Springfield when she was spotted from an army watchtower. She was arrested and taken to Springfield Road police station where, she says, she was beaten because she refused to reveal where she was taking the rifle. She was sentenced to two years, a comparatively light sentence for that offence. At the age of seventeen she was sent to Armagh jail, the women's prison where she said she was a prisoner of war not a criminal and refused to wear prison clothing. One of her first visitors was Sister Genevieve.

With the exception of Rose Curry and Patricia McKay who were killed and 'Bernadette' who was never charged, all of Genevieve's pupils who are known to have joined the IRA in the early seventies served time in Armagh jail. They were sentenced for membership of the IRA or for possessing illegal weapons or both. One girl was initially charged with murder because she stayed with the killers after handing over the weapon.

Brenda was nervous when she heard that Genevieve was going to visit her but she found her former headmistress 'very motherly' and outraged at the treatment that Brenda had received after her arrest. According to Brenda 'there was a deep sadness in Genevieve' over the girls' involvement with the paramilitaries but whatever Genevieve thought of their actions and however much she was opposed to the IRA, they were still her girls. She not only visited them; she sent them letters and books and encouraged them to study and to remember their faith. 'Even in prison you can make something of yourself,' she told Brenda, and when she sent the novels that Brenda had requested, she slipped in a volume on St. Therese of Lisieux.

In 1977, Brenda was arrested again and charged with taking part in a bombing which she denies. With insufficient evidence on that charge, she was sentenced to four years for membership of Provisional IRA and returned to Armagh jail. Although she was pregnant, she renewed her protest against being treated as a common criminal so the prison authorities offered her a deal. If she would give up her protest, she would be allowed to keep her baby for a year. Brenda rejected the deal and her baby daughter was taken away to be brought up by Brenda's mother. In 1980, Brenda joined other IRA women prisoners in the so-called 'dirty protest', smearing the wall of the cell with faeces and menstrual fluid.

When she was released in 1981, Brenda left the IRA. 'It is a movement of volunteers,' she explained. 'I just said that I wished to resign. There was no difficulty.' She is now a writer. Her first play about the Troubles, *Bin Lids*, was performed at the West Belfast Festival and on Broadway in New York in 1998. She has two daughters and sent them both to St. Louise's.

While she was in Armagh jail, Brenda met Peggy Fisher, another of Genevieve's former pupils who had been sentenced for the possession of illegal weapons. Peggy Fisher was never convicted of being a member of an illegal organisation but says 'I was active in the Republican cause from the age of twelve'. In 1975, at the age of fifteen, she was arrested for the possession of a sub-machine gun and sent to a juvenile training school. Two years later she was arrested again, this time for being in the possession of two armalite rifles and was sentenced to six years in prison. When Brenda Murphy told her that Sister Genevieve was visiting, Peggy replied, 'She's definitely not going to send for me', and she was right. Genevieve almost certainly did not know that Peggy was a former pupil because she had left St. Louise's at the start of her fourth year and had dropped out of the education system altogether.

Peggy lived in the Divis Flats which was the latest in a long line of temporary homes for her desperately poor family. Her father was one of the long-term unemployed. As the eldest daughter, Peggy was expected to help her mother with her younger siblings even if that meant missing school. Not that Peggy cared much whether she missed lessons: what the teachers had to offer seemed irrelevant to the twelve-year-old as she walked to school past the burning barricades. She says she regarded school as 'just another oppressive authority'.

Girls like Peggy Fisher from the Divis Flats did not fit easily into Genevieve's well-ordered world. They missed school or were often late, they were caught smoking in the toilets, and they seldom appeared in the correct uniform. Rebellious and disaffected they may have been but they were not unintelligent. After serving her prison sentence, Peggy went to Queen's University, Belfast, and obtained a degree in politics and information studies. But at the age of fourteen she could not have cared less for Genevieve's emphasis on qualifications and jobs. When an exasperated senior mistress told her to go home and stay there because she was not wearing the school uniform, Peggy was only too willing to oblige. The education authority never came knocking at her door and she assumes that the school never reported her departure. She was just fifteen when she found herself with no schooling and the vacuum was filled by her involvement in the armed struggle. Peggy is now a theatre administrator. She has twin daughters who attend an Irish medium school.

If the girls who were active in the armed struggle had anything in common, it was perhaps that unlike the girls in the sixties who made another form of commitment by joining a religious order or congregation, they did not identify with Genevieve or with her priorities. The girls who joined the Daughters of Charity or the Presentation Sisters were not only on Genevieve's religious wavelength, they were keen to serve the school in other ways as head girl or captain of the netball team. That could not be said of the girls who committed themselves to the Republican cause.

The girls who chose the religious life and the girls who chose the armed struggle were small minorities in a very large school. There is no way of knowing how many girls who might have joined the IRA were dissuaded from doing so by Genevieve's indoctrination. Some who appeared to have followed Genevieve's advice about not joining a political organisation until they were eighteen, such as Patricia Cahill who did not join Sinn Fein until she was twenty-two, were influenced by parents as well as by the school. Those who observed what was happening from outside the school, however, had no doubt Genevieve's influence was crucial. Cardinal Cahal Daly spoke with admiration of Genevieve's 'remarkable success in resisting paramilitary groups'; he thought that the girls at St. Louise's were under great pressure to join the paramilitaries and that it was Genevieve who gave them the self-confidence to refuse. Jim Kincade, the head of Methodist College in Belfast, who knew Genevieve and St. Louise's well, believed that Genevieve did more than anyone to keep her girls out of the IRA because the Christian values she had established in the school were so strong; and British politicians who served in Northern Ireland, such as Brian Mawhinney and Nicholas Scott, were convinced that it was Genevieve's teaching and example that kept many of her girls from joining the paramilitaries.

Not knowing how many girls were at risk makes it difficult to assess the effectiveness of Genevieve's indoctrination. Eight girls who are known to have joined the IRA at the time of maximum pressure to do so from a school of over a thousand pupils does not sound very many, but then it is probably true that for most girls at St. Louise's joining the IRA would have been unthinkable even in the extraordinary circumstances of the early seventies. That is not to suggest that Genevieve's policy of indoctrination had little impact; there are women who were at the school in the early seventies who now say of their contemporaries who joined the IRA, 'there but for the grace of God . . .' Genevieve's achievement was to create a climate in the school that made it easier for those who were tempted to stop short of lifting a gun.

In the late seventies and eighties other girls from St. Louise's joined the IRA but as far as it is possible to tell when there are no records of membership there was never again a group of eight in the organisation at the same time. At any time it would have been difficult for Genevieve to predict which girls would join the paramilitaries. Although she seems to have anticipated where Brenda Murphy's political commitment was leading, in some other cases there was no obvious correlation between a girl's attitude and behaviour in school and subsequent membership of the IRA. Contemporaries of Patricia McKay, the dedicated revolutionary, remember her as 'the girl with laughing eyes' who loved singing; a 1968 photograph shows her as one of the principals in the school's production of *The Gipsy Baron*. Of Rose Curry, who was killed by the bomb on which she was working, teachers say she was 'a quiet, unassuming, lovely girl'. Rose's father had been interned (and was released on compassionate grounds to attend her funeral) but Republicanism in the family was not a good predictor of how the children would react. Not only did some Republican parents discourage their daughters from getting involved but siblings brought up in the same Republican atmosphere could react in entirely different ways – some joining the IRA and others continuing with their normal lives.

While some girls from Republican backgrounds were convinced that Genevieve was hostile to the Republican cause, 'Bernadette' believed that Genevieve as an Irish patriot sympathised with the feelings that drove some of her pupils to join the armed struggle in the early seventies. Her evidence for this is that at the worst of times Genevieve would say at assembly, 'I realise your frustration but please don't get involved'. Genevieve *was* angry about the way the British army and the RUC behaved and she was openly sympathetic to the victims. On the first anniversary of Bloody Sunday she prayed for the victims at morning assembly: 'In your mercy God, remember all who died in Derry a year ago and comfort relatives and friends.' And from her notes for assembly it appears that she prayed for a girl's brother in prison who was refusing to wear prison clothes.

It must have been difficult for Genevieve to express the sympathy she felt for individuals and their families without giving the girls confusing signals. There was nothing confusing about her decision to visit former pupils in prison because that did not imply support for the IRA, but her decision to allow a whole class from St. Louise's to attend Patricia McKay's funeral was open to more than one interpretation. The funerals of Rose Curry and Patricia McKay in St. Peter's Pro-Cathedral were both major events in the West Belfast, community, with large congregations – two thousand attended Rose Curry's funeral – and paramilitary ritual including shots fired over the coffin. These girls had been Genevieve's pupils and they had been brought up in the Lower Falls where Genevieve lived. Patricia McKay's younger sister was still in the school. Genevieve's decision to allow the young sister's class to attend the funeral is understandable but it could have encouraged some girls to wonder whether Sister Genevieve was as opposed to the armed struggle as she appeared to be.

There is no doubt however, that Genevieve was unequivocally opposed to the IRA. She was a blunt and consistent critic of that organisation. She did not have to be. Headteachers are not expected to engage in public controversy and are frowned on when they do; it is assumed they are neglecting their responsibilities. But for Genevieve, publicly opposing the IRA *was* one of her responsibilities. She was trying to prevent the girls joining by encouraging them to think for themselves. What sort of role model would she have been if she had toned down her criticisms of the IRA or suppressed them altogether? Most of her criticisms were expressed in talks she gave in Northern Ireland, in England and in the United States. Some of her friends must have wondered whether she needed to be quite so critical of the IRA in public but in private she used even stronger language.

What divided Genevieve and the girls who joined the IRA was the use of violence. When Genevieve visited Brenda Murphy in Armagh jail their talk often came round to this question. Genevieve insisted, as she had always done, that the injustices suffered by the Catholic population would be overcome by peaceful means, especially by education – 'education, not by lifting a gun, Brenda'. But Brenda replied that the civil rights movement had proved that peaceful methods did not work; the violent course had been forced upon her by the violent state. 'You'll end up dead,' said Genevieve. 'I accept that,' Brenda replied. The answer, according to Brenda, was deeply disturbing to Genevieve because life was a gift from God that should never be thrown away. Brenda liked and admired Genevieve as an inspiring example of what a strong woman can achieve but she found her former headmistress's faith in the power of education to change society naïve. Whereas Genevieve argued 'the futility of violence', Brenda asks now whether the British government would ever have tackled the injustices in Northern Ireland if some Catholics had not been prepared to lift a gun.

'Bernadette's' belief that Genevieve was sympathetic to the Republican cause would have come as a surprise to Republicans in West Belfast, many of whom regarded her as pro-British. There were times when she seemed to go out of her way to offend Republican opinion. She turned down an offer from Gerry Adams, Sinn Fein's West Belfast representative, to talk to the senior girls but invited British politicians to do so. Genevieve would have had no difficulty defending these decisions. Visits by British politicians enhanced the school's standing but Adams represented the political wing of an organisation she condemned. As one of her former pupils put it: 'She was playing to an audience outside West Belfast.'

Genevieve prevented Gerry Adams, the Sinn Fein politician, talking to the sixth form but she could not prevent the younger girls being dazzled by Gerry Adams the celebrity. When Adams stood as the Sinn Fein candidate for West Belfast in the 1983 Westminster election, he took his young relative, Marie-Terese Hannaway, canvassing on one occasion. The thirteen-year-old, who as a new girl at St. Louise's had not wanted to be known as Alfie Hannaway's grand-daughter, was proud to be seen with her father's famous cousin. Her friends from school were amazed. 'How do you know *him*?' they cried. 'I was a star then,' Marie-Terese remembers, 'I was a goddess then.'

Republican criticism dogged Genevieve throughout the Troubles. It was most frequently expressed in the columns of the *Andersonstown News*. This weekly paper had started life as *Internment '71* and had developed into the local paper for Catholics in West Belfast. When it criticised Genevieve, she dismissed it as 'the local IRA publication' but it was not; as the community paper it reflected both the Nationalist and the Republican sympathies of its readership.

Genevieve was impatient with Republican criticism and she sometimes deliberately portrayed it as an attack on the school rather than on herself. But the Republicans had no quarrel with what she was doing at St. Louise's; on the contrary, they were generous in their praise. Their quarrel was with her attitude to the 'British presence' in Northern Ireland; for a prominent head-mistress on the Falls Road to be friendly with the occupying power was at best insensitive and at worst a form of collaboration with the enemy. The Republican case against Genevieve was that she was too friendly with the British, that she accepted a British honour and that she allowed herself to be used as part of the British propaganda machine. Genevieve's answer to all these charges was the same; everything she did as principal of St. Louise's was for the sake of the school.

Direct rule of Northern Ireland from Westminster, introduced in March 1972, meant that control of education policy and education money was in the hands of British ministers stationed in Belfast but answerable to London. Genevieve was quick to spot that there would be advantages in getting to know the key players. According to one of the senior school inspectors of the time, 'Sister

Genevieve had a great capacity for fingering the right people'. The first British politician she fingered was the junior minister responsible for education in Northern Ireland in Callaghan's minority Labour government. Peter Melchett was a young Old Etonian peer who had cast his lot with the Labour party and who shared Genevieve's opposition to the 11+ and the grammar schools. Genevieve invited him to visit the school and he became the first British minister to venture this far into the Republican heartland. When his armour-plated official car drew up at the wrong entrance, he met several girls leaving the school by the back door. He says that when he asked them where they were going, they replied: 'Some big wig is coming, we're not well enough dressed so we've been sent home.'

Despite his patrician English background Melchett became a friend and supporter of Genevieve. Genevieve made sure that she was also on good terms with subsequent British ministers responsible for education including Nicholas Scott, Richard Needham and Rhodes Boyson. Her friendship with Brian Mawhinney in the late eighties was particularly close. She won friends in high places for the school rather than additional resources; her high profile in political circles enhanced the school's reputation and her own. But it annoyed Republicans.

Genevieve's acceptance of a British honour, the OBE, in 1978 antagonised a wider constituency. Her name had probably been put forward by Lord Melchett and she seems to have had no hesitation in accepting. But for many Catholics in Northern Ireland, whether or not to accept a British honour was a difficult question. 'Most Catholics of integrity have refused to accept them,' declared the *Andersonstown News*, and when Billy Steele accepted the OBE he found that he was congratulated by the heads of Protestant schools but by none of the priests on his own governing body. Accepting a British honour was accepting the legitimacy of the 'British presence'. Both Nationalists and Republicans were angry that an Irish woman educating Irish girls in the Falls when the streets were occupied by British soldiers should agree to become an officer of the Order of the British Empire. Genevieve said that the honour was for the school not for herself, but she accepted it as 'Mary O'Farrell' not as 'Sister Genevieve O'Farrell', the name by which she was known at St. Louise's. Although Genevieve regarded much of this Republican criticism as small-minded, it is not difficult to understand why some Republicans in the Falls do not share the British politicians' good opinion of her character and her policy. One incident in 1983 illustrates well how her single-minded concentration on the school led her to ignore the Republican point of view.

Over lunch at Hillsborough, the official residence of the British Secretary of State, Genevieve met Jane Prior and invited her to visit the school. For security reasons, the visit of the Secretary of State's wife to the Falls was not publicised beforehand. When Republican parents heard that the visit had taken place, they were angry and complained to the *Andersonstown News*. The next issue of the paper reported the parents' complaints and claimed that the visit had been kept secret because of its political nature. In Republican eyes, Jane Prior's visit was part of the British government's counter insurgency policy. 'Things are in a sad state,' one of the parents was quoted as saying, 'when this woman who is involved in publicity work for a government responsible for the murder by plastic bullets of seven innocent children should be invited to the Falls Road School.'

Genevieve left it to two of her senior girls to reply. The following week, the *Andersonstown News* published a long letter signed 'Two Upper Sixth Formers from St. Louise's'. It is an interesting letter for a number of reasons, not least because the paper was willing to publish it. The girls rebutted the criticism of Mrs Prior's visit point by point and derided the Sinn Fein spokesman, who had been quoted in the original report, for being 'totally blinded by his narrow-mindedness and bigoted viewpoint'. The two sixth formers attacked the whole mind-set of the Republican movement. What Sinn Fein really objected to was that the girls at St. Louise's were articulate and could think for themselves:

> We have realised that there is only one way out of this
> stalemate situation in Northern Ireland and that is through
> Education. We are the future of Northern Ireland and we

will have it within our power to claim our rights more
vociferously and forcefully than any bomb or gun can
do . . . We have not betrayed any so-called Irish Cause but
we are determined to embrace it with new vigour and in
the proper manner. It is only too apparent that violence has
exacerbated the Northern Ireland problem.

The influence of Genevieve's indoctrination is clear but the letter
does not read like an exercise in pleasing the principal. The tone
throughout is that of a younger generation tired of the Troubles
and fed up with the role of oppressed Catholics. 'We want the best
for ourselves and for our school, and if the people of West Belfast
are prepared to consider themselves second-class citizens, we are
not.'

Genevieve must have known that Jane Prior's visit would anger
some Republicans; she was not so much insensitive to their feelings as unconcerned about them. If the visit benefited the school,
it was no one else's business. But that argument was less convincing as an answer to Republican accusations that she allowed herself
to be used by British propaganda.

From the point of view of the British government's Northern
Ireland Office, an intelligent and articulate Roman Catholic sister
from the Falls Road, who was scathing in her criticism of the IRA
and who argued that the priority for her girls was employment not
the end of British rule, was something of a godsend. Nicholas
Scott, who served as a junior minister in the province in the eighties, acknowledges that it was always helpful to have Genevieve to
lunch when there were visiting delegations from overseas.
Foreigners who were inclined to be sceptical of what British officials told them, were surprised and impressed by what Genevieve
had to say.

Lunching at Hillsborough was harmless whether the Republicans
liked it or not. Lobbying against the McBride principles in the
United States was a much more controversial step. The nine
McBride principles aimed to ensure an end to discrimination against
Catholics in employment in Northern Ireland. The principles were
promoted by the Irish National Caucus, a Nationalist organisation

one of whose roles was to lobby against Britain in the United States. If the Caucus could persuade an individual state to adopt the McBride principles, investment by that state in Northern Ireland was effectively blocked unless the company concerned put the principles into practice in every detail.

The British government argued that its own fair employment and equal opportunities legislation made the McBride principles irrelevant but the American states needed some persuading. Genevieve was invited to go to the United States at the suggestion of Jim Eccles, a Catholic member of the Fair Employment Agency in Belfast. On previous visits Eccles had been questioned about discrimination against Catholics in education, hence his wish to have Genevieve at his side.

Genevieve made two visits to the United States while she was principal of St. Louise's in 1987 and 1988. The trips were paid for and sponsored by the British government; Genevieve kept the 1987 invitation which is from the Department of Economic Development in Belfast and specifically asks her to speak at a hearing on the McBride principles in Illinois. She made a third visit in 1989, the year after she retired. Although she went to speak about education and employment, she also expressed her views on the IRA. She told her audiences that the Fair Employment Agency 'has done marvellous work' and that Catholics 'have now reached the promised land because there is no way that any employer in the public or private sector will get away with discrimination'. As for the IRA, it thrived on unemployment and did not represent the true hopes of the Catholics of West Belfast.

When she first went to the United States, Genevieve had worked in the Falls for thirty years and she probably knew more about the problems of finding employment for Catholic school leavers than anyone in Northern Ireland. She believed that the McBride principles would stop investment and make it harder for young people to find jobs, a view held by many prominent Catholics including Bishop Cahal Daly and John Hume. She saw no reason why she should not put the case against the McBride principles to Americans, particularly to Irish Americans who she described as 'abysmally ignorant of the present situation'. Her

comments on the IRA were part of that case and were no different
from the views she had often expressed at home.

Reports of Genevieve's visits to the United States were not
well received by Republicans. Father Sean McManus, director of
the Irish National Caucus, publicly accused her of allowing herself to be used in the British campaign against the McBride
principles. It is difficult to believe that Genevieve, who had
invested so much time and effort in preventing her girls being
used by the Republican movement, would have allowed herself to
be used by the British government. She was too independent-
minded to be manipulated by anyone. But while she may not
have consciously allowed herself to be used by the British there is
no doubt that she was useful to them and Republicans could be
forgiven for suspecting that the devious British had found a way
of turning her independent-mindedness to their own advantage.
A British honour received at Buckingham Palace, lunches with
leading politicians and foreign dignitaries and invitations to speak
in the United States would have tested the humility of the most
dedicated follower of Vincent de Paul. But while Genevieve may
have been flattered by the British, she was not duped by them.
Every step that annoyed Republicans she took with her eyes
open. She was in her way as calculating as any politician and
more single minded than many. She had her long-term plan and
clearly believed that a degree of co-operation with the British was
in the best interests of the school and of her girls. Accusations of
lack of humility and lack of sensitivity to Republican opinion did
not worry her as long as she believed that she was fulfilling her
mission.

Genevieve's decision to encourage openness to Protestants and
Protestantism was also part of her strategy to liberate her girls
from the narrow perspective of the ghetto. It had less to do with
ecumenism, despite her close friendship with Protestant heads
and ministers, than with her ambition for her girls. The Troubles
convinced her that Catholic suspicions of Protestants were just as
much a barrier to her girls' advancement as Protestant discrimination against Catholics.

Her attempts to indoctrinate the girls against religious bigotry date from the early eighties and were mirrored in some other Catholic and Protestant schools. Middle-class schools less affected by the Troubles found it easier to advocate tolerance than schools in the working-class ghettos, so to that extent St. Louise's was unusual, and it is no surprise that the Protestant schools with which Genevieve built the closest contacts were voluntary grammar schools in the more affluent parts of the city. The fact that openness to the other religious tradition was on any school's agenda in Northern Ireland was one of the few unqualified benefits of the Troubles.

Before the Troubles there was little contact between Catholic and Protestant schools and the idea that children should be educated in the same school was anathema to both religious traditions. Sport which might have been expected to help bridge the divide acted as a form of apartheid. The Catholic schools played Gaelic sports, such as Gaelic football, while the Protestant schools preferred sports with a British pedigree such as cricket and rugby football. The Gaelic Athletic Association banned its members from playing or even watching 'foreign games'. For a few neutral sports such as netball, an inter-school league operated but with cries of 'Fenians!' greeting Genevieve's pupils when they ran onto the court, even this limited contact can hardly have been a source of mutual understanding.

Catholic schools were, if anything, more fearful of what might happen if school pupils were encouraged to step outside the ghettos of the mind. When Jim Kincade was head of Dungannon Royal School in the sixties, all that separated his school from the adjacent Catholic school, St. Patrick's Academy, was a high hedge, but his suggestion that the hedge should be removed and that the two schools should have sporting and social contacts was bluntly rejected. Catholics believed that Protestant schools taught their pupils to hate the Catholic faith; Protestants believed that Catholic schools taught their pupils that Protestants were heretics and would burn in hell. That these mutual suspicions were not entirely unfounded is suggested by Genevieve's frank admission, in a paper she wrote on 'Ecumenism in Education in Northern Ireland' in 1982, that 'the idea that a Protestant could be called a

Christian was initially a huge shock to the Falls Road Catholic girl'.

There is nothing in Genevieve's early life and career to suggest that her own attitude to Protestants was any different from that of the Falls Road Catholic girl but once the Troubles had forced her to reconsider her attitude, she took up the challenge of countering religious bigotry with typical thoroughness. She was fortunate to have the support of her chairman of governors, Father Padraig Murphy, who in this, as in other matters where his traditionalism might have been expected to clash with Genevieve's policy, proved himself to be surprisingly open-minded. But she did not at first have the support of British ministers who were cautious about enlisting the help of schools to improve community relations. 'Education for mutual understanding' on the school curriculum did not have official blessing until 1989, twenty years after the Troubles started.

Many headteachers, including Genevieve, did not wait for the government. In the early eighties, St. Louise's introduced a cultural studies course aimed at developing acceptance of cultural diversity, the first school in Belfast to do so. Ministers from Presbyterian and Methodist churches were invited to address the sixth form and the school was one of the leading supporters of PRISM, Peace and Reconciliation through Inter-school Meetings, a weekly discussion group for sixth formers from Catholic and Protestant schools. Morning assemblies, whether taken by Genevieve or by the senior girls, often had religious tolerance as a theme and Genevieve had a slogan for the occasion: 'A Catholic does not have to be a Nationalist; a Protestant does not have to be a Unionist.' Genevieve's constant emphasis on the importance of thinking for yourself as a way of countering paramilitary propaganda could also be used as an argument against religious bigotry.

Thinking for yourself did not however include questioning Catholic doctrine. Eilish Weir, who was at the school in the seventies and returned to teach in the eighties, recalls that while Genevieve was emphatic on the importance of being open-minded, she was uncompromising in her Catholicism. The girls

Mary O'Farrell (centre) aged 17, with her school friends Bridie Byrne (left) and May McFadden.

Genevieve (left) aged about 34, soon after she arrived in Northern Ireland, with Sister Mary.

8 January 1958. The sisters lead the girls down St. James's Road to the new school.

Sister Ita and Genevieve (back right) with colleagues and senior girls in 1958. IRISH NEWS

The 'Brown Bombers' with Genevieve (right) and Sister Mary on a school trip to the continent, 1961.

The Falls August 1969. At first the Catholic population welcomed the British army as protectors. HULTON GETTY

The Falls July 1970. A year later, British soldiers are seen as an army of occupation. HULTON GETTY

Would you Please PRay ✳
for a 1st. years daddy
Who Was Shot & dead
Last night. Eterneal rest grant
on to him O Lord + Let PerPeturaL
Light Shine upon him May he rest in Peace
amen

Note handed to Genevieve before morning assembly in the early 1980s.

The Falls Road during the Troubles. For many of Genevieve's pupils this was the way to school. HULTON GETTY

Genevieve (centre) at Buckingham Palace to receive the OBE, 1978, with Sister Ita (left) and Sister Mary.

Genevieve in 1983 aged 60.

'A haven of peace and normality' during the Troubles. The end of afternoon school in the late 1970s.

Genevieve with senior girls in her office at St. Louise's in the early 1980s.

Genevieve returns to the school in November 1988 for a retirement presentation.

Genevieve with Mary O'Hara in Cambridge 1991. Mary had just received her degree.

Still working. Genevieve in her late 60s in her study in Balmoral Avenue.

were left in no doubt that mutual understanding between
Catholics and Protestants did not mean fudging their own distinctive beliefs or diluting the Catholic ethos of the school. In
1980, there were only two Protestant teachers in a staff of one
hundred and sixty and Genevieve freely admitted that she would
always appoint a Catholic in preference to a Protestant. She was
particularly scathing about the suggestion that the Troubles could
have been avoided if Catholic and Protestant children had
attended the same schools. Injustice not segregated schooling was
the cause of the conflict in Northern Ireland, and she described
the campaign for integrated schools as 'a middle-class answer to a
working-class war'.

Speaking to the older girls at the Senior Prize Giving in 1985
Genevieve said: 'I have every reason to believe you students will
never allow yourselves to be steeped in narrow bitter bigotry. You
want a normal society and it is not normal to choose your friends
on grounds of religion. So get out and change the world and
remember you can do it.' But the girls' opportunities for making
Protestant friends were limited. The few Protestant families in the
Falls had long gone. Before the Troubles, the Falls had a population of 35,000 of whom only nine per cent were Protestant. The
neighbouring Shankill was the reverse – a population of 32,000 of
whom only nine per cent were Catholic. The Troubles had quickly
cleansed both districts of their religious minority so that for most
girls the only chance of meeting a Protestant was at one of the
uncontentious conferences for sixth formers organised by
UNESCO or on one of the joint trips to England that Genevieve
arranged. Friendships were made but seldom lasted. It was not
bigotry that kept the young people apart but the practical difficulty
of sustaining a relationship across the so-called 'Peace Line'.
Jennie Shannon, who was head girl in 1987, said that despite the
sixth form contacts she never really met a Protestant until she
went to Queen's University. For those who did manage to sustain
a relationship, religion was not an issue, but when the older girls
were asked whether they would marry a Protestant, the affirmative
answer was qualified: 'only if he promised to bring up the children
Catholic; they have to make that promise if you marry them.' As

Genevieve would have wished, the girls were loyal to Catholic
teaching but open to Protestant friendships. One girl's relationship
with a Protestant boy survived even her father's murder by
Loyalist gunmen.

There is something refreshingly direct about the way
Genevieve set about trying to influence her pupils during the
Troubles. She urged them to think for themselves but she did not
pretend that she would be indifferent to the decisions they made.
It was wrong to use violence even if the structures of society were
unjust. It was wrong to hate people because they held different
religious beliefs but that did not mean you had to modify your
own. She used some of the techniques of propaganda so that the
girls would be in no doubt how she wanted them to think and act
but she knew that slogans without self-confidence would not protect them from the pressures of the ghetto. Cahal Daly was right.
It was the self-confidence that Genevieve developed in the girls
that enabled them to resist the paramilitaries. Self-confidence also
enabled them to meet Protestants on equal terms. When a group
of sixth formers from a Protestant school visited St. Louise's for
the first time and trotted out stereotypical prejudices about
Catholics, they were taken aback by the confident and articulate
manner in which the girls replied. The Protestants, who had been
brought up to think of Catholics as inferior, found themselves
face to face with Genevieve's elite who were a match for any of
their contemporaries.

The Troubles exposed another failure of understanding that
Genevieve tried to do something about. Pupils and teachers in
schools on the mainland were well aware of the conflict in
Northern Ireland, especially when the IRA's bombing campaign
brought the violence closer to home, but they were inclined to
think of it as someone else's war and probably knew little about the
years of discrimination against Catholics that had given the
gunmen their opportunity. When Genevieve was invited to speak
to pupils in England, at Huyton College in Liverpool, for example, or at Charterhouse, a well-heeled public school in Surrey, she
confronted these two issues. She told the boys at Charterhouse: 'If
the British government had realised that the local government in

Belfast was practising discrimination against Nationalists in Northern Ireland for fifty years prior to 1969 the present blood bath might have been avoided.' And she reminded them that the blood bath was happening in their own country not in some remote part of the world. 'You are lucky in the situation of your school,' she said, 'in the secure world that surrounds you. Make the most of it, but be conscious that there are children of your age who are suffering, and not just in India and South America but in part of the United Kingdom.'

Many people on the mainland had difficulty coming to terms with the fact that Genevieve's troubled world was indeed part of the United Kingdom, a difficulty that may be illustrated by a personal recollection. In 1981, the annual meeting of public school headmasters in Oxford was held just a few weeks after the death of the tenth and last hunger striker, Michael Devine. The hunger strikes and the reaction to them had caused and would continue to cause exceptional difficulties for Genevieve. Although the headmasters gathering in Oxford could hardly have been expected to have the situation in Northern Ireland on their agenda, I do not think it would even have crossed our minds that the predicament of a fellow headteacher trying to run a normal school in that guerrilla war was anything to do with us. The Falls Road in Catholic West Belfast may technically have been part of the United Kingdom but as far as we were concerned it might just as well have been in a foreign country.

Thousands of girls passed through St. Louise's in the years between the outbreak of the Troubles in 1969 and Genevieve's retirement in 1988. Genevieve believed they had faced unique difficulties: 'Never has a generation been up against so much,' she wrote, 'never has a generation had to undergo such a severe test to survive as ordinary decent young adults striving to live fulfilled and happy lives.' The girls themselves were not always keen to be regarded as different. They wanted to be seen as the same as their contemporaries and some of them objected to media portrayals of St. Louise's as 'the school behind the barricades'. In 1989, Fidelma Harkin, an inspirational drama teacher and former pupil, told a journalist:

Don't insult these girls by suggesting that they live in a
dangerous, embittered place. The Troubles barely impinge
on their lives – in fact they are just like teenagers anywhere
else. We're sick and tired of negative images about where
we live and we don't want to be patronised or felt sorry for.

The way Genevieve's pupils experienced the Troubles depended
on a number of factors, including their family's politics, where
they lived and when they were born. It could not have been said of
the girls who were at the school in 1971 or 1981, the year of
Internment and the year of the hunger strikes, that the Troubles
barely impinged on their lives. But the constant factor seems to
have been the girls' strong desire to lead normal lives and thanks
to Genevieve's policies most of them were able to do so. Whether
the girls were directly affected by the Troubles or just had to live
with them, their outstanding memory is the contrast between the
chaos on the streets and the calm normality of the school. If
Genevieve had achieved nothing else, her leadership of the school
in this period and her creation of a safe haven when death and violence were literally at the gates, would make her one of the most
remarkable headteachers of her time.

1969–1988
The largest girls' school in
Western Europe

10

*'I told Canon Murphy that if he went
along with the idea I was leaving'*

The early years of the Troubles coincided with the expansion of the school. In ten years, the numbers more than doubled, from 1,000 in 1969 to 2,400 in 1979. New buildings could not keep pace with the increase so that for much of the time Genevieve and her senior colleagues had to improvise; classes were taught wherever a space could be found. Yet the school's clear sense of direction never faltered. Despite all the distractions, Genevieve remained focused on her mission to create a school that would enable girls of all abilities to fulfil their potential.

The rapid expansion of the school began in 1965. The Diocesan Education Committee decided that another girls' secondary school was needed in St. John's parish, which included the new estates of Ballymurphy. St. Louise's could not help because it was committed to two other parishes, St. Peter's and St. Mary's, and was already outgrowing its original buildings, as Genevieve persuaded more girls to stay on after the school leaving age. Genevieve did not see the new school as a threat, it would help to ensure that her own school could be kept to a manageable size. Over the next three years the planning went ahead. The only land that the Church had available was what remained of the plots between St. Louise's and the Milltown cemetery so that the new school would have to be built next door to St. Louise's. An architect was appointed. The

Daughters of Charity agreed to provide the headmistress and the school would be named after the Vincentian Saint, Catherine Laboure. By 1968, planning permission had been granted and the new school was set to admit its first pupils the following year. Then at this late stage, the Ministry of Education, which would be providing most of the money, had second thoughts. Did it make sense to build a new school next to an already successful one? Why not create one big school instead?

The letter from the Ministry proposing that one very large school should be created arrived at the sisters' house in Clonard on a Saturday morning. Genevieve was immediately opposed to the idea. It had taken ten years to establish St. Louise's as a school where discipline was good, where the girls got jobs and where enthusiastic young teachers wanted to teach. If the school was now forced to more than double in size, it would lose its distinctive ethos and become more difficult to control. Stories of the break-down of discipline and of low academic standards in large schools in England re-enforced her determination to resist the Ministry's proposals. She had only recently visited a large London comprehensive school and had been appalled by the slovenliness of the pupils who wore no uniform, failed to stand when she entered the room and smoked openly in the corridors. On receiving the Ministry's letter, Genevieve decided to confront the chairman of the school committee, Father Padraig Murphy. He was on retreat at Glasnevin, outside Dublin, but she was impatient to make her opposition known. 'I got into the car and I never stopped until I got to Glasnevin and I told Canon Murphy that if he went along with the idea I was leaving.' Murphy assured her that he too was opposed to the expansion of St. Louise's and Genevieve returned to Belfast confident that the Ministry's proposal would be rejected. Yet within a few weeks both Murphy and Genevieve had changed their minds and agreed to go ahead with the creation of the largest girls' school in Western Europe.

The key figure in bringing about this change was Father McCaughan, the secretary of the Diocesan Education Committee. McCaughan, a pragmatist, was persuaded that the Ministry of Education would pour money into the large school and provide

facilities that no other secondary school could match. He recognised that the enlarged school would be difficult to manage but he
had seen Genevieve stamp her authority on the existing school and
believed that she was one of the few people capable of managing a
school twice the size. The question was how to sell the idea to
Genevieve herself.

He first won over the parish priests and then Father Murphy.
His argument was that this was an opportunity Catholic education
could not afford to miss because the Ministry was prepared to
make resources available on such a generous scale. But Genevieve
was not persuaded. The real risk of destroying the school she had
created was far more convincing for her than the apparent folly of
looking a gift horse in the mouth. It was one of the unhappiest
periods of her career. Sister Vincent supported her and so did
most of her staff but she felt isolated nevertheless and under pressure from the Church hierarchy to agree to a step she believed
would undermine everything she had achieved. It was at this time
that Michael Murphy, the head of St. Peter's Boys' Secondary
School, who liked to drop in at the end of the school day for tea 'in
good china cups', found Genevieve sitting alone in her office in
tears. She cried quite openly as she explained to him her anger and
frustration at the determination of the priests to accept the
Ministry's proposal.

At this point someone in the Diocesan Education Committee
or the Ministry of Education must have decided to change the
thrust of the argument. It was not just a question of resources,
Genevieve was told; the enlarged school would also be the first
step towards comprehensive education for the poor children of the
Falls. As neither body had any plans to introduce comprehensive
education (the description 'comprehensive' did not exist as far as
the Ministry was concerned), there was more than a touch of
disingenuousness about this argument. Neither the Diocesan
Education Committee nor the Ministry was opposed *in principle* to
ending selection at eleven but they feared the hostility of the
grammar school lobby which was far more influential in Northern
Ireland than in the rest of the United Kingdom. The Catholic
church had additional reasons for wanting to keep its grammar

schools. If the Catholic grammar schools disappeared, some of the more able Catholic children would go to the academic Protestant schools that welcomed Catholics, such as the Methodist College, and the Church might lose control of the next generation of Catholic leaders. So whatever educational or social benefits there may have been in 'going comprehensive', the Church's pragmatism argued strongly for retaining the status quo. Both the Church and the Ministry looked on St. Louise's as an experiment to see how far a large and well-funded secondary school could go towards developing academic courses and a sixth form. They never intended it to be the first step towards abolishing selection at eleven in the Falls or anywhere else.

Genevieve was won over nevertheless. 'The deciding factor in this change of heart,' she wrote some years later, 'was the realisation that the establishment of such a school would be a possible way of promoting the ideal of comprehensive education.' In other words, she read more into the experiment than the priests and the civil servants. Whereas they thought the enlarged school was a way of making a gesture towards comprehensive education without provoking the grammar school lobby, Genevieve thought she could go further and use the resources of a large school to fulfil the comprehensive ideal and prove the grammar school lobby wrong once and for all.

The story of how Genevieve tried to achieve this goal while leading the school through the trauma and disruption of the Troubles is the story of her life from 1969 until her retirement in 1988. Although in this account the impact of the Troubles has been described separately, in reality the problems of running and expanding the school and the problems posed by the guerrilla war all had to be dealt with as they arose. A common experience of headteachers is that the pressures of the job are uneven; on some days he sits in his study and wonders what he should be doing while on others the problems come so thick and fast it is difficult to do justice to any of them. For Genevieve in the early seventies, days without problems were rare. Teachers who needed reassurance, girls who broke the rules, and parents who wished to complain did not time their knock on Genevieve's door to coincide with periods of comparative calm on the streets. The IRA did her one favour however; burning buses, riots and gun battles meant the inspectors called less frequently.

Genevieve was tireless. She was in her mid-forties when the expansion and the Troubles started. She had had no serious illness. In the photographs of the period she has aged little though the features that in early photographs were beautiful and stern are now more relaxed. Perhaps it is just the effect of not wearing the white cornette (a casualty of Vatican Two) which had framed her face and made her look so tall and forbidding. She now wore a blue veil that covered the back of her head and rested on her shoulders.

Physically and psychologically fit and strong as well as confident in her faith and her vocation, Genevieve was able to absorb the pressure more easily and to devote more time to the diverse problems than a lay headteacher. Her training in the seminary had taught her that there was no such thing as spare time; in their service of the poor, the early sisters had driven themselves to exhaustion, even death. 'People expect sisters who have made the sacrifice of motherhood and family life to be totally dedicated to prayer and work and not to seek a soft lifestyle,' Genevieve wrote, 'to give and not to count the cost pays dividends for our own fulfilment – a fulfilment that will not come from a 35 to 40 hour week.' Her own working week was open-ended; her extra-curricular activities such as visiting her former pupils in Armagh jail had to be fitted in on Saturday or Sunday. Like many other leaders of whom multiple demands are made, she developed the knack of being able to switch from one subject to another many times a day and to give each new problem her full attention. But she could be impatient with those who lacked her zeal for getting things done – 'You've no sense of urgency' was one of her standard criticisms – and she did not suffer fools gladly. When an angry father whose daughter had been suspended drew a handgun and placed it on the desk between them, a clumsy reminder perhaps of his paramilitary status, Genevieve told him to put it away; his daughter was in enough trouble without her father behaving like a fool.

Genevieve worked well under pressure and deliberately left tasks, such as writing a speech for prize night, until the last minute so that she would have to work against the clock, but for all her resilience and restless energy she was not super-human. As the pressures intensified, her quiet times at the beginning and the ending of the day became more precious. So did her summer holiday in her beloved Scotland. It was her practice to spend the first two weeks of the summer break in the school, dealing with business for which there had been no time during the term and seeing members of staff who had something to get off their chests. At the end of July she escaped across the Irish Sea. The sisters were given long leave every summer and Genevieve usually spent two weeks at the Daughters of Charity house at Kingussie in the Spey Valley or with the Sacred Heart sisters at Bridge of Earn near Perth. When she was staying at Kingussie, she liked to leave the house early in the morning and spend the whole day alone in the hills, solitary walks that must have been wonderfully refreshing after the demands of the term and the claustrophobic atmosphere of the ghetto.

After her two weeks holiday in Scotland, Genevieve exchanged the peace of the hills for the tensions of West Belfast. Clonard was a potentially dangerous area at any time, not least because the British army was convinced that the superior of the Redemptorist monastery sympathised with the IRA and allowed IRA weapons to be hidden in the monastery cellars. The Redemptorist fathers remained in Clonard throughout the Troubles but by the early eighties, Genevieve and the other sisters were thinking of moving. They were reluctant to leave the house where the community had begun its mission to the Falls in 1900 but it made no sense for those who were teachers to be living in an area where it was unusual to have an uninterrupted night's sleep. In 1983, Genevieve, Ita and Declan moved to a house in Balmoral Avenue in South Belfast, outside the ghetto but an easy drive to the school. The *Andersonstown News* briefly noted Genevieve's departure under the heading: 'The Queen moves to Balmoral!'

Genevieve, who had wept tears of frustration when her objections to the large school were being ignored, drove a hard bargain as the price for changing her mind. She would accept the proposal of the Diocesan Education Committee and the Ministry but only on certain conditions. St. Louise's must continue to take the girls from its original parishes of St. Peter's and St. Mary's, it must honour all family ties and it must be free to take girls *from any parish* who had qualified for the grammar school but preferred to come to St. Louise's.

By insisting that the school remain loyal to its families from Lower Falls, Genevieve shrewdly ensured that as the school expanded there would be a high proportion of girls whose families knew the school and knew the standards of behaviour that she expected. In the eighties, two-thirds of the girls at St. Louise's were the daughters of former pupils, a higher proportion than at even the most traditional public schools in England, such as Eton and Harrow, where sons had been following fathers for generations. And by insisting that St. Louise's should be allowed to accept any girls who had qualified for the grammar school, Genevieve was ensuring that St. Louise's would have a chance to be truly comprehensive in its intake and to throw off the image of a secondary school which in Belfast meant a school for failures. With this in mind, she refused to countenance the enlarged school being described as 'secondary'. It must be called 'comprehensive' and, so that its equal status with the grammar school was clearly signalled, it should be called a college not a school. In vain, the education authorities in Belfast protested that 'comprehensive' was not on the list of recognised terms. Genevieve, supported by Father Padraig Murphy, would not back down. In 1969, St. Louise's Girls' Secondary Intermediate School became St. Louise's Comprehensive College.

For the first two years the plan for a gradual expansion went smoothly. Only a proportion of the eleven-year-olds from the primary schools in St. John's parish joined St. Louise's while the rest continued to go to the Dominican Secondary School in the Lower Falls, St. Rose's. But in June 1971, the Dominicans announced without warning that they would take no more girls from the two primary schools in Ballymurphy. Genevieve was presented with a *fait accompli*. The Daughters of Charity of all people could not refuse to take the extra ninety girls who were from the poorest

homes in Ballymurphy, even though the school was already bursting at the seams.

Between June and the start of the new school year in
September, Genevieve and Father Murphy had to find a way of
accommodating this unexpected increase. No period better illustrates the way in which the expansion of the school and the
Troubles combined to test Genevieve's resolve. While she and
Father Murphy were arranging with the education authorities
for extra classrooms to be airlifted onto the site, the Falls
erupted. Internment – Operation Demetrius – began in the early
hours of 9 August; girls' fathers, brothers and uncles were seized
by the British army often on the basis of inaccurate information
about active Republicanism. (It was also the day on which the
senior girls' Advanced Level exam results were published.)
Internment provoked widespread rioting and prolonged gun
battles between the IRA and the army. In the three days following its introduction, 22 people were killed and 7,000, mostly
Catholics, made homeless. When the new term started, some of
the older girls had already decided to join the IRA, while others
returned to school restless and resentful.

For Genevieve and her staff that September, pastoral and logistical problems overlapped. There were now seventeen mobile
classrooms clustered round the original buildings but teachers
found themselves taking classes in corridors, under the stairs and
in the school store as they had had to do when the school first
opened. Three classes were taught at the same time in the assembly hall. Meanwhile the army must have decided that mobile
classrooms were just the sort of place that the IRA would choose
to hide their weapons because Genevieve found soldiers searching
the site without her permission and angrily told them to 'Get out!'
Unlike the Redemptorist monastery, schools were not off limits to
the army and some officers stationed at Macrory Park reckoned
they could enter the school grounds whenever it suited them. It
was several years before the mobile classrooms could be dispensed
with altogether. When the contractors moved in and started pile
driving to sink firm foundations into the Bog Meadows, the school
became a building site as well as a mobile classroom park. The first

phase of the building was completed in 1975. The second and third phases were completed in 1979. In September of that year, the school reached a total of 2,400 pupils.

Quite apart from the logistical problems associated with the increase, Genevieve had to adapt her very personal style of leadership to the larger school. She had developed the ethos and reputation of St. Louise's by the force of her personality and by the clarity of her vision of what sort of school she wanted it to be. Her fear that it would prove impossible to inspire a much larger school in the same way was understandable. It had never been tried before. There were very large schools in other countries but in these schools the head or principal was an administrator with little or no personal contact with the pupils. Genevieve would never have been satisfied with that role. In accepting the proposal to create a school of 2,400 pupils she was gambling that she would be able to run an efficient administration while retaining her personal influence over her girls.

11

'Ultimately the principal must remain in control'

Genevieve believed that God had given her a talent for leadership. When she prayed on her way to school, 'Lord help us to use the talents you have so generously given us', this was the talent she had in mind. She knew she possessed some of the qualities of a successful leader, notably single-mindedness of purpose and the ability to inspire others with her vision. But her leadership of St. Louise's up to this point had been largely a question of stamping her authority on the school; it was by no means certain that a religious sister, trained in obedience not in business administration, would have the more sophisticated skills needed to lead a school of 2,400 pupils and 160 teachers. Genevieve had never been known to read a book on management and she was critical of what she described as 'the uncontrolled application of management theory to schools', yet within a few years she had set up an organisation at St. Louise's that was a model of how a very large school should be managed.

It was not just the size of the school that encouraged Genevieve to modify her autocratic approach. By the early seventies, the old-style headteacher who ruled the school as a more or less enlightened despot was going out of fashion. Heads still exercised real power but they were now expected to delegate some part of their authority and to consult their colleagues. The absolute monarchs of the past were

becoming much more like the chief executives of organisations outside the school world. Surprisingly in view of the way she had been
running the school, this change appears to have presented few problems for Genevieve. She was a realist. 'The day is gone,' she told
parents in 1971, 'when the principal could without blinking an
eyelid talk about *my* school, *my* pupils as if he or she made every
decision.' Some years later she explained to student teachers how for
her the role of the head had changed.

> In spite of the existence of Trustees, School Committee,
> Education and Library Board and Department of
> Education, the headteacher really has the responsibility of
> running the school – at least this head does. She defines the
> policy, determines the standards that are acceptable from
> staff and pupils and is the main public relations officer.
> Having said all that, let me add I believe in the changing
> role of the head today. No longer can the head shut herself
> away in an office and make arbitrary decisions without
> consultation. The head must bring her staff along with her
> and can only do this by real delegation and the
> encouragement of involvement and initiative. She sets the
> tone of the school and sets up structures whereby
> management is shared and teachers have responsibility.

The concept of the head bringing her staff along with her was very
different from that of the head who treated teachers as 'sheep who
must be led', and in the early seventies some of Genevieve's staff
must have doubted whether her autocratic instincts would allow
genuine consultation and delegation to occur. Teachers are understandably sceptical about initiatives that purport to give them a
role in the management of the school and are easily persuaded that
the head's new enthusiasm for committees and working parties is
only window-dressing.

Genevieve was not window-dressing. She saw clearly that a
school of 2,400 girls would not become the exemplar of the comprehensive ideal unless there was an effective management
structure through which she, as principal, could work. People who

were surprised how easily the autocrat became the chief executive underestimated her intelligence. She was determined to overcome every barrier to the fulfilment of her vocation. The new structures she set up were not original; there are only a few variations on the theme of delegation and consultation. What was unusual in the school world was the extent to which she was able to make consultation and delegation work. In that sense, she was ahead of her time.

Genevieve's cabinet was called the Administration Team. It consisted of eight members: her two deputies, five colleagues and herself. Reporting to the Administration Team were a number of 'weekly working parties' that were responsible for every aspect of the school's operation from discipline to the curriculum. Genevieve insisted that the working parties had a formal agenda and kept proper minutes. Every Friday, the Administration Team met to consider matters raised at the weekly meetings. Some critics thought this was all too bureaucratic but Genevieve was adamant that the weekly meetings were 'the essence of administering a school of 2,400' and that the minutes were needed because 'communication cannot be left to chance as it so often was in the past'.

Like other headteachers who were adapting to a more managerial style, Genevieve kept her hands on the levers of power. In the much larger school, she was prepared to delegate authority to those she called her 'middle managers', the heads of years and the heads of academic departments, but only on the condition that they were prepared to take on the burden of responsibility. If they were going to exercise authority in her name, they had to be leaders too and could not shy away from the tough decisions that leaders have to make. In her 1983 address to student teachers she made her fullest statement of what she understood this to mean in practice. She was talking about the heads of academic departments.

First, they must have leadership qualities not just academic qualifications:

> The ability to lead others, colleagues and pupils, is an
> essential quality for any head of department and if it is
> missing teachers suffer and pupils suffer.

As leaders, they must have clear objectives which are understood and put into practice by the members of the department. Genevieve had been teaching long enough to know that many teachers were reluctant to exercise authority over their colleagues, yet the effective management of a large school depended on their being willing to do so. On the sensitive question of going into colleagues' classes, she had no doubt where the head of department's responsibility lay:

> The major part of their role is their responsibility for the teaching within their department. They are managers. In industry they would be referred to as middle managers. As managers they differ from other teachers in that they work through others. It must be obvious that a head of department must know what is happening inside the classroom if she is to do her job properly. Before this can happen she must create the correct climate, so that her presence is accepted by pupils who must not see it as spying on the teacher and also by the teachers themselves who should not see it as an attack on their professionalism.

Genevieve's experience had also taught her that some heads of department thought their responsibility was solely for academic matters and that discipline was someone else's problem. She abhorred that attitude. In a school of 2,400 pupils, every middle manager, whether academic or pastoral, had to take responsibility for good order:

> It must be remembered that without discipline education is impossible, even with the most relevant and imaginative objectives. There may be a tendency on the part of the more trendy heads of department to get away from this as they become so involved in their academic role. However, I firmly believe that discipline is the cornerstone of everything we do, and a head of department must be expected to play a leading role well above that of ordinary teachers in this as in other aspects of education. One cannot teach a subject in the midst of chaos.

Genevieve's attitude to discipline was out of step with the times. From the late sixties onwards, schools throughout the United Kingdom had been busy dismantling the compulsions, such as the wearing of school uniform, that were associated with traditional discipline. In some educational circles 'discipline' had become a dirty word and it is unlikely that any of Genevieve's contemporaries, in state or independent schools, would have publicly asserted that 'discipline is the cornerstone of everything we do'.

Genevieve had welcomed the liberating spirit of the sixties, particularly as it affected the religious life, but she did not make the mistake that was made by some headteachers of equating traditional school discipline with oppressive regimes. Far from oppressing pupils, good discipline helped to liberate them from the ignorance, poverty and discrimination that held them back. On her regular visits to England she was amazed at the lack of discipline in the inner-city comprehensive schools and at the teachers' apparent inability to recognise the harm chaos was doing to the pupils' chances. To her it was obvious that the poorest and most marginalised children had the most to gain from an orderly environment and the most to lose when authority was undermined. Throughout this period, from the late sixties until her retirement in 1988, she did not modify her view that discipline was the cornerstone of a good school. St. Louise's was living proof that a very large inner-city school taking children of all abilities could be run on well-disciplined lines. Visitors to the school in the eighties, including the author, were surprised at how quiet it was and at the orderly way in which 2,400 girls moved about the school at the changeover of lessons. It was like watching a well-oiled machine yet the girls were not automata but lively individuals.

Visitors were also surprised by the absence of litter and graffiti. The school was spotless. A woman who worked as a cleaner at the school for thirty-five years described how Genevieve would run her finger along the ledges in the corridor to check for dust and wield a brush herself to demonstrate how the tops of the lockers should be cleaned. In Genevieve's eyes the cleaners made an important contribution to good discipline and in the school magazine they were listed by name just like the teaching staff.

Discipline was good at St. Louise's because Genevieve made it a priority. She expected heads of department to make it their priority too. When she advised young teachers joining the staff, she adopted the same approach that Sister Philomena had used in the seminary – a little theory and a lot of practical advice. Her advice is worth quoting at length because it helps to illustrate why she was so successful where many heads of large, inner-city schools failed, in creating the disciplined environment that disadvantaged children needed.

The children are products of factors over which they have no control and they have not created the social malaise in society which is responsible for their difficulties. A teacher's best attitude is sympathy without softness and understanding but not indulgence of unacceptable behaviour. Discipline is the be-all and end-all of teaching. The most brilliant teacher who has bad discipline is a failure and the most unhappy of human beings. No group of people can be as cruel as children. If they detect one chink in the armour of a teacher, they will exploit it to the full. And once *they* have got control the teacher can never regain control.

Genevieve knew that as students the young teachers had received little practical advice on how to control a class so she provided it herself.

When you open the door of your first class in your first school you are under intense scrutiny from 30 pairs of eyes – they are deciding if you are nervous or confident and how far they can go with you . . . The greatest antidote to discipline problems is hard work – no hiatus at the beginning of the class, in other words no time for thinking up means of disruption. Realise the tricks that pupils try out: forgetting tools of the trade, pen and pencil etc; getting 'sick' and asking to go out; choral answering; chewing, talking and distracting others. Realise the value of

getting to class in time as three to five minutes can cause
havoc with an unsupervised group. Do not feel self-
conscious or discouraged when clearly laying down rules,
you are in charge and the pupils want you to play your part.
Good discipline results from attention to detail: always
follow up what you say; if you make threats see you carry
them out; if you give homework do the child the honour of
correcting it; above all, never go to a class without knowing
how you are going to spend every minute. If you demand a
high standard, set a high standard for yourself; in work, in
speech and in personal presentation.

Attention to detail showed that the teacher respected the pupils.
'Before we start complaining about children let's ask ourselves a
few questions', she told a staff meeting in 1978. 'What respect do
I give pupils before asking for respect from them?' When a male
teacher complained to the head of department about a particularly
disruptive class, Genevieve went along to observe. In her presence,
the girls were subdued but the teacher did nothing to hide his lack
of interest in them. At the end of the lesson, Genevieve gave him
a piece of advice: 'If you get off your backside and take your hands
out of your pockets and treat them with a bit of respect, maybe
you would get it back.'

Genevieve expected heads of department to be able to deal with
lazy teachers. Even the best schools may have some teachers who
do the minimum required to avoid censure. Their colleagues
resent the fact that these teachers 'get away with it' but are very
reluctant to tackle the problem themselves. 'This is an unpleasant
subject,' Genevieve acknowledged, 'and one that teachers tradi-
tionally shy away from, but if our profession is going to develop we
must face up to it.' Ideally, the head of department would create
such a strong team spirit that 'the lazy teacher will feel uncomfortable and inadequate in the face of the dedication and industry
of her colleagues'. But if that did not work, the head of department
'will at times have to be unpleasant'.

This was the deal Genevieve offered. If the heads of department were given real responsibility they would have to show the

leadership qualities, including 'a touch of ruthlessness', that she herself had needed to establish the school's reputation.

> The picture I have painted is one of heads of department
> acting very much as mini-heads in their own domain. That
> domain may have two teachers or ten – it is irrelevant.
> While there is considerable potential for job satisfaction in
> this role, it also brings responsibilities. It demands decision
> making which may be popular or unpopular. It demands
> that the good of the pupils always be kept uppermost in
> one's mind. To achieve this, the head of department must at
> all times be conscious that the children may suffer if she
> fails to meet her responsibilities and this may call for a
> touch of ruthlessness. She cannot remain 'one of the girls'.

The structure of weekly meetings enabled Genevieve to monitor the performance of these middle managers and although her instincts may still have been those of an absolute monarch she had the sense not to interfere. 'Ultimately the principal must remain in control,' she concluded her talk to the student teachers, 'but the intelligent principal will only step in when there is a breakdown in relationships within the department or when children are being neglected by a teacher.'

The new style Genevieve was still the boss. Andy Dougal, the school's registrar or bursar, who worked closely with Genevieve when the school was expanding, described this new style as 'not dictatorial but highly directional', a nice distinction between the autocrat Genevieve had been in the early years and the no-nonsense chief executive she became. In common with many successful headteachers, she was not an original or profound thinker about education. She was a jackdaw, picking up ideas here and there, in articles she read and at conferences she attended, and then demanding of her middle managers 'why aren't we doing this?' In this way she created an atmosphere sympathetic to innovation. The word soon reached the teacher training colleges and those in the education world who wanted to pilot a new syllabus or a new teaching method.

The result was that from the teachers' point of view St. Louise's became an even more exciting place to work. It also became more demanding. Teachers who thought they could leave at the end of the afternoon school or who expected to be given time to do their marking in school hours were swiftly disabused. Youth was no bar to promotion. The average age of heads of department was seldom over thirty. Carmel Gallagher was appointed head of history in her early twenties and with only two years teaching experience. From time to time, Genevieve also appointed a young teacher to the Administration Team, ostensibly to gain experience but actually to demonstrate that the school was not going to be run on strictly hierarchical lines. If older teachers found this preference for youth unsettling, Genevieve probably regarded that as a bonus.

As the number of teachers rose to 120 in 1975 and 160 in 1979, it became more difficult for Genevieve to be certain that all the staff shared her commitment to the comprehensive ideal and to the school's Vincentian ethos. She used staff meetings to empha-sise the importance of her mission but the sheer size of the meeting and the growth of union membership meant that she no longer had things all her own way. There were times when Genevieve came back to her office fuming because she believed some teachers were putting their own interests before those of the pupils. She publicly supported union claims for better pay (her own salary went straight to her religious community) but she remained as unsympathetic as ever to those for whom teaching was not a vocation. One way in which she tried to ensure that the staff shared her sense of vocation and loyalty to the school's aims, was to appoint former pupils as teachers. It was an approach adopted by the heads of traditional English public schools and by a very different type of headmaster, her hero Padraig Pearse, whose former pupils lived in the school and taught part-time while they were at university. Some of Genevieve's former pupils were loyal guardians of her dream but others did not stay long, com-plaining that Genevieve continued to treat them as pupils when they were on the staff.

Despite the fact that Genevieve's personality still dominated the school, she had to rely more and more on a few trusted lieutenants to interpret her policies to the rest of the staff. Every headteacher needs allies who are close enough to give frank advice yet not so close that they lose credibility in the eyes of their colleagues. In the early years, Genevieve had relied on Sister Ita and Maire McFadden. As the school expanded, so did the number of her trusted lieutenants. The most important of these, in order of their arrival at the school were, Mairead O'Halloran, Aidan Hamill, Andy Dougal and Sister Declan Kelly.

Mairead O'Halloran was appointed in 1966 straight from teacher training college. Her interview with Genevieve, for which she wore a hat (this was Belfast not swinging London), was brief, almost perfunctory, and she was offered the job on the spot. By luck or instinct, Genevieve chose the woman who would be her closest friend outside the religious community and an ideal lieutenant, loyal, hardworking and willing to take responsibility. In a career of over thirty years at St. Louise's, Mairead filled many roles including head of year and vice-principal but none so important as taking over from Genevieve responsibility for ensuring that the leavers had jobs or places in higher education.

Genevieve's instinct for identifying potential allies was also at work in the appointment of Dr Aidan Hamill, an experienced teacher who applied for the post of head of science in 1971. He did not get the job but Genevieve liked his enthusiasm for the comprehensive ideal and his interest in curriculum development (about which she knew little) and decided to offer him a job anyway. He was responsible for the reform of the school's curriculum and was eventually appointed a vice-principal.

Andy Dougal was not appointed by Genevieve but by the Belfast Education and Library Board. The rapid expansion of the school and the complex building operation needed someone on the spot to be responsible for the day-to-day management of the project. Andy Dougal was called Registrar but his role was very similar to that of the bursar in an independent school. He looked after the finances, the fabric and the non-teaching staff. Genevieve welcomed the division of labour. 'My area is by and large teachers and pupils,' she explained, 'in a word, education not business.' It is unusual in an independent school for the headteacher and the

bursar to have a trouble-free relationship; the separation of education and business is not as easy in practice as the school's
governors think. But Genevieve and Andy Dougal hit it off from
the start. The secret of their successful collaboration was mutual
respect; they knew what the other did best. Genevieve was the
strategic leader, Andy Dougal the staff officer who made sure the
resources were available; she provided the vision and drive, he the
administrative back-up. On the new building, she said what she
wanted and left it to him to trouble-shoot with the architect and
the contractor. When he left in 1983, Genevieve told him: 'I personally am tremendously indebted to you. You brought style and
professionalism to the business side of the school.' He was also,
like Aidan Hamill, a reassuring presence at her elbow during the
Troubles. At times when British soldiers were blocking the Falls
Road and the way home, it was often Andy Dougal not Genevieve
who telephoned army headquarters.

Genevieve praised Andy Dougal's 'loyalty to the ideals of this
form of education'. She would have found it impossible to work
closely with someone who did not share her commitment to both
the Vincentian and the comprehensive ideals. Of all her lieutenants none was more committed to these ideals than Sister
Declan Kelly. Sister Mary, 'the gentle and kindly sister' died young
of cancer in 1978 and Sister Declan replaced her on the staff the
following year. Declan had been working in Ballymurphy and
living in the sisters' house in Clonard so Genevieve already knew
her well. Though she was appointed to teach religious education,
she quickly became one of Genevieve's most loyal collaborators,
taking charge of the first year girls and, like Mairead O'Halloran
and Aidan Hamill, eventually becoming a vice-principal. Like
Genevieve, she came from the Irish Republic and had trained in
the seminary at Blackrock and although very different from
Genevieve in style and character, possessed the same capacity for
hard work.

The true measure of a headteacher is not whether she motivates
her pupils but whether she motivates her staff. It is the most difficult aspect of the job not because teachers are naturally lazy but
because teaching day-in and day-out demands such resilience.

There are no walk-on parts in a school; every teacher, however inexperienced, has to accept a starring role alone in the classroom with an audience who would rather not be there. Even dedicated professionals may experience a temporary loss of nerve or just a sinking heart at the prospect of facing the head-bangers on a Friday afternoon. Motivation is everything.

Genevieve was a great motivator. Though fear of her may still have been a potent factor – 'the staff were all terrified of her', Carmel Gallagher claimed – her ability to motivate her staff owed more to the feeling she had created that St. Louise's was a school on the move, a place where anything was possible for the enterprising teacher. She went out of her way to help teachers develop their careers and, unlike some headteachers who do not want the trouble of finding replacements, she encouraged them to spend time away from the school on courses or secondments. As with her preference for promoting young teachers, her enthusiasm for professional development helped to keep disillusionment and cynicism at bay in the staff room. Her vision of the sort of school St. Louise's was going to be and her talent for releasing the energies of her staff provided the dynamic that drove the school forward in the seventies and eighties.

For those who did not share her vision or respond to her leadership there was little point in staying. Genevieve made it clear that as far as she was concerned those who were not with her were against her. Her style was less dictatorial than in the past but she could still at times be high-handed and unpredictable, even with those who were her strongest supporters. Eddie McArdle was one of twenty-eight new teachers joining the staff in 1974. Married to one of Genevieve's former pupils, he had no difficulty identifying with Genevieve's vision but he recognised the contradictions that some of his colleagues found disconcerting. She could be inordinately sensitive and understanding with a teacher who had personal problems but brusque and rude if she decided, sometimes on slender evidence, that a teacher was not fully committed to the cause. She was a driven woman whose emotions sometimes got the better of her reason and at the same time a woman of great spirituality, who went to the oratory just inside the main

entrance at the beginning and the end of school day to say a
decade of the rosary with those pupils who were present. She
believed passionately in the importance of a Catholic education
but refused to take into account the effect of her aggressive marketing of St. Louise's on other Catholic schools. When McArdle
referred to the characteristics of other Catholic schools in the area
at a meeting of prospective parents, she was furious. His job was to
sell St. Louise's.

McArdle admired Genevieve's single-minded pursuit of her
goals. He had 'never met anyone as tenacious'. In Genevieve's
long-running battles with the education authorities, her tenacity
defeated all but the most resilient officials. Whatever she may
have said to parents about school principals no longer speaking of
'my school' and 'my pupils', she continued to think in those terms
and to see herself as the school's champion battling against forces –
the priests on the school committee, the officials in the education
authority – who refused to give her what she wanted. She chose
confrontation where other heads would have adopted a more indi-
rect, diplomatic approach. If she usually got her way in the end
there was a price to pay in hostility to the school and to herself.
Peter Melchett, the British minister responsible for education in
Northern Ireland in the late seventies, was told that her tactics had
made her 'intensely unpopular' with officials and with the Catholic
hierarchy. When ten years later Brian Mawhinney told her final
assembly that he had come to meet the woman his staff in the
Department of Education was terrified of, he was only half in jest.
By 1988, there were officials in the Department and in the Belfast
Education and Library Board who were glad to see Sister
Genevieve retire.

Genevieve's confrontational style can partly be explained by
the impatience an all-powerful headteacher feels in having to go
cap in hand to officials. But confrontation seems to have come naturally to her, as though her instinct when faced with any difficulty
was to attack. The hostility she provoked never appears to have
worried her. Melchett thought she actually enjoyed being unpopular, an observation that echoes others made at different stages of
her career, from the young sister who was said to enjoy 'ruffling

feathers' to the sister with attitude whose problems with clergy 'were of her own making'.

Her dealings with the Belfast Education and Library Board were mostly about the provision of equipment and the maintenance of the buildings. Problems arose because she wanted more than officials were prepared to give. Some officials, like some senior girls, decided that the only way to deal with Sister Genevieve was to stand up to her. Jim Caves, a senior official at the Board throughout the seventies, became a friend but of his early meetings with Genevieve he said, 'You had to be tough not to be bludgeoned'. Another official, Jimmy McCulloch, described her as 'a juggernaut'. If browbeating did not work Genevieve appealed to higher authority, using her contacts with British politicians to put pressure on civil servants. According to Caves, 'she was relentless in going over your head'.

Headteachers are not by and large saintly people; if they are not unscrupulous by nature, the job soon inclines them to be so. Genevieve was not more unscrupulous than other headteachers; she was more tenacious. According to Mawhinney, when she spotted a weakness in the official position she exploited it. 'If there was an exposed toe and she needed something she would have no hesitation in treading on it.' She was prepared to charm those male officials who found it difficult to refuse an attractive nun and to play the religious card by accusing Protestant officials of discriminating against Catholic girls from a deprived area. Like her staff, the officials found her unpredictability disconcerting. One of the sisters in her own congregation described how Genevieve 'could charm the birds off the trees one moment and be intimidating the next', behaviour that civil servants were not accustomed to. But Jim Caves thought there was a lot of role playing in Genevieve's performance and that she had probably thought out in advance which role would be most effective. In the middle of a fierce argument – 'You're doing your damnedest to make it impossible for me to run this school!' – an official from the Board might be surprised to see a mischievous twinkle in her eye. But knowing what she was up to did not make her easier to resist; her determination to have her own way was the same.

She was certainly calculating when she planned how to receive those officials who were not afraid to venture into the Falls Road. She would give them the impression that they were coming for a discussion with her over a glass of sherry in her office and then confront them with a large formal meeting, with herself in the chair, flanked by senior members of staff, all of whom wanted to know why more money was not being made available. 'It was like going for a job interview,' Jimmy McCulloch complained. Returning from one of these meetings, Caves was asked by a colleague how he had managed to keep his temper. 'I prayed to God to give me patience,' Caves replied. If Genevieve thought she could get away with it, she tried to bypass the education authorities altogether. 'Better to apologise afterwards than to ask permission,' was one of her favourite slogans, though it was not one she shared with her pupils.

Genevieve did not adopt the same tactics in her dealings with the governors of the school. The members of the school committee, like the old-style priest manager they had replaced, had authority over Genevieve and the power to frustrate her plans. A more politic approach was required. The fact that priests constituted half the membership of the committee and occupied the key positions of chairman and vice-chairman made this more difficult to achieve. The normal disagreements between the headteacher and the governing body were exacerbated by Genevieve's barely disguised hostility to the male domination of the Church.

The new school committee was set up in 1968 but its first meeting did not take place until 1969. The chairman was Father Padraig Murphy, Administrator of St. Peter's pro-cathedral and later parish priest of St. John's. The vice-chairman and secretary were also based at St. Peter's. Of the twelve members of the committee, six were priests and only two were women. Genevieve was not a member but was in attendance at meetings. Eight of the twelve members had been appointed by the Trustees of the school and four by the Belfast Education and Library Board, the two-thirds to one third ratio required if Catholic schools were to have the benefits of being maintained by the local authority.

The role of the Trustees complicated the work of the committee and fuelled Genevieve's suspicion that for the Church
hierarchy the education of girls who had not qualified for grammar school was not a priority. The Trustees were the legal owners
of the property and proprietors of the school notwithstanding the
fact that the Department of Education had put up most of the
money. The Trustees not only nominated the majority of the
committee members but by their ownership of the property could
veto improvements and additional building. Everyone knew that
the Trustees represented the interests of the Church hierarchy
but, in a way that Genevieve regarded as typical of the male ethos
of the Church, the identity of the Trustees was not publicly
revealed. Three of the priests on the school committee, including
the chairman, spoke on behalf of the Trustees but refused to say
who the Trustees were. When lay members of the committee
complained that their work was 'hampered by the veil of secrecy
surrounding the identity of the Trustees', the chairman suggested
that they should write to the bishop or the bishop's solicitors. To
someone of Genevieve's outlook and temperament it must have all
seemed very childish. Not surprisingly, there are numerous references in the minutes of school committee meetings to the lack of
communication between the Trustees and the committee.

Genevieve had good reason to resent the Trustees' role. In
1979, they effectively blocked a scheme to provide sports facilities,
including a swimming bath and playing fields, next to the school.
According to Peter Melchett, the Department of Education would
have paid the full cost on the condition that the facilities would
also be used by the community, but the Trustees refused to release
the land. The Trustees said they needed the land for an industrial
development that would provide employment in the area but the
land was left derelict and soon become so rat-infested that it was a
health hazard to the school.

For a woman who believed that developing St. Louise's was
her vocation, the power of the Trustees to thwart her plans must
have been hard to bear. With Father Murphy as chairman, she
could at least feel that there was one priest who understood what
she was trying to achieve. After his death in 1986, she described

him as an 'enlightened chairman' who had supported her pursuit of the comprehensive ideal. As a Catholic priest Murphy was not in favour of abolishing the 11+ exam and the grammar schools, but he was happy to see Genevieve create a family school that was comprehensive in style. The relationship between the feminist sister and the gruffly courteous priest was good in parts. The mutual respect that had been forged at the start of the Troubles was strengthened in the difficult years of the school's expansion. When they disagreed it was usually about money. Murphy, a Falls Road man through and through, was sensitive to the fact that the parishes would have to contribute to the cost of the improvements Genevieve wanted on top of the repayment of the debt incurred when the original school was built. Genevieve, the outsider who had won the respect of the people of the Falls, was inclined to see expenditure solely from the point of view of her mission and her girls. But their disagreements do not appear to have been personal despite the fact that they were both strong characters who liked to be the boss.

Father Murphy could not have worked with Genevieve for ten years if he had felt threatened by her. She must have made other priests in the diocese feel insecure however, because when Murphy retired in 1978, two priests were appointed to the school committee, one as chairman, whose clear intention was to assert the authority of the Church over the school and over Genevieve herself. Genevieve was accused of exceeding her authority by taking decisions that should have been taken by the committee and the new chairman announced that in future he alone would decide what items appeared on the committee's agenda. In vain, the lay members protested that this was an undemocratic way of proceeding.

The struggle for power between the lay members and Genevieve on one hand and the priests appointed by the Trustees on the other continued for several years, flaring up over particular issues and then dying down again. When feelings ran high, the normal courtesies of committee meetings could be forgotten. 'Some strong exchanges took place,' the minutes record of a meeting in 1978, 'and the issue tended to become personal. Some members of the committee objected to the principal being insulted in the presence of the chairman'. At another meeting a few years later, a lay member 'was appalled by this attack on the integrity of the principal'.

Genevieve could look after herself even in the roughest meetings but she must have been aware that this was not just a routine power struggle. Her perceived feminism was also a target. She had alienated a number of priests in the diocese by the blunt manner in which she had made it clear that she was not going to be treated as a second-class citizen by the Church. She was not a militant or radical feminist; on the contrary, she accepted that because women possessed different qualities to men they would play different roles in the life of the Church. What she demanded was equal respect for those roles and a recognition by the clergy that equality did not derive from or depend on ordination.

One priest who took a detached view of Genevieve was the secretary of the diocese's maintained schools' committee, Father Colm McCaughan. In 1982, when he attended a meeting of the St. Louise's school committee, he tried to resolve a typical dispute over whether Genevieve had the authority to appoint part-time staff without reference to the governors. McCaughan's advice recorded in the minutes was characteristically pragmatic: 'Father McCaughan said that normally speaking power should be delegated and that the principal should be left to do her own job with as little interference as possible.' But the priests on the school committee did not consider that they were interfering and they continued to challenge Genevieve's actions when they saw occasion to do so. During the eighties two major disputes occurred, one over Genevieve's policy on enrolment, which was said to involve 'poaching' girls from other parishes, and the other over her policy for the expulsion of disruptive pupils.

After Genevieve retired in 1988, the influence of the priests on the school committee declined. By 1998, forty years after the school was founded, the governing body of St. Louise's was made up almost entirely of lay men and women, with one or at the most two priests as members. The Trustees still owned the school but the Church hierarchy had deliberately backed away from a policy of trying to establish clerical control. The battles Genevieve had fought had not been in vain.

12

*'She loves those smart girls; she doesn't
have any time for the ordinary ones'*

Headteachers are good at giving the impression that they know
every pupil by name. It is one of the tricks of the trade. In a school
of 2,400 pupils, Genevieve did not pretend. 'It is not important I
should know every pupil,' she wrote of the enlarged school, 'what
is important is that each pupil is known very well by some person
and be able to approach that person.' She knew a remarkable
number of the girls nevertheless, and not just those at the top of
the school and those most often in trouble. Unusually for a headteacher, she lived for many years in the same area as most of her
pupils so that even when the Troubles drove many Catholics out of
the Lower Falls, the younger sisters who came to the school from
new addresses were still from families Genevieve knew well.

When Father Padraig Murphy spoke of St. Louise's as a family
school, he was identifying one of its defining characteristics; the
family networks that meant it was comparatively rare for a new girl
to arrive who had no relatives among the present or former pupils.
Knowing these networks, Genevieve could probably place more
pupils in their family context than the heads of much smaller
schools. By the early eighties, the networks included the daughters
of her first pupils so that Genevieve, like Mr Chips, was able to
enjoy remembering. 'You and I have known one another for
thirty-one years – do you realise that?' she wrote to Anne Graham

who had first met Genevieve in St. Vincent's primary school and
had then followed Genevieve to St. Louise's, 'You were a lovely
seven-year-old and you are still as lovely as then. Can I say more?
I think you have another girl coming in September. If she is as nice
as Paula is she will do very well.'

Paula, like her mother, became one of the head girls. The relationship between the headteacher and the head pupil is often close
and can be the basis for a life-long friendship. 'Love from one
friend to another,' Genevieve ended her letter to Anne Graham.
From the start, Genevieve had taken the traditional view that the
head girls (of whom she had as many as six at one time) must set an
example to the rest of the school and as the school expanded, the
leadership role of the head girls became even more important.
Using language that was going out of fashion elsewhere, she
explained this to parents in 1972: 'Character training with stress
on leadership has always been the ideal put before the senior
pupils.'

In the enlarged school, her attitude to the sixth form was in
some respects straight out of Dr Arnold who looked to the senior
boys at Rugby to set the moral tone of the school. Within the sixth
form there was an elite of the more academic girls who most
closely identified with her ideals. When an American writer,
Elizabeth Shannon, visited the school in the eighties, she recorded
her impressions in a book, *I am of Ireland*. Genevieve introduced
Elizabeth Shannon to the elite:

> This is the cream of the crop . . . You can talk to them and
> get a good idea of what goes on in the school. But they
> aren't representative. All these girls will be going on to
> university next year. They are all senior prefects. They are
> the school leaders.

Although Genevieve sometimes seemed to be trying to create an
English public school in the Falls, her head girls and prefects bore
no relation to the old-style public school elite who were primarily
interested in privilege and power. Genevieve's idea of leadership
was fundamentally different. It was based on the Vincentian ideal

of service. 'There is no better way for developing character,' she argued, 'than to get involved with others, to feel responsible for someone less fortunate than yourself.' Her senior girls' responsibilities were more pastoral than authoritarian. They had the routine jobs, such as taking assembly and supervising the canteen, that senior pupils might be expected to do in any school, but the upper sixth also acted as student counsellors, a more sophisticated version of the practice of placing naughty girls as 'lodgers' for the day with senior girls. They were attached to one of the year groups lower down the school and, according to Genevieve, often proved more effective than the adults at sorting out the day-to-day problems of the younger girls. Jeanette Halfpenny, a sixth former in the mid-eighties, recalls that when she was a counsellor to the third years, the younger girls called her 'miss' and that her role was to be a friend at court, mediating between the girl in trouble and the teacher on the warpath.

The senior girls were also expected to set an example by their devotion to the Vincentian ideal of self-forgetfulness. As leading members of the school's religious societies they dedicated themselves to the service of others. They gave up their free time and some of their holidays to work with families even poorer than their own, giving mothers a break by looking after the children in the home or spending their afternoons with children in the Play Centre in Ballymurphy. In Genevieve's vision of what it meant to be a Vincentian school, leadership and religious commitment were inseparable. As in the early days, it was the senior girls, not the staff or Genevieve herself, who led a cross-section of the school in prayer before the Blessed Sacrament during the lunch hour. 'Oh yes, this is a Christian school with very Christian sixth formers,' Genevieve told parents in 1985, 'How many other seventeen- and eighteen-year-olds understand the Divine Office of the Church and pray it so beautifully?'

The cream of the crop had been trained by Genevieve to be confident, poised and articulate. These were the keys to their liberation, hence Genevieve's enthusiasm for drama and public speaking and for slogans that drove the message home: 'Keep your own accent but speak correctly; then people have to listen.'

Visitors to the school were impressed by how smart these girls were in both senses of that word. A journalist from the *Belfast Telegraph*, visiting the school in 1980, met 'articulate' sixth form-ers 'looking like air hostesses in their immaculate uniforms of brown skirts and cream blouses'. 'They had a certain self-confi-dence that gave them a quiet dignity,' Elizabeth Shannon recorded, 'when they spoke it was with a seriousness and intensity that is unusual in a girl of sixteen or seventeen.' Genevieve's belief in the importance of social training, which included such compar-atively sophisticated topics as distinguishing between professional, casual and formal dress, was mocked by some as social snobbery. But Genevieve had the last laugh. At a time of high unemploy-ment, it was her girls who got the jobs.

Genevieve's concept of leadership was not confined to the role of the senior girls. In the context of a ghetto controlled by the IRA, she contrasted being a leader with being a follower, and the one thing she did not want her girls to do was to follow the crowd. The artic-ulate sixth former who was not afraid to express her own opinion was also Genevieve's answer to society's assumptions about a woman's role. Too many people, she said, think of girls as followers rather than leaders. For her girls, therefore, leadership was a form of assertiveness training. 'It was drummed into us that we were leaders and could achieve anything,' Eileen Boyle remembers. Even with the sixth formers, Genevieve used slogans, 'Stand up straight, walk tall', 'Get off your knees', and for some years she gave each leaver a laminated card with the name and dates at the school on one side and on the reverse a short, Kipling-style poem entitled, 'Don't quit!'

Given the size of the school and of the open sixth form, it is easy to see how some people gained the impression that Genevieve was only interested in the girls at the top. When Elizabeth Shannon told a friend about her visit to St. Louise's, she received this response:

She's a tyrant, that Sister Genevieve. She's also a shrewd
politician. She knows what she wants for the school and she
knows how to get it. But she loves those smart girls; she
doesn't have any time for the ordinary ones.

It is common to hear adults complain that when they were at school the headteacher was only interested in the most able pupils or in those who were prepared to conform in order to win promotion. In the literal sense, Genevieve did not have time for every girl but to imply that she was not interested in the ordinary ones is to ignore the evidence of the battles she fought on behalf of all her girls, her insistence that all girls should be treated with equal respect and the pastoral structures she put in place to ensure that no girl could be overlooked. The very idea that some girls were special while others were ordinary would have been alien to someone who had been trained as a Vincent de Paul sister.

There were, as in any school, senior girls who reacted against the head's style and personality, including those who declined the position of head girl because they wanted to concentrate on their work, and others, like Anne Donegan, who refused to join the Children of Mary because they preferred not to be part of the school's religious elite. According to Anne Donegan, the Genevieve of the late seventies accepted the fact that some senior girls did not share her vision but insisted characteristically that the dissenters state their case in a clear logical argument. To this extent Genevieve had mellowed over the twenty years since the school opened but for most girls she remained a driven woman who they respected but were careful not to cross. 'She was very, very strict but you loved her,' said Brenda Macgowan, a contemporary of Anne Donegan. Jennie Shannon, a second generation St. Louise's girl, who was a head of school in 1987, emphasised how unwise it was to provoke Genevieve. 'A good strap would have been preferable to facing her wrath,' she said.

The Troubles both re-enforced Genevieve's belief in the importance of strict discipline and increased the number of disciplinary problems she had to face. There had been 'bold girls' in the early intakes, 'undisciplined and extremely wild' she had called them, but she had soon brought them under control. In the seventies there appears to have been an upsurge in the number of younger girls who Genevieve described as 'emotionally disturbed' and whose disruptive behaviour was more difficult to deal with. The

new school committee minutes contain numerous references to
the behaviour of girls from 'disturbed homes' who were 'completely uncontrollable' and 'totally disruptive'. Genevieve's
treatment of these girls was criticised in the popular press and is
still a subject on which her critics and supporters disagree. One
view is that she was 'trigger happy' about expelling girls who
threatened the school's reputation for good discipline and that in
her haste to be rid of them she did not always follow the correct
procedure. A very different view is held by those who believe that
as a Vincentian sister she was reluctant to give up on any girl and
went to extraordinary lengths to keep the disruptive girls in the
school.

Sheila Chillingworth who was the educational psychologist
responsible for the schools in the Falls at this period believes that
most of these disturbed and disruptive girls were in effect casu-
alties of the guerrilla war. Where they lived on the housing
estates of Moyard and Ballymurphy and in the Divis Flats, violence and intimidation were part of everyday life. If father had
not been killed or imprisoned he was almost certainly out of
work. In 1983, 80 per cent of all adults in Ballymurphy were
unemployed and the figure for Moyard was 79 per cent. The
housing estates were afflicted by other social ills: child abuse,
wife beating, alcoholism, one-parent families, paramilitary
involvement, beatings by the security forces, beatings by the
IRA, debts that could never be paid and petty crime. Bringing up
children in this atmosphere of fear and despair was too much for
some mothers left to cope on their own. Genevieve's pupils who
lived in the Divis Flats would have known about the mother who
told her eight-year-old to run up to her uncle's flat while she
made a telephone call and then went to the top of the Divis Flats
and jumped off.

The disturbed and disruptive girls at St. Louise's covered the
whole ability range from those who had qualified for the grammar
school to those who in the unattractive terminology of the day were
deemed to be 'educationally sub-normal'. Their behaviour in class
took the form of violence and aggression or throwing tantrums or
just weeping continuously. Even Genevieve's critics acknowledged

that many of these girls could not be helped or contained in a normal school. All the secondary schools in working-class districts of Belfast had to deal with some exceptionally difficult pupils during the Troubles. When Jim McCabe, at his Protestant secondary school, suspended a boy for hitting a teacher, he received a telephone call from the police shortly after. During his time off, the boy had attempted an armed robbery and the police suggested he would be less trouble back in the school.

From the earliest days, persistently disruptive girls at St. Louise's had been taken out of school and sent to 'Room 21' to cool off while they worked under strict supervision. In 1975, this *ad hoc* arrangement was formalised with the creation of the Tutorial Centre with a head of department in charge and accommodation for thirty-five girls. The Centre, which was also known as the Withdrawal Unit and, to the girls, as Long Kesh, the H-Block and the Loony Bin, received no funding from the education authority but proved to be an effective way of containing disruptive behaviour. The girls seldom spent longer than a week in the Centre; what they disliked and what encouraged them to suppress their rebellious and truculent mood was being cut off from their friends and the normal life of the school. Some girls returned to the Centre many times but even these recidivists eventually gave up or grew out of their urge to misbehave. Geraldine Brannigan, who was head of the Tutorial Centre from 1979 to 1992, estimated that in a school year there were about three hundred admissions to the Centre, including girls on repeat visits, and that all but a very few settled down in the end and completed their school career. Genevieve was proud of the Centre's success: 'Our philosophy is that rather than institutionalise these children in separate schools, we keep them in the normal educational environment and with patience and motivation eventually return most of them into the normal class structure.'

The success of the Tutorial Centre does not suggest that Genevieve was over-eager to expel the disruptive girls and the minutes of the meetings of the school committee in the seventies and eighties confirm that, far from trying to rush expulsions through the committee, she approached the subject cautiously.

The treatment of girls who were said to have been expelled from St. Louise's nevertheless became a subject of public controversy. Genevieve, who usually had no difficulty brushing aside criticism in the press, now worried about the effect of this publicity on prospective parents. The minutes of a staff meeting on 10 January 1983 reflect her anxiety:

> Sister Genevieve said she was going to tell staff how the school came to be the size it is today. She was doing it because of the publicity. She felt someone, somewhere was determined to destroy what was happening in St. Louise's. St. Louise's was dragged into every article about expulsions. Canon Murphy had always said to ignore that sort of thing. Sister Genevieve said that up to a point that was right but parents read the *Sunday World*. How many ever questioned the continuous sniping in the *Sunday World*? At this time of year parents were making choices about post-primary schools. All schools were trying to save themselves.

Criticism of expulsions from Catholic schools was not confined to the pages of the *Sunday World*, a Dublin-based tabloid widely read in West Belfast. Nor was the criticism aimed at St. Louise's alone, though Genevieve's undisguised ambition for the school encouraged her critics to say that she was skilful at passing on her problem children to other schools. In 1976, there were allegations that St. Louise's had been 'channelling' its disruptive and less academically inclined pupils to St. Rose's, the Dominican school in the Lower Falls. The allegation was made at a public enquiry into education organised by Father Des Wilson at his Upper Springfield Resource Centre.

Father Des Wilson was a radical community priest in Ballymurphy who was out of favour with the Church hierarchy and who shared some of Genevieve's concern about the way the Church was run. Initially supportive of Genevieve's work, he became disenchanted by what he perceived to be her determination to make St. Louise's more elitist at the expense of other Catholic schools. He was a friend of Gerry Adams, at whose marriage he had officiated, and had antagonised the bishops by speaking out against the way state violence was used in Catholic areas. As a result he had been stripped of his parish duties (though subsequently allowed to say Mass in public) and had devoted much of his time to community education. It was in this latter role that he found himself at odds with Genevieve over the question of expulsion.

Wilson was drawn into the controversy in the late seventies by the arrival at his Springfield Community Centre of girls who claimed that they had been expelled from St. Louise's. He arranged to provide a teacher for them in what became a small, alternative school. At about the same time, the Divis Education Project started a similar alternative school in a converted garage at the Divis Flats. This school, known as Crazy Joe's, also attracted girls who said they had been expelled from St. Louise's. Many years later, a description of Crazy Joe's and of Genevieve's former pupils who went there was given by John Conroy in his book *War as a Way of Life*. Conroy was an American journalist from Chicago who in 1981 spent a sabbatical year in Belfast reporting on the social and economic consequences of the Troubles. He took lodgings in Clonard just round the corner from where Genevieve was living. Of her former pupils he wrote:

> Their formal schooling was terminated by Catholic authorities who told all six girls that they were no longer welcome in Catholic schools. The six had attended St. Louise's, a local Catholic girls' secondary school with a national reputation for its fine programs. They had been dismissed for committing a variety of offences including cutting classes, smoking in the washrooms, hopping on the back of lorries while wearing the school uniform and being disruptive in class. One of the girls was sent home after only three weeks in the school and she spent the next four years getting no education at all. There is no doubt the six were difficult kids. What is considered normal behaviour in Divis Flats is considered wildly aberrant by some of the nuns and middle-class students at St. Louise's. On the face

of it, the expulsion of some of the girls seems routine. The
principal told me she had done all she could for them, that
they are now the state's responsibility.

The truth about pupils who said they had been expelled was more
complicated than at first appears. Pupils claimed to have been
expelled when they had only been suspended or were playing
truant. On the other hand, suspension could be a *de facto* expulsion
if the headteacher imposed an indefinite or 'rolling' suspension.
The term 'expelled' was also sometimes used to describe pupils
who had been recommended for transfer to a special school by the
schools' psychiatric service. The confusion over whether or not
girls had actually been expelled from St. Louise's prompted one of
the priests on the school committee to imply that Genevieve was
expelling girls in an arbitrary manner, but when he produced a list
of girls who were said to have been expelled, Genevieve was able
to point out that a number of these girls were still in the school.

The girls on the priest's list and those who turned up at Des
Wilson's or Crazy Joe's might have been expelled or suspended or
have been playing truant but the most likely explanation is that
they were girls who were waiting in vain for a place to be found for
them at another school. In theory, the so-called educationally sub-
normal girls were recommended for transfer to a Catholic school
for children with special educational needs. In practice, that
school, like St. Rose's, refused to be used as a dumping ground for
Genevieve's difficult pupils. In theory, girls who could not be controlled went to the Jaffe Centre, a special school for children with
emotional and behavioural difficulties but once again in practice
some of the most disruptive girls left St. Louise's with nowhere to
go.

There was, therefore, a small number of girls from St. Louise's
who were, in Father Des Wilson's words, 'outcasts tossed out of
the system'. Though Genevieve may have regarded these girls as
the state's responsibility, the state took little or no interest in them.
The Catholic church was reluctant to acknowledge that there were
pupils its schools could not handle and the education authorities
were reluctant to antagonise the bishops by drawing attention to

the problem. The outcasts lived in an educational no man's land and not surprisingly, sometimes made common cause with the hoods. These girls were not victims of Genevieve's arbitrary use of expulsion but of a school system that did not know what to do with its most difficult pupils.

The continuing inability of the school system in the United Kingdom to find a constructive and effective way of dealing with its most disruptive pupils helps to put what happened to Genevieve's pupils in perspective. In 1994, long after Genevieve had retired, the Belfast Education and Library Board reported that almost half the pupils expelled from Belfast schools had been expelled 'illegally' and that in many cases no alternative schooling had been arranged. Five years later, the Audit Commission in England found that local education authorities had lost track of a third of the pupils who had been expelled – pupils were 'simply disappearing from the education system' – and that schools were refusing to accept difficult pupils from other schools.

Genevieve was herself part of a bad system for whose failings she cannot be held responsible. She must have been aware that a few of her girls had become outcasts living off what scraps of education they could pick up in the alternative schools. As a Vincent de Paul sister she may have worried about these lost sheep. As a headteacher she had no choice but to devote her energies to the many who remained in the fold.

Much of the criticism levelled at Genevieve over expulsions implied that she was willing to sacrifice the most difficult girls because they did not fit in to her plans to make St. Louise's the best school in the area and an effective rival to the grammar school, St. Dominic's. If this really was her motivation she would never have agreed to admit two groups of 'pupils' whose presence could easily have alienated parents. The welcome she gave both to the children of travelling families and to adults who wanted to join classes in order to obtain qualifications gives the lie to those who said Genevieve was only interested in the smart girls and the school's image.

The policy of the Department of Education in Northern Ireland was that the children of travelling families should be fully

integrated into the mainstream schools but like many official policies on marginalised children it bore little relation to what
happened in practice. Travellers, whether Irish or Romany, had no
tradition of formal education and their nomadic lifestyle prevented
regular school attendance, with the result that many of the children were illiterate. When travellers' children did attend school
they encountered prejudice and provoked hostility. Aspects of the
distinctive travellers' culture were difficult to accommodate in
mainstream schools. 'Traveller children have a different approach
to property,' as one report put it. Other children complained of
the smell and their parents complained about the nits. In West
Belfast, the large number of traveller children attending St.
Patrick's primary school resulted in a boycott of the school by the
local community. Despite the official policy of integration, traveller children in that part of the city would now be taught in a
school of their own.

In 1984, Anne Fitzmaurice, the principal of St. Paul's primary
school for travelling children in the Lower Falls, went to see
Genevieve. She needed help to provide classes for the few traveller
boys and girls who were prepared to attend school after the age of
eleven. Given the prejudice the children had experienced in the
past, she was amazed by Genevieve's positive and unconditional
response and by the warm welcome the traveller children received.
'They were treated like lords and ladies at St. Louise's,' she said.
About twenty traveller children were bussed to St. Louise's twice
a week to study home economics, art, typing and word-processing.
When they passed their Royal Society of Arts exams, as some of
them did with distinction, 'they walked up as proud as punch to
get their certificates on prize night'.

It is difficult to interpret Genevieve's willingness to help the
traveller children in any other way than as an expression of the
Vincentian ideal of serving the most marginalised members of the
community. The same ideal contributed to Genevieve's initial
enthusiasm for creating a community school at St. Louise's that
would serve another marginalised group – the adults who had
been denied a good education and who now wanted a second
chance. Allowing adults to join classes during the school day to

work for the same qualifications as the girls would also enhance St. Louise's reputation as an enlightened and progressive school. Genevieve presented the experiment as a way of making the school more truly comprehensive and she claimed, in a talk to careers officers in 1982, that she had always dreamed of reaching out to parents in particular 'to make up for the formal education they missed'. What she did not foresee was that an experiment that involved a few mothers joining classes would grow into a large Community Education Project that had its own momentum.

Much of the drive and vision needed to develop the Community Education Project came not from Genevieve but from a member of her staff, Mrs Pauline Murphy. In the late seventies and early eighties Pauline Murphy transformed a Sunday Club offering a few courses for adults which were run by the senior girls into a community school offering twenty-four academic subjects, with a thousand adults enrolled in Twilight and Evening Classes and about a hundred and fifty studying for public exams alongside the girls. As an experiment in second chance education it was an outstanding success and it met a real need in the area. The majority of adults who benefited were women. Margaret, the mother of twelve children, had been forced by family circumstances to leave school early and had watched her friends going to school with tears in her eyes. Now at the age of sixty she successfully took two Advanced Level exams at St. Louise's. Among the men who obtained qualifications were a former member of the IRA who became a teacher, a boy who had been refused permission to take an exam at his own school because he was not wearing the correct uniform and a Ballymurphy man who had been unemployed for sixteen years and who passed eight Ordinary Level exams in his first year at St. Louise's.

Although Pauline Murphy was the Project's inspiration, Genevieve's openness to the idea and continued support were vital. In public, Genevieve was proud of what the Project was doing for the people of West Belfast but as the numbers grew she began to have private doubts. From the adults' point of view, being able to attend classes during the school day was a godsend but whether it helped the girls to have their mothers and other adults learning alongside them was less certain. Typically, educationalists thought up a theory to underpin the practice; it was said that teacher, adult and pupil formed 'a powerful learning triangle', a striking phrase whose exact meaning remained obscure. In 1980, advocates of community schools claimed that 'adults learning alongside children in school classrooms will become a common phenomenon in the next decade' but they were wrong. Neither the theory nor the practice survived for long at St. Louise's or elsewhere.

Increasingly, Genevieve and Pauline Murphy found themselves in disagreement about the way the Community Education Project should develop. Pauline wanted to open the school even more to the local community while Genevieve worried about the impact of more adult activity on the life of the school and on its principal task which was the education of the girls. It was a clash between two different visions of how St. Louise's should serve the local community. By 1984, the disagreement was such that Pauline Murphy decided to leave. Three years later, the education authority opened a community school offering adult education in a former boys' school on the Whiterock Road and Genevieve took the opportunity to bring the experiment at St. Louise's to an end on the grounds that it was no longer needed. Evening classes in such subjects as basic literacy continued but adults joining classes during the day was phased out.

Adults learning alongside children was one of those educational fashions that was bound to fade because it had no clear rationale, but at St. Louise's it helped to meet a specific need. Genevieve was criticised for 'pulling the rug from under the Community Education Project', but by 1987 the Project had served its purpose. Her relationship with the Project and its most enthusiastic protagonists had not always been easy but she deserves at least a share of the credit for giving so many adults a second chance.

The traveller children and the adults had good reason to be grateful to Genevieve but the success or failure of her mission depended on what happened to the St. Louise's girls. At the two extremes of fortune were the smart girls, poised and articulate, who were heading for university, and the outcasts huddled in their overcoats against the cold in Crazy Joe's converted garage.

Between these two extremes were hundreds of girls, overwhelmingly from families that had suffered for generations from poverty, unemployment and discrimination, who looked to Sister Genevieve and St. Louise's for a way of escape from the past. With these girls in mind, Genevieve was fond of quoting Yeats:

> But I, being poor, have only my dreams;
> I have spread my dreams under your feet;
> Tread softly because you tread on my dreams.

13

'We don't believe Christ endorsed a segregated system at eleven plus'

By the mid-seventies, Genevieve had successfully defied the Northern Ireland establishment and created at St. Louise's a school for children of all abilities. To the leaders of the Catholic and Protestant communities, the very idea of a 'comprehensive' school, where intelligent and well-motivated pupils would have to rub shoulders with children who were thought to have little or no interest in education, was anathema. While the rest of the United Kingdom was 'going comprehensive', Northern Ireland remained stubbornly convinced that children with different abilities had to be taught in different schools. On the mainland, Genevieve's outspoken opposition to the separation of children at the age of eleven would have been unremarkable but in Northern Ireland it was a sign of contradiction.

Those who advocated the introduction of comprehensive schools did not all have the same motive. Some identified the separation of children into different types of school with the class divisions that bedevilled British society. Others believed that the separation resulted in a waste of talent that Britain could ill afford. Many people suspected the 11+ exam was far from foolproof; affluent parents could increase their child's chances by paying for private coaching while intelligent children from poor families failed to qualify.

Genevieve's motivation was Christian. All human beings were
of equal value in the sight of God and as members of society and
must therefore have an equal opportunity to make the best of
themselves. Drawing a direct connection between Christ's teaching and comprehensive schooling, she argued that a Christian
could not support an education system that selected some children
and rejected others. 'Christ tells us that every person is allotted
different talents and it is our job to see that our children get the
opportunity of developing these talents' she told parents in 1983.
'We believe that only in a school that caters for all the different talents of pupils and values all equally, can this Christian precept be
carried out.' There was no doubt whose side Christ was on. 'We
don't believe Christ endorsed a segregated system at eleven plus,'
she said. By the time she retired in 1988, she clearly believed she
had won the argument against those Christians in Northern
Ireland who supported the grammar schools: 'We have proved
that a comprehensive type of education which caters for all, irre-
spective of ability or social background, is the only really Christian
form of education.'

Some members of the Catholic hierarchy strongly objected to
Genevieve's attacks on selective schools, especially when she called
Christ as a witness and stated publicly her opinion that 'the
Church upholds a system that is quite close to apartheid'. They
thought her Christian arguments simplistic and her demands that
the Church should wholeheartedly embrace the comprehensive
ideal unrealistic in a society where the grammar schools had political influence and popular support. The hierarchy took the
pragmatic view that it would be a mistake to move ahead of public
opinion on this issue, not least because many Catholics believed
the 11+ exam was their best chance of making progress in an
unequal society.

As we have seen, the Catholic church and the Ministry of
Education were content to let Genevieve develop St. Louise's as a
school that was comprehensive in its style and aspirations, never
imagining that she would be able to make it comprehensive in
reality. To do that she would have to attract the more academically
inclined girls away from the grammar school and in the context of

Northern Ireland that must have seemed an impossible task. The mistake that the Church and the Ministry made was to underestimate Genevieve's dedication to the comprehensive ideal and the ruthlessness with which she would pursue her goal.

There had always been a few girls at St. Louise's who had qualified for the grammar school but whose parents had decided that Genevieve's school would suit them better. Now as the school expanded throughout the seventies and acquired new facilities, she set out to increase that number so that St. Louise's would become truly comprehensive, catering for children of all abilities. In theory, a comprehensive school has 20 per cent of its intake from each of five ability bands though in practice a number of factors, such as the proximity of academically selective independent schools, may deny a comprehensive school its fair share of the more able children. Genevieve was competing for the more able girls not only with the Catholic grammar school but also with Protestant independent schools that were prepared to take bright Catholic children. Yet by 1980, she was able to claim that between 20 per cent and 25 per cent of the intake to St. Louise's at eleven was made up of girls who had qualified for the grammar school.

Genevieve made this claim to a journalist who wrote a long piece about St. Louise's in the *Belfast Telegraph* of 2 October 1980. Officials of the local education authority, while acknowledging that Genevieve was astonishingly successful in attracting talented girls to St. Louise's, doubt whether the percentage was ever that high. But even if Genevieve was exaggerating, there is no doubt that she attracted enough girls in the top ability bands to give St. Louise's a strong academic stream most of whose members would go on to third level education. She achieved this by a characteristic combination of single-minded recruiting and skilful public relations.

The first step was to persuade Father Padraig Murphy and the school committee that if St. Louise's was to be truly comprehensive, it was necessary to recruit able Catholic girls from anywhere in the city regardless of her own school's catchment area. This would mean taking bright girls from parishes that had no connection with St. Louise's and might undermine other Catholic schools, but that did not worry Genevieve. She was, as ever, focused on her mission and her vocation. Father Colm McCaughan, not given to overstatement, described these recruiting tactics as 'totally ruthless' and the parish priests used their pulpits to tell parents to send their children to local schools not to St. Louise's.

Genevieve remained determined to fight off any attempt to stop her recruiting bright girls from anywhere in the city as long as their parents made St. Louise's their first choice. Priests on the school committee complained that this might mean refusing entry to girls from the parishes St. Louise's had been set up to serve but Genevieve was unmoved. In 1986, the local education authority entered the fray by announcing that it would only pay fares when children went to the nearest school. Genevieve was outraged and urged parents to unite against what she described as 'the most flagrant act of injustice ever perpetrated by the local education authorities'. When, in the same year, the Diocesan Education Council produced a report on the Re-organisation of post-Primary Education in West Belfast, she interpreted this as 'a thinly veiled threat' to cut St. Louise's down to size, both literally and metaphorically, so that it would no longer be a truly comprehensive school. Neither the secular nor the religious education authorities succeeded, however, in stopping Genevieve attracting bright girls to St. Louise's regardless of where they lived.

The conflicts over Genevieve's admission policy would not have occurred if she had not been so successful in selling the school and the comprehensive ideal. She was one of the first state school headteachers to recognise the importance of marketing her school. Whether she was talking to visiting journalists or to prospective parents, her message was the same: a comprehensive school was better for all children; whatever their ability, they were more likely to realise their potential at St. Louise's than if they were separated into different types of school at the age of eleven. Her skilful use of the media and her contacts with British politicians annoyed her opponents but helped to ensure that St. Louise's was the most talked about school in the North. She even managed to turn the Troubles to the school's advantage. The world's journalists were always looking for a new angle on the conflict and a Catholic girls' school operating normally at the heart of the war zone provided the press and the television cameras with an interesting story. The journalists may have thought they were dealing with an unworldly nun but the newspaper articles and the television programmes of the eighties gave the school the sort of entirely favourable publicity other headteachers could only dream about.

'St. Louise's has caught the imagination of the world,' Genevieve pronounced. Exasperated critics, envious of the attention she was receiving, accused her of the sin of pride. There *was* something incongruous about a high profile religious sister successfully manipulating the media, especially as Genevieve seemed to relish her public role, but being a well-known public figure was not inconsistent with the view of humility that the Vincentian community adopted after Vatican Two. Humility was 'the realisation that we are no better or worse than the rest of men and women'. For Genevieve's contemporaries in the community and presumably therefore for Genevieve herself, humility was the virtue that made them open to the needs of the poor and willing to accept their talents as God-given gifts to be used in His service. One of Genevieve's closest friends in the Daughters of Charity argues that exposing herself to accusations of lack of humility by exercising her gift for public relations, was one of the sacrifices Genevieve had to make in order to serve the girls of the Falls effectively.

How Genevieve reconciled humility and celebrity was a matter for her own conscience. From the school's point of view, her fame as a headmistress had the advantage of encouraging more parents of girls who had qualified for the grammar school to choose St. Louise's instead. 'The 11+ passes came rushing in from everywhere', Genevieve reported to the Provincial of the Daughters of Charity. But Genevieve was shrewd enough not to be dazzled by her own publicity and she knew that her public relations were only effective because there was a good story to tell. St. Louise's reputation was based on the reality of what was happening in the school not on the fame of its principal or on the images presented by the media.

The most difficult aspect of that reality to assess retrospectively is the academic performance of Genevieve's pupils. Were the bright girls who were attracted to St. Louise's pulled down by the more modest ambitions of the majority as the grammar school lobby was convinced would happen? Or did the development of a strong sixth form with girls taking Advanced Level courses and aiming for university help to raise the expectation of the school as a whole? Even if there was detailed evidence available these questions would be hard to answer. As it is, global totals of exams passed and certificates gained only provide the basis for speculation.

The best indicator of whether the bright girls did as well at St. Louise's as they would have done at the grammar school would be their performance in Advanced Level exams and university entrance. In a typical year in the eighties, there were about 400 girls in the sixth form, the majority of whom were taking a one or two year mixed academic and commercial course. Only about a hundred were studying for Advanced Level exams and, of those, about half would eventually qualify for university entrance, in most cases at Queen's University, Belfast or Ulster Polytechnic. The hundred girls, fifty in each of the years in the sixth form, were Genevieve's academic stream. Some of these girls are known to have failed the 11+. When Anne McGreevy sent her twin daughters to St. Louise's one had passed the 11+ and the other had failed, but both flourished in Genevieve's sixth form and went on to university. Marie McIntyre and Eilish Weir were 11+ failures who, thanks to St. Louise's, won places at Queen's University, Belfast. Mary McAleese, herself a product of the grammar school down the Road, believed that Genevieve had 'shattered the myth of the 11+'. Had the school kept accurate records of all the Marie McIntyres and Eilish Weirs, that case would have been easier to prove. All that it is possible to say on the basis of incomplete exam results and anecdotal evidence is that the bright girls do not appear to have suffered from attending Genevieve's comprehensive school and that a number of girls who had failed the 11+ positively benefited from doing so.

The real beneficiaries of Genevieve's approach to comprehensive education were the many girls who in an ordinary secondary school would have left when they reached the school leaving age but who at St. Louise's were persuaded to stay on to obtain better qualifications. It was estimated that about 75–85 per cent of the year group were staying on and this estimate is borne out by the numbers in the sixth form. To put this figure in perspective, in the majority of Northern Ireland's secondary schools, no pupils were staying on after the leaving age. Even some of the grammar schools had a less impressive 'staying on rate'. Across the water, where comprehensive schools were becoming the norm, St. Louise's 'staying on rate' would have been regarded as impossible to achieve. Even today when comprehensive schools in England are well established, a typical inner city school has a staying rate of under 50 per cent.

Genevieve's success in persuading so many girls from an inner city, working-class population that it was worth staying on at school when they did not have to do so had no parallel in the United Kingdom. She was inclined to give the credit to the girls themselves. 'Girls are more far-seeing than boys,' she said. 'Easy money and then the dole does not appeal to them. They will not sacrifice qualifications, the passport to real freedom.' But it was her creation of an open sixth form and her constant propaganda in favour of staying on that won over the girls and their parents.

An open sixth form where any girl was welcome as long as she was working towards some qualification had been a feature of St. Louise's since the early sixties. The secret of its success was that every course, academic or commercial or a mixture of the two, was given the same status. Inevitably, some girls thought the academic stream was favoured, but St. Louise's came close to establishing that elusive 'parity of esteem' that enabled the girl who was studying for a commercial qualification to feel just as valued by the school as the academic high-flyer. Genevieve did not believe that every girl should receive the same education but that every girl's education should be accorded the same respect and that this could only happen if they attended the same school.

Parity of esteem was a crucial factor in persuading girls to stay on. So was the variety and nature of the courses on offer. Girls whose aim was to get a job rather than to go to university could combine academic subjects with practical skills such as typewriting, shorthand, word processing, accounts and office practice, a combination that was not available at any other school. For the girls' parents, many of whom were unemployed, the key question was whether staying on would result in a better job. From the start, Genevieve had taken the view that it was the school's responsibility to find jobs for its pupils. Where other schools gave careers advice, St. Louise's acted as a job centre, matching pupils to the vacancies that had been identified. When it became impossible for Genevieve to oversee this task which involved close liaison with employers in the city, she enlisted the help of Mairead O'Halloran who became as skilful at guiding a girl into the right clerical job as she was at advising on university entrance. It may not have been true, as was sometimes claimed, that no girl left St. Louise's and went straight on to the dole (a common occurrence at the boys' schools in the Falls and the Shankill) but St. Louise's record of finding jobs for the girls was extraordinary in an area where the majority of adults were unemployed. It was not just the qualifications that made the difference; employers were surprised and delighted to find young people who were so well mannered and confident.

If one of the aims of a comprehensive school is to encourage all pupils to believe in their own potential, then Genevieve's version of a comprehensive school was a triumphant success. At St. Louise's most girls stayed at school longer, and got better qualifications and jobs than they would have done if they had attended an ordinary secondary school for 11+ failures. That alone would have justified Genevieve's faith in the comprehensive ideal. But St. Louise's with its open sixth form also encouraged girls who had started with modest aspirations to aim higher. Here is a former pupil giving evidence to Des Wilson's Public Enquiry into Education in 1976:

I was a pupil at St. Louise's Comprehensive College for seven years and as is the usual tradition I was asked at the end of third year to make a choice as to which courses I wanted to follow. I decided I wanted to do shorthand and typing, that is the commercial course. Fortunately enough

at the end of my fifth year I had a job as a part-time
summer typist in an office in town. After a while in that job
I walked out of the building and said to myself, I never
wanted to see a typewriter again. And I meant it. I went
back to school at the start of my sixth year and I hadn't a
clue what I wanted to do. I knew I did not want to be a
typist because it was not for me. I went to my counsellor
and had a good long chat with her and at the end of it all I
decided to take up A levels and try for a place at college. I
selected the subjects that I wanted to do, that is economics
and politics, and at the end of my seventh year when I
completed my A levels, I was successful and managed to get
a place in the Northern Ireland Polytechnic to do a degree
in Business Management. If St. Louise's had not been a
Comprehensive College I would not be where I am today.

Although Genevieve exposed the limitations of the 11+ and
demonstrated that children of widely differing ability could flour-
ish in the same school, the Northern Ireland establishment was
not won over. As the province begins the new millennium, children are still divided at the age of eleven, the grammar schools still
dominate the educational landscape and the Catholic church is still
reluctant to move ahead of public opinion and embrace wholeheartedly the comprehensive ideal. What Genevieve did prove,
however, was that the alleged shortcomings of comprehensive
schools – the poor academic standards, the lack of discipline, the
low expectations of the pupils – reflected failures of leadership
not fundamental flaws in the concept. A comprehensive school did
not have to have any of these shortcomings. She made a comprehensive school work for all its pupils because she was an
exceptionally strong, visionary and single-minded leader. Her ability to attract able girls away from the grammar school, her success
in persuading so many 'average' girls to stay at school to obtain
better qualifications and jobs and her establishment of good discipline and high morale in such a very large, inner-city school were
all remarkable achievements.

Genevieve thought she had proved the case for comprehensive

schools beyond doubt and she was critical of those in Northern
Ireland who still refused to put the comprehensive ideal into practice. Meanwhile in the rest of the United Kingdom comprehensive
schools became the norm so that by the new millennium the great
majority of secondary school pupils were being educated in these
schools. Arguments about the performance of comprehensive
schools continue nevertheless. Despite the fact that the league
tables of public examination results show some comprehensive
schools competing effectively with all but the most academically
successful independent and grammar schools, the suspicion per-
sists that a very large school trying to cope with a wide range of
ability is unlikely to bring out the best in the more able pupils,
especially if the school is serving a deprived inner-city population.

Both sides in the debate could call Genevieve as a witness. She
did prove that a comprehensive school could be successful for all
its pupils in the most difficult circumstances but even the champi-
ons of comprehensive education would have to admit that she was
exceptional. Running a large comprehensive school in a deprived
area is one of the most demanding jobs in contemporary society so
that the number of men or women who can do it successfully is
bound to be small. The difficulty encountered in recent years by
so-called 'superheads' parachuted in to save failing inner-city comprehensive schools underlines how very rare headteachers of
Genevieve's calibre are. The irony of her career is that her remarkable achievements in West Belfast could be regarded as the
exception that proves the rule. If all comprehensive schools were
as good as the school she created, the case for keeping selective
grammar schools would be undermined. But they are not and it is
the exceptional nature of Genevieve's talent for leadership that
makes one wonder whether they ever will be.

The public recognition of her achievements must have made it
easier for Genevieve to give up a job to which she had devoted
herself for thirty years. In 1982 she had received one honorary
degree, a Master of Arts in Education from Queen's University in
Belfast. At the time of her retirement in 1988, she was given an
honorary Doctorate of Letters by the University of Ulster. In his

oration, the Dean of the Faculty of Education praised Genevieve's 'unfailing energy, constant compassion and fearlessness in speaking her mind on educational issues' as well as her courage in troubled times which had caused her to be described as 'the best man on the Falls Road'.

Other tributes marked the end of her reign at St. Louise's. One described her as 'a legend in her own lifetime', another as 'an internationally recognised educationalist'. When Brian Mawhinney, the British minister of education in Northern Ireland decided to turn up unannounced at Genevieve's last assembly, it was his admiration for her outstanding qualities of leadership as well as his affection for her as a person that persuaded him to ignore the advice of his officials and plunge deep into Republican territory. The school committee passed a formal vote of thanks: 'The success of the school is due to the tremendous leadership given since the foundation and the Board should express its gratitude to the outgoing principal, Sister Genevieve, to whom the school is a monument.' Even her old adversary, the *Andersonstown News*, devoted its front page to an interview in which Genevieve was allowed to speak for herself. 'I have always tried to live by the teaching of my order of St. Vincent de Paul,' she told the paper, 'and to have respect for the dignity and individuality of every child.'

Shortly before she retired, Genevieve had entered the school for one of the annual awards given for educational achievement by the Jerwood Foundation, and shortly after she retired it was announced that in competition with 573 schools across the United Kingdom, St. Louise's had won one of the five awards of £50,000. What had impressed the representatives of the Foundation had been 'the brand of leadership provided by Sister Genevieve' and the fact that 'amidst riots, social and political unrest, and the collapse of communities, St. Louise's Comprehensive offered a refuge of educational and social development under the most difficult circumstances'.

Welcome though this public recognition must have been, nothing would have been more important to Genevieve than the knowledge that she had helped to make Sister Vincent's dream

come true. The granddaughters of the doffers and weavers were
receiving as good an education as the children from the most affluent parts of the city. Some had become the doctors and lawyers of
Belfast, though most of Genevieve's pupils who went on to higher
education followed different careers, teaching and journalism being
two of the most popular. One of the future journalists was Mary
O'Hara whose time at St. Louise's coincided with Genevieve's last
years and whose story illustrates better than any other how
Genevieve and the school she created helped to liberate girls from
the prison of poverty and low expectations into which they had
been born. As the first girl from St. Louise's to go to Cambridge,
Mary was exceptional, but in so much else she was typical of the
girls who were the beneficiaries of Genevieve's vocation.

Mary O'Hara was the third of seven children of a bricklayer and
his wife who lived on the Grosvenor Road in the Lower Falls.
While she was at St. Louise's her father lost his job and has been
unemployed ever since. When Mary failed the 11+ her primary
school teacher encouraged her to go to St. Louise's because there
her potential would be recognised. Mary started at St. Louise's in
1981 during the aftermath of the hunger strikes by Republican
prisoners in the Maze. That autumn the Falls Road was often
blocked but Mary got up early while the rest of the family was
asleep and walked to school, a diminutive figure in school uniform
picking her way through the debris of the previous night's rioting.
She shared with a number of Genevieve's pupils a determination
never to miss a day's school, partly because of a hunger for education but also because for some girls from the poorer parts of
Ballymurphy and the Lower Falls, a day at school was preferable
to a day at home. 'School,' said Mary, 'was my solace, my escape.'

As a young girl, Mary found Genevieve a rather terrifying presence, tall and dominating and wearing tinted glasses like a mafia
boss but as she moved up the school she came to know and admire
the woman behind the intimidating exterior. Genevieve liked
Mary's independent mind, and she enjoyed engaging Mary in
debates, often prompted by the badges of Marx, Lenin and Che
Guevara that Mary had pinned to her head girl's sash. She liked
Mary's feminism, too, and was delighted when in a debate on

women priests, Mary dismantled the traditionalist case put forward by the school chaplain. Being small, Mary stood on a chair to
speak and saw Genevieve giving her arguments a thumbs-up from
the back of the hall. But it was as an unlikely academic star that
Mary played her part in the fulfilment of Genevieve's mission. To
send a girl, particularly one who had failed the 11+, to Cambridge
would vindicate Genevieve's attacks on that qualifying exam and
fulfil the high hopes that she had always had for the girls of the
Falls.

Mary's academic ambitions, nurtured by the school, had to run
the gauntlet of ignorance and even hostility at home. 'My parents
were not educated people. Their generation lost out on the
chances I was being given. Sometimes, their lack of understanding
was taken out on me. They simply couldn't understand why I
wanted to write essays which made my life harder. They couldn't
grasp why my dreams were so lofty. They thought achievement
was a good secretarial job. Only middle-class people became doctors and lawyers and journalists. I needed to know my place and
not listen to stupid ideas.'

When Mary told her parents she was applying to a university in
England, her mother said she would not be able to cope without
her, and when Mary accepted a place at Cambridge, her father
refused to speak to her for five months. By going to Cambridge,
Mary would be betraying her roots – not Irish roots or Republican
roots but working-class roots and the way things had always been
done in a working-class family.

'No one from the family had gone away before and no one else
intended to. They simply couldn't comprehend my motivations.
My Da really believed at that time that daughters would leave his
house only when it was time to walk them up the aisle. By their
standards, I was rebelling. By the standard of a conventional
middle-class family, I was an ideal child trying to better myself but
to them, moving away made them vulnerable. I couldn't be relied
upon to help them anymore. The fact was that they needed me
and instead of telling me this, they rejected me. The goals of education were simply not important enough to leave home for.'

Long after Mary had left Cambridge, a public debate still raged about whether Britain's elite universities really were open to boys and girls from poor homes and inner-city comprehensive schools. Mary's contemporaries at Cambridge from more privileged backgrounds would have found it difficult to imagine the circumstances in which she had had to work for her exams. She did her homework in the bedroom she shared with her three sisters. Outside the window the daily drama of the Lower Falls unfolded. In the early evening, her friends, some of whom were also from St. Louise's, started to gather like gulls on the low wall across the street. Around eight o'clock the hoods drove up in their stolen cars, soon followed by other disaffected youths whose dislike of discipline kept them out of the paramilitaries. As they revved their cars and drank beer from cans, the hoods and rogues kept a wary eye open for IRA punishment squads. They were wise to do so because Mary's street had been the scene of numerous punishment beatings. 'I looked up from my work,' said Mary of one occasion, 'and three men in balaclavas were beating a man up and down the street.' By nine o'clock on most evenings, it was impossible to concentrate any longer.

Mary had to belong to both worlds. She knew the hoods who stole cars and drove them round the estate and she often talked with them late into the night, trying to persuade them that life was not as utterly hopeless as they imagined. They regarded her as an eccentric. As for the other girls – 'I'd be in the street later in the evening and even though I'd get the piss taken out of me for even bothering to do my homework, there was a quiet acceptance that that was what I did. As long as I still hung out I was OK. I had to manage the balance between being streetwise and accepted and pursuing my unusual goal of passing exams.'

The girls who spent the evenings hanging around on the street outside Mary's window included some of Genevieve's most difficult pupils. Like the hoods, they had no hope of ever escaping from the ghetto. 'Their environment took their chances away from them,' Mary wrote, 'and not even a great school and an inspirational nun could help them.' To the critics who say that Genevieve had no time for these girls, Mary replies: 'One of the loveliest things I ever witnessed at school was Genevieve hugging one of the girls renowned in the school for trouble making – she was from a violent home in a dire part of the city. Genevieve spent a lot of time with girls like this. I think she knew that many of them were hopeless cases, doomed to violence in their own adult lives. But what is important is that she did not write them off.'

Mary obtained the Advanced Level grades she needed for Cambridge but when she told her parents, they asked, 'Is that good?' They still did not understand what she had achieved or why she wanted to go. 'All the more reason for you to be proud,' Genevieve said. In October 1988, Mary entered Magdalene College, Cambridge. 'From the moment I closed the door to my room I felt that finally here was somewhere I belonged'. A year later Genevieve heard that Mary had been placed in the first class in the first part of the Cambridge Social and Political Sciences Tripos and that, in her politics papers, the girl who had failed the 11+ had scored the highest marks in the university. The following year, Genevieve, now retired as principal of St. Louise's, decided to visit Mary in Cambridge. Mary had devised, directed and taken the lead in a production for the theatrical dance society and at the end of the performance, Genevieve strode forward and, to the astonishment of the audience, lifted Mary in her arms and swung her round, saying, 'This is the proudest moment of my life.'

1988–1994

14

'I shall go on trying to be the voice of the voiceless'

Genevieve left St. Louise's at the end of the summer term 1988. Six years later she suffered a severe stroke that left her paralysed on her right side, unable to speak or to look after herself and confined to bed or a wheelchair. Sometimes she seemed to understand what was being said to her and joined in the laughter when former pupils who came to see her recalled incidents from their schooldays but at other times the look in her eyes suggested she was very far away.

When Genevieve retired from St. Louise's she could have devoted herself exclusively to the many public and charitable bodies who were keen to invite a well-known and independent-minded Catholic sister to join them. She did accept some of these invitations, too many in retrospect; in 1991, she typed out her own curriculum vitae and listed no fewer than fifteen public bodies on which she was serving, including the Senate of Queen's University, the Northern Ireland Curriculum Council and the Secretary of State's Standing Advisory Commission on Human Rights. But much as she appeared to enjoy these public responsibilities, committee work could never provide the new focus she needed for her vocation. She had retired as a headmistress but she was still a Vincent de Paul sister. For thirty years, her commitment to the Vincentian ideal had found expression in her dedication to the girls of West Belfast but while she kept in touch with many of her pupils and was happy to be known as 'the former head of St. Louise's Comprehensive College' when she wrote for the newspapers (she was for a time a guest columnist on the *Sunday Life*), that phase of her religious life was over.

Even before she had retired from St. Louise's, she had developed a concern for men serving long sentences as a consequence of their paramilitary activity. Help to prisoners was very much in the mainstream of the Vincentian tradition. Vincent de Paul himself had asked Louise de Marillac to train the early sisters to be 'the servants of the galley slaves', men who were held in appalling conditions in the Conciergerie and other Paris prisons awaiting the departure of the chain gang to man the galleys at Marseilles. Genevieve was no stranger to prisons; in the early seventies she had often visited her former pupils in the women's jail at Armagh. But it was the father of one of her pupils who opened her eyes to the needs of the long-term prisoners. Writing to a commonwealth High Commissioner on behalf of one of these prisoners, she explained: 'I got interested in the fathers of the children who were serving long life sentences and were in some cases abandoned by their families.' In 1985, she started visiting one of these abandoned fathers, a member of the Provisional IRA serving a life sentence for murder, and her experience of this case persuaded her that help for long-term prisoners was a cause to which she should devote herself when she left St. Louise's.

Genevieve helped twenty long-term prisoners over the period 1988–1994. Twelve of these men were Catholic and eight Protestant. The majority had been members of Republican or Loyalist paramilitary organisations and were serving one or more life sentences for murder. Genevieve did not go fishing for men to help; she built up a network of contacts by responding to the recommendation of one prisoner that another prisoner would welcome a visit. Her first visits were to prisoners in the Maze (as Long Kesh was now known) but all her subsequent visits were to men in Maghaberry, a new prison built twenty miles south of Belfast. The H-Blocks of the Maze housed Republican and Loyalist prisoners in separate compounds but paramilitaries who renounced violence were, from the late eighties, transferred to Maghaberry where there was no separation and all men were subject to a normal prison regime.

Genevieve received a mixed reception in the Maze. When she visited a Loyalist prisoner, people in the visiting room were at first taken aback to see a Catholic nun. 'Who's she visiting?' they asked. The man she was visiting had already cleared her visit with the UVF officer commanding the compound so there was no trouble but when Republican prisoners heard she had visited a Loyalist they were highly critical. That sort of criticism never worried Genevieve but her treatment at the hands of Protestant prison officers did and eventually she complained to the Northern Ireland Office. Her religious habit was a red rag to some of the prison officers who regarded her with a hostility they did not attempt to hide and kept her waiting as long as possible. Critics who had thought her proud and a publicity-seeker did not see her sitting alone in the prison waiting-room long after all the other visitors' names had been called. 'There is a vindictiveness and nastiness on the part of the security men which is impossible to describe,' she wrote to the permanent secretary at the Northern Ireland Office in 1988. 'I belong to an international community, our sisters work in prisons all over the world. In Brixton and Holloway, to take two examples, they are not subjected to this barbarous treatment.' Reluctant though she was to draw attention to her British honour, she decided that this was an occasion when it could be useful. When she started signing herself in as 'Sister Genevieve OBE', the attitude of the prison officers became more deferential, a minor victory for snobbery over prejudice.

Genevieve's visits raised prisoners' morale. 'Even when I was down in the dumps,' one former IRA man recalled, 'she would have me laughing in ten minutes.' A former Loyalist paramilitary still cannot get over how amazed he was that Genevieve was so warm and easy to talk to and that he always felt so happy in her company. Young Loyalists, raised in the Shankill, had been taught from an early age to abominate the Pope and all his works – some had their arms and legs tattooed with symbols of violence and messages of hate – and yet here was a Catholic sister, one of the

Pope's elite troops, treating them as equals and as friends and by her love helping them to reject whatever hate and bitterness was left.

Genevieve wanted to be more than just a prison visitor. The contemporary version of the Vincentian mission, confirmed by the congregation's Irish province in 1990, committed the sisters to 'helping our brothers and sisters who are poor to get back on their feet, keeping in mind our aim of making the poor person less and less someone who needs help'. Getting former paramilitaries back on their feet once they had renounced violence meant above all giving them an ambition, a stake in the future, and, typically, Genevieve thought in terms of academic qualifications. 'Even in prison you can make something of yourself,' she had told her former pupil, Brenda Murphy, and this was the message she took to the men in Maghaberry.

Six of the men Genevieve helped obtained first class degrees at the Open University. Three went on to work for a Ph.D. when they left prison. Catholic and Protestant boys, who had left their secondary schools in working-class districts with few or no qualifications, discovered in prison and with Genevieve's encouragement that they were capable of achieving academic distinction. For Genevieve it was further evidence that the selective system that had labelled these men as non-academic at the age of eleven was fundamentally flawed.

Genevieve did not restrict her work with prisoners to those who had academic ambitions. One of the Loyalist paramilitaries she helped had been totally illiterate when he was sent to prison at the age of eighteen and only learnt how to write his own name when he was twenty-three. Genevieve took as much trouble to get this man back on his feet as she took with the academic high-flyers, providing practical support when he was released – secondhand furniture for his flat, money to pay the electricity bill and references for a job. As long as a man had renounced violence and had asked to see her, she tried to help. The nature of their crimes and their religious allegiance were irrelevant as far as she was concerned. It made no difference to her whether a man was serving one life sentence for murder or fifteen. That had always been the Vincentian way. 'Our

Lord,' Louise de Marillac reminded the sisters who were going into the prisons, 'helped the most miserable sinners without considering their crimes.'

Genevieve did, however, consider their motivation. 'Are you political?' she would ask the prisoners she was proposing to help. She was wary of helping men who had killed for personal rather than political reasons because there was a chance that these men would kill again, whereas with former paramilitaries she could be reasonably sure that their renunciation of violence was for good. Although she did help one man who had committed a crime of passion, she found it easier to justify to herself and to her Catholic community helping men who had been motivated by some form of idealism, however narrow or wrongheaded that idealism may have appeared to the outside world.

Some of Genevieve's friends were puzzled by her attitude nevertheless. One of the last letters she wrote before her stroke was to a Republican prisoner telling him of her meeting with a Loyalist prisoner called Robert Bates. Robert 'Basher' Bates was a leading member of the infamous Shankill Butchers, the UVF murder gang that terrorised the nationalist community in the late seventies by a series of gruesome cut-throat killings of innocent Catholics. In 1977, when Bates was arrested he confessed to ten murders and was sentenced to sixteen life terms. The judge said the crimes would 'remain for ever a memorial to blind sectarian bigotry' and recommended that Bates should spend the rest of his life in prison.

This was the man for whom Genevieve now said she 'felt full of compassion'. Genevieve's friends understood why, as a Vincentian sister, she wanted to help Republican and Loyalist prisoners 'get back on their feet' but they found it hard to understand how she could feel compassion for men who had carried out the most horrific murders of Roman Catholics. In addition to two former Shankill Butchers, she befriended another Loyalist who had been one of those responsible for a notorious anti-Catholic atrocity. When the sisters questioned Genevieve about this, she refused to listen to any criticism of men she often referred to as 'my boys'.

Vincent de Paul told the early sisters that they should see Jesus Christ even in the most ungrateful and unprepossessing people they were called to help, but translating this ideal into practice can never have been easy. A number of factors may have made it easier for Genevieve, however, than for the early sisters who probably knew nothing about the galley slaves they encountered in the Conciergerie. Genevieve knew that the prisoners she was visiting had renounced violence, a crucial point for her. She also knew that it had required courage on their part to turn their back on their paramilitary past. 'I am very, very fond of him and admire his courage enormously,' she wrote to the parents of the other former Shankill Butcher she was trying to help.

For some of the Loyalist prisoners, including Robert Bates, the renunciation of violence was associated with their becoming 'born-again Christians', a form of conversion that was greeted with scepticism by the relatives of their victims but that undoubtedly changed the lives of the men concerned. One Loyalist in the Maze told the officer commanding his compound that as he was now a born-again Christian, 'I'll not be taking any more orders'. The officer was sceptical. 'Give him time,' he told other prisoners, 'he'll be back to his old self.' But the officer was wrong. The man renounced violence, moved to Maghaberry and with Genevieve's help, found a job when he was released. Thirteen years on he is still an enthusiastic born-again Christian. Born-again Christianity with its literal biblicism and evangelical fervour was not to Genevieve's theological taste but she accepted the men's conversion as genuine. There was never a hint in her dealings with Protestant prisoners that she questioned their particular brand of Christianity or tried to persuade them to consider Roman Catholicism. Proselytising was not on her agenda.

The more Genevieve learnt about how 'her boys' had been drawn into violence, the more she sympathised with them. She never condoned their crimes but she saw them as the victims of the extraordinary circumstances that had existed in working-class districts at the start of the Troubles when the pressures on young men in their teens to join the paramilitaries had been very difficult to resist. Living in the Falls in the early seventies she knew all about the pressures on young Catholics; now she discovered that the pressures had been every bit as hard to resist for the young

Protestants growing up in the Shankill a few hundred yards from her home in Clonard.

'What he did in the past was due to many factors,' she wrote in a reference for a Loyalist from the Shankill who was serving life sentences for two murders, 'not least the lack of pastoral care in his school where he played truant at will and also the fact that in his early teens the Troubles were at their worst.' The failure of schools and parents to provide a framework of discipline for these youngsters was a theme to which she returned often though she would have known better than anyone that these were precisely the sort of pupils whose 'unauthorised absence' few headteachers were keen to follow up. Of another Loyalist lifer who had been thrown out of every school he had attended and who was now a born-again Christian, she wrote: 'His life as a child and adolescent was tragic. He was a waif on the Shankill, in and out of borstals with no education and no parental control. His only world was one of violence. He could not escape being involved in murder as that was the only world he knew.'

Genevieve argued that men who had been drawn into the Republican or Loyalist paramilitaries in the early seventies should receive special concessions, by which she meant early release, especially if they wanted to pursue educational goals. Her problem was how to persuade the authorities that she was not just another bleeding-heart nun but someone whose recommendations should be taken seriously. She sought the advice of Brian Mawhinney and of one of his senior civil servants, John McConnell, head of the political division at the Northern Ireland Office. Both these men helped to establish Genevieve's *bona fides* and themselves came to trust her judgement as far as individual prisoners were concerned. Nevertheless, Genevieve felt the need to emphasise when writing to officials that she was not the sort of naïve prison visitor who was taken in by the first hard luck story she heard. 'I am a Religious, a sister of St. Vincent de Paul, I am not a social worker nor, hopefully a sentimental do-gooder.'

When officials in the Northern Ireland Office were being particularly obdurate, she reminded them that she had stuck her neck out for them in the past:

> May I remind you that I did not hesitate to go to the USA
> at the request of the Northern Ireland Office in the
> interests of employment in West Belfast – a journey which
> was exploited by the Republican press and which caused
> some stress. I do not regret having done so and it is in this
> spirit I am now involved with this long-term political
> prisoner.

Although Genevieve was able to call on her influential contacts, she found that persuading the authorities – the Northern Ireland Office, the Life Sentence Review Board and the prison governors – that her prisoners should be given special consideration proved very difficult. In some cases she was instrumental in bringing forward the date of a prisoner's review or in having a definite date set for release. In one case, she persuaded the authorities that a prisoner could do his six-month 'work-out' in England in order that he could begin his university course and she helped to overcome the fears of a number of universities that were reluctant to have former paramilitaries studying for higher degrees. She stood as a sponsor for men during the transition year from prison to university, providing financial help and seeing the men on a regular basis even though that meant trips to the mainland, and she persuaded one university to waive the tuition fees for a former IRA man who had failed to get a grant. There were inevitably some disappointments. Men hoping for release on license were 'knocked back' for two or more years despite her pleas and had to abandon all hope of going to university. Others were not offered a place because the prison authorities refused to allow them to go for interview even though the men were close to release. Genevieve argued that these men were not murderers in the normal sense of that term – 'He got involved in violence for altruistic reasons', she wrote of one former Republican – but the authorities never accepted her distinction between those who had been swept into the paramilitaries in the early seventies and those who joined later and in her words 'knew perfectly well what they were doing'.

'I shall go on trying to be the voice of the voiceless in my way but I hope in a constructive way,' Genevieve wrote to the

Northern Ireland Office after receiving one more disappointing response. In the broad definition of 'les pauvres' accepted by the late-twentieth-century sisters, those who could not speak for themselves had an important place. Genevieve's work with long-term prisoners was a continuation of her work as a headmistress. She had enabled the girls of the Falls to speak for themselves by giving them confidence and teaching them to be articulate; the long-term prisoners were not inarticulate but they had no way to make their voices heard. Even if her pleas on the prisoners' behalf fell on deaf ears, the men became her friends for life; and just as she had visited them in prison, so they in their turn when they were released visited her in the prison imposed by her stroke.

This part of Genevieve's life and vocation more than any other would have encouraged people to think that perhaps she did indeed possess some of the qualities of a saint, especially in her uninhibited Christian love for men who had been sectarian killers. But her work with prisoners was unpublicised and unknown except to those directly involved. Genevieve's reward was the gratitude of the men and their families and the knowledge that she had successfully adapted the example of Louise de Marillac to the prisons of Northern Ireland. Though she never drew attention to it herself, she had also transcended religious prejudice in a remarkable way. No finer tribute was paid to her in all her years in Belfast than when the former officer commanding the Ulster Volunteer Force in the Shankill described this Catholic sister as 'the greatest person I have ever met in my life'.

By the early nineties, some of the prisoners Genevieve was helping were eligible for three days parole at Christmas. Before going home on Christmas Eve, they made their way to the sisters' house in Balmoral Avenue to see Genevieve and with her at the centre of their circle, the former Republican and Loyalist paramilitaries had a few drinks together and wished one another the compliments of the season. Surrounded by her 'boys' and joining in their camaraderie, Genevieve must have enjoyed these occasions as much as any in her long career as a Sister of St. Vincent de Paul.

Early in 1994, Genevieve decided that she should cut down on her many public commitments. According to her doctor, she often worried about her blood pressure, which was at the upper end of normal though if she worried specifically about having a stroke she does not appear to have discussed this anxiety with anyone else. Strictly speaking, a stroke is not caused by overwork but overwork may contribute to high blood pressure which in time damages the blood vessels that control the flow of blood to the brain. Genevieve was seventy-one and was still driving herself hard, often going from one meeting to another or straight from the London plane to Maghaberry prison. She seemed to have inexhaustible energy but the years of running St. Louise's, of fighting battles with various authorities, of demanding more of herself because she was a religious sister without family commitments, must have taken their toll.

In May she was in England and she arranged to meet a former prisoner she had been helping before flying back to Belfast. They met at Heathrow and had a meal together in Garfunkels Restaurant in Terminal One. The former prisoner remembers that she looked tired and stressed and that she appeared to be worried about the reaction of the Catholic community to her willingness to visit Loyalist killers in Maghaberry. At the end of May, she attended a conference in the Wellington hotel on the Malone Road. She was among friends, including a former senior colleague from St. Louise's and Dr Sheila Chillingworth who had been the educational psychologist responsible for schools in the Falls and who had remained on good terms with Genevieve even though they had not always seen eye to eye over 'expulsions'. At some point during the conference, her friends noticed that Genevieve had stopped talking and saw her papers slip off her lap onto the floor. Sheila Chillingworth called an ambulance. On the way to the hospital, Genevieve was seen to be crying as though she knew only too well what had happened and that, having fought so hard to be the voice of the voiceless, she had become one of the voiceless herself.

A few days later on the 9 June, when the severity of Genevieve's stroke was more widely known, a special prayer was written for the sixth form service at St. Louise's:

In our Mass today we remember very specially Sister
Genevieve who is ill. No printed word or message could
begin to tell what she has done for St. Louise's and indeed
the youth of West Belfast. She gave her girls purpose and
pride no matter what their background was, she taught
them to think for themselves, she accepted them fully with
all their talents, faults, strengths and weaknesses. She
gently guided childish eleven-year-olds and helped them
grow into confident young women . . . We ask God to
guard her, to bless her every day for her faithfulness, her
patience and her courage.

It was nearly a year before Genevieve was moved from hospital
back to the house in Balmoral Avenue she shared with Sister Ita
and Sister Declan. The two sisters looked after her with the help
of carers and former pupils. One of her many visitors was her
brother, John, who had accompanied her to Dublin on the day she
became a postulant in the Daughters of Charity. On that rain-
swept day so long ago he had pleaded with her to come home but
Genevieve had shaken her head – she would give the religious life
a try. Whether Genevieve was able to remember that day or to
reflect on her religious life, we cannot be sure but not long before
she lost the power to speak or write, she jotted down on a card
words that suggest she had no regrets: 'You have dealt with me
extraordinarily well, mon cher Seigneur, why I shall never know.
Please teach me how to show my thanks.'

Index